50

LEAN FOR THE CASH-STRAPPED LEADER

The Path to Growth and Profitability

LEAN FOR THE CASH-STRAPPED LEADER

The Path to Growth and Profitability

John E. Madigan • Todd C. Maher • Mohammad Ali

CRC Press
Taylor & Francis Group
Boca Raton   London   New York

CRC Press is an imprint of the
Taylor & Francis Group, an **informa** business

A PRODUCTIVITY PRESS BOOK

CRC Press
Taylor & Francis Group
6000 Broken Sound Parkway NW, Suite 300
Boca Raton, FL 33487-2742

© 2016 by Taylor & Francis Group, LLC
CRC Press is an imprint of Taylor & Francis Group, an Informa business

No claim to original U.S. Government works

Printed on acid-free paper
Version Date: 20150918

International Standard Book Number-13: 978-1-4987-3896-5 (Paperback)

Visit the Taylor & Francis Web site at
http://www.taylorandfrancis.com

and the CRC Press Web site at
http://www.crcpress.com

Contents

Preface: The "Why" of This Book vii

Acknowledgments ix

Authors xi

Introduction: About This Book xiii

1   Brief Overview of Lean and Elimination of Waste 1

2   A Different Way of Thinking 9

3   Rationalizing the Inventory 21

4   Kanban Signals 33

5   Deriving Dependent Demand for Kanban 43

6   Documenting the Current State in a Process Map 55

7   Creating the Future State Process Map 65

8   Understanding Kanban–Heijunka Card-Flow Process 77

9   Kanbans and Heijunkas..93

10 Continuous Improvement, the Kaizen Event............................105

11 Beginning the Kaizen and Documenting Reality.......................117

12 The Percent-Loading Chart 133

13 Using the Percent-Loading Chart.. 147

14 Dependent-Demand Manufacturing Kanbans..........................163

15 The Total-Value Flow with Standard Work and Visuals............ 177

16 Tying Up Loose Ends in the New Total-Value Flow...................193

17 Competition and Continuous Improvement............................211

Recommended Readings **219**

Index **221**

Preface: The "Why" of This Book

Created by Lean practitioners with real-world, results-proven track records, *Lean for the Cash-Strapped Leader* is designed to help owners of small businesses or senior managers of large ones make their enterprises more efficient, more productive, and, ultimately, more profitable. At once a how-to manual and a strategic management guide, the book lays out, in simple English, all the steps in implementing Lean, from formulating a strategy and managing organizational change, to establishing a kanban-driven, level-loaded production system.

Without acronyms or esoteric jargon, *Lean for the Cash-Strapped Leader* provides a plain-English how-to guide for understanding and implementing a Lean total-value flow. It presents Lean as a substantive business strategy and all-encompassing manufacturing philosophy, not just a temporal, tactical method. Although written to describe manufacturing processes, astute readers can substitute their own particular process (hospital or medical flows, office flows, distribution flows, etc.) to gain insights on what is needed to implement Lean strategies and methods in their particular enterprises.

Along the way, the book gives detailed attention to the need for the "soft message" that underwrites and supports actions required for a business to achieve the transformation that Lean can bring. *Lean for the Cash-Strapped Leader* emphasizes the messaging and the degree of management involvement required to have a successful Lean result.

Throughout their careers, the authors have been struck repeatedly by the number of companies embarking on a Lean conversion who were reluctant to move from beginning housekeeping events ("5S" in Lean speak) into the meat and potatoes of Lean. This book is intended to help those struggling souls, convinced of Lean but bereft of budgets to hire live-in consultants, to overcome their fears, start substantial change in their businesses, and begin to reap the benefits of Lean.

Acknowledgments

Lean is a journey, and we acknowledge our debt to all who have taught us along the way. This goes to the expert Lean leaders and teachers who entered our lives and the dedicated employees and managers who served on the never-ending kaizen events. Enlightenment is a thousand points of light and not simply one all-illuminating manifestation. We are indebted to you all.

A special acknowledgment goes to Mary Madigan, without whose help, patience, wisdom, counsel, criticism, and encouragement, this book would not have happened.

Authors

John E. Madigan earned his BA from the University of Denver. While at Wiremold's Chicago manufacturing plant, he held management positions in both materials and operations. Madigan likewise benefited from Lean training delivered by Shingijutsu and Moffitt Associates. After Wiremold, Madigan did Lean implementation consulting and training in the Midwest for seven years at various companies—from small privately held companies to several Fortune 500 companies.

Todd C. Maher's educational credentials include a BS in industrial engineering from the University of Illnois and an MBA in operations management from DePaul University. He worked for Wiremold during their Lean transformation and held leadership positions in both operations and engineering. At Wiremold, he also benefited from 10 years of training delivered by Shingijutsu Ltd. in both the United States and Japan. After Wiremold, Maher spent the last 13 years helping both private and public companies with their Lean initiatives. Maher has participated in or led over 500 different kaizen events since learning this philosophy.

Mohammad Ali earned a BS in electrical engineering from the University of Illinois at Chicago. He has also received hands-on training in PMP, CCNA, and is Security+ certified in information technology.

Ali has participated in numerous kaizen events during his tenure at Wiremold's Chicago plant. He is an expert in creating VBA-based Microsoft Access applications with user-friendly graphical interfaces. He has successfully designed, tested, and implemented a number of such applications for many small- to medium-size manufacturers for their kanban cards' creation process.

Introduction: About This Book

In *Lean for the Cash-Strapped Leader*, we reinforce the idea that Lean is a substantive strategy and an all-encompassing manufacturing philosophy rather than a temporal tactic or method. From deriving kanban-card population to percent-loading chart manning analysis, the serious reader learns step-by-step how to set up his or her first production cell, which can serve as a success story and internal "learning lab" to speed the Lean transformation process along. We recommend starting small and getting an incremental gain. There is no going for the "grand slam" with a first effort. Unless you have people on board who truly know what they are doing, trying to Lean up your factory in one "can't fail" event is folly and only for those souls who do not want to sleep at night. We believe you should start with some secondary process, smaller in scope, but still an excellent candidate to begin the Lean transformation, and create a learning lab to see results, build confidence, and train employees in Lean. Expand out from there as rapidly as your freed-up resources will allow.

This book grew out of years of hands-on Lean practice experience, opening up our factories for "missionary work," helping to train guest visitor companies and vendors, and consulting experience. We were always struck by the fact that many companies starting out with Lean were reticent to move from endless housekeeping events ("5S" in Lean lingo) into the meat and potatoes of Lean: level loading of the shop, rationalizing inventory, and process-focused kaizen (focused waste-eliminating improvement activity) events, such as setup reductions, forming cells for product lines, and total productive maintenance. These housekeeping concepts were ideas and methods that, intuitively, were readily understood and could be applied. The benefits of the greater application of Lean methods and philosophy (e.g., level loading the shop floor, one-piece flow, Lean inventories to support one-piece flow, etc.) were not so "intuitive" and thus not attempted for want of an expert "guiding hand" to help them along the way, or absolute fear of disastrous results if applied incorrectly without expert help. From these observations of smaller businesses and talks with operations personnel, this book found its reason for existence and focus.

For those fearful of starting substantial Lean change on a "lean" budget, *Lean for the Cash-Strapped Leader* gives a low-cost roadmap to a successful start. For those struggling with profitability and productivity issues and fighting to remain on their feet in the global market, the book offers a "paradigm shifting" manufacturing philosophy and strategic vision, utilizing existing workers and minimal cash outlays in equipment and programing to rapidly make the transition to Lean and improve profitability and productivity.

Factory-wide 5S efforts and continuous plant-wide personnel training in Lean concepts without creating a level-loaded model line to work from are, in the words of Lean, a waste of time better spent. If enterprises are going to have success with Lean implementations, they need to get to level-loaded, signal-driven scheduling methods as soon as possible. This will serve as the stake in the ground whereby change and improvement can be measured. More importantly, it will become the learning lab where the champions of Lean get a practical understanding of Lean concepts and methods and can then spread the gospel more rapidly throughout the plant.

The Lean efforts we discuss in this book utilize readily available Microsoft® Office Suite programs—Word, Access, and Excel—coupled with VBA programming language to get results. Most companies already have these programs installed on their networks. By simplifying and democratizing information processes, information technology transforms from "gatekeeper" to "door opener." Most importantly, by taking the "consultant-ese" and layers of strange words out of explanations, the book provides the willing reader, bedeviled by minimal budgetary resources, with clear context and understanding to begin doing Lean with reduced fear and minimal or no reliance on outside consultants.

American companies have been studying and implementing Lean since the introduction of Deming and the Toyota manufacturing systems in the postwar years. American automobile manufacturers have been the leaders in Lean implementation in the manufacturing area. By reducing inventories and the number of labor hours required for producing a car, American car factories have remained competitive both domestically and globally due to Lean practices. Lean also works for smaller manufacturing enterprises.

Recently, Lean philosophy and methods have entered into the food, office, distribution, and healthcare arenas. Hospitals are using Lean practices such as kanban surgical room instrument kits (think factory inventory) to cover patient demand (think factory sales order), and posting standard work and protocol checklists (think factory process sheets, prints, and engineering standards) to insure consistency in staff hygienic and operational practices and outcomes (think quality metrics). If you are not a manufacturer, this book will still probably help you. Keep your eyes and ears open and your imagination alive!

The bottom line is this: Companies will have to learn to do more with less in the global economy. This is the message at the heart of Lean.

(*Note*: In this book, we will use the terms *total-value flow* and *production cell.* The production cell term refers to the more specific aspects of producing a part; the total-value flow is the more general term encompassing all activity from product selection for the cell to production of the product to recycling of the kanban card, to, as needed, replenishment of inventory.)

Chapter 1

Brief Overview of Lean and Elimination of Waste

What is meant by the term "Lean" when used in manufacturing? The most austere definition might be "making or doing something after as much waste as possible—time, distance, space, and material—has been removed from the process and making or doing it one piece at a time as demanded by the customer." This tends to be counterintuitive and contrary to the computer-driven, "economy of scale" thinking, and standard cost-accounting practices that permeate traditional manufacturing thought.

Lean *is not*

- A means for cutting staff so that the resultant zombie workers, tied to unrealistic time standards, do the work of four people, have no time to think or be creative, and have no input into their quality of work life
- An inventory-free system
- A "beat up your vendors" system
- A system managed and implemented only by Six Sigma black belts
- A "flavor-of-the-month" addition to the other mishmash of manufacturing requirements planning (MRP)/enterprise resource planning (ERP), employee empowerment-, management-by-objective-, quality-is-free-, and employee-suggestion-box-driven programs
- An "app" you download that lets you become an absentee manager

Lean *is* an all-encompassing business strategy and manufacturing philosophy that provides the foundation for sustainable company-wide results in

- As waste-free and productive business practices as possible
- A more satisfied, committed, and productive workforce
- Business growth potential with existing workforce
- Potentially larger profits by continually focusing on market-driven costs
- Potentially better cash flow resulting from minimizing inventories and simplifying processes and machinery

Much has been written about the origins of Lean. It draws from many sources. Leaving room for debate and editing of our selections, following are some that come to mind. Frederick W. Taylor put a scientific basis to measuring and quantitatively reporting work and productivity. Henry Ford contributed standardized processes, designing for manufacturability, integrated supply chains, and supplying workers with materials at point of use. Taiichi Ohno of Toyota is credited with putting first Lean concepts on a solid footing in modern manufacturing with the pull system, one-piece production via the Toyota Production System, and the concept of continuous improvement. Shigeo Shingo gave the Toyota Production System its continuous flow and stockless production due to minimizing changeover times. W. Edwards Deming contributed quality at the source, the role of enlightened management, the need for process metrics, and employee empowerment. Even the accounting methods follow the same monthly checkbook-balancing rituals families have used forever—period tracking of actual revenues and expenses.

What this book will do for you is provide you with a clear understanding of Lean philosophy, methods, and implementation steps, in jargon-free, easy-to-understand language. We show how readily available computer programs can be used for kanban analysis and the source of a kanban-card database that drives your whole system. We provide commonly used examples and show how to create flowcharts that document typical processes. Examples and cases are typical. You will have to assess your company in light of where you are on your Lean journey. There are many ways to do things in Lean. You know your business best, and you, with your team, will have to make decisions based on the realities of your company. As long as you stay true to the Lean principles described in this book, you should achieve success.

Embedded within the methods and tools of Lean is the activity-driving kaizen event, a focused, waste-eliminating productivity improvement activity. If done right, ordinary workers and management, in the spirit of the great pioneers above, make extraordinary contributions to eliminate waste and streamline processes at the company level. The genius of the kaizen event is that the previously powerless, who had to deal with the problem or challenge, now are given the power to recommend and implement solutions to that very problem or challenge. Following the objective facts to implementable conclusions in kaizen events is transfigurative—both for the company and the individuals who now sense they have become change agents whose opinions and thoughts matter. Once a company begins Lean, the continuous improvement only ends by a failure of imagination and capitulation to the ordinary.

The best way to understand the essence of a Lean process is to know what it attempts to eliminate: waste. Or, to put it in different words, the ideal Lean process is one wherein all or most activities in the process are considered "value-added" activities that contribute directly to a qualitative and functional product the customer wants. Value added is what the customer is willing to pay for and expects. Anything not value added is a form of waste. In today's global economy, elimination of waste is also a company survival necessity. If you want to know where your cash flow, your lifeblood, is going, search out your waste.

Lean and waste, as applied to processes, are reciprocals—opposites. Where Lean is rationalized and readily measureable, waste can be subtle and unapparent. Waste can even result from what historically were viewed as accepted business practices—for example, maximum utilization of machinery, especially high-cost and high-volume designed "monument" assets, to insure productivity measurements remain high and cost of monument asset justified; MRP system programing pushing shop order releases to the factory floor; buying economic order quantities or large lots for favorable purchase price variance; standard cost accounting driven activities centering on justifying variances to standard or product absorption of costs; making company maintenance departments solely responsible for preventative maintenance, etc. (A monument is the super machine, usually expensive and "high-volume" oriented, which insures lowest part cost at the expense of high-inventory levels; in other words, a machine not "right sized" to the task at hand.)

In any process, there are many distinct activities. When a process mapping exercise of a product (we will discuss in depth in Chapters 6 and 7) is completed and activities are classified, the result is that there are value-added steps, steps that are "absolute waste," steps that are "wasteful but temporarily necessary," and steps that we will call "administratively necessary." It will be enlightening to discuss each of these activities.

Value-added activities, as we said above, are processes that a customer is willing to pay for. Punching and forming sheet metal, welding the metal into a cabinet frame, applying pop rivets to door hinges on cabinet, vacuum sealing prepared foods for distribution, electrical test for continuity of circuits, leak testing for pressure vessels, etc., are all examples of value-added activities. When a customer buys a product, he expects the purchased product to deliver a level of quality, safety, and suitability for application.

Absolute waste is what should be removed from any Lean process as soon as possible—some may be considered wasteful but temporarily necessary (see next paragraph) in the short term. Examples of absolute waste are walking to a central tool crib to retrieve tools routinely required for setup or product changeover, cycle counting, adding mezzanines or renting buildings to hold "extra" or "overflow" inventory, basing purchasing practices only on unit purchase price, releasing multiple MRP shop orders to allow "foreman flexibility" to schedule line as he or she sees fit, researching standard-cost work-center efficiency or productivity variances for monthly management "who shot John" blame meeting, issuing individual purchase orders for repetitive purchases of the same part numbers, elaborate system of sign-off requirements for routine tasks, etc. These activities contribute nothing to the final product the customer is willing to pay for and are, instead, a reflection of internal process and control breakdowns or lack of trust or confidence in employees.

Wasteful but temporarily necessary actions will be eliminated when the process is improved to the point that they are no longer necessary. In most cases, these are due to the legacy systems—either formal or informal—which are in place in a company. In many MRP-based companies, expediters and cycle counters are "most valuable players" when it comes to keeping the place running every day. They compensate for activities that are not done efficiently by defined process. Once inventory is rationalized and the shop is level loaded, the need for expediters and cycle counters goes away. Accounting systems also require actions like plant-wide, multiday inventory-counting shutdowns, which will probably go away when the inventory is rationalized and kanban-driven inventory quantities (a "kanban" is a signal to purchase or produce a part) are defined for the auditors.

When it comes to Lean implementations, these wasteful but temporarily necessary practices are always kept in place until process improvement eliminates the need for them. A Lean process improvement does not put any existing process or product line in jeopardy by arbitrarily cutting away a safety net without a proven process to put in its place.

"Administratively necessary" activities are processes required by law or safety concerns that are built into the process. The Food and Drug Administration (FDA) has certain requirements that must be met when dealing with products like foods and pharmaceuticals. Underwriting agencies, insurance companies, and the Occupational Safety and Health Administration (OSHA) have requirements in place for other products. Since the product cannot be sold without compliance, these activities are necessary.

Most of the Lean literature discusses seven major sources of waste: (1) overproduction, (2) excess inventory, (3) waiting time, (4) transportation, (5) excess motion, (6) defects, and (7) overprocessing. These were forms of waste identified and singled out for elimination by Taiichi Ohno in his writings. In the course of this book, we will address the Lean tools and methods that help eliminate waste. In the short term, we will give examples of each type of waste.

Overproduction: Simply stated, this is making more than the customer wants. In many companies, overproduction is driven by "economy of scale" thinking or exorbitant changeover or setup times. Whatever the reason, overproduction ties up cash in inventory not needed, wastes production time, and lengthens lead times, producing things you cannot immediately sell. Overproduction is often considered the most serious form of waste, because it has all the other forms of waste in it. In a Lean company, inventory is only replaced as it is sold, and the inventory in total is rationalized (we will deal with this in Chapter 3). In some companies, overproduction is also driven by mandates for utilization of equipment to justify acquisition costs, or it is driven by "piece rate" worker compensation schemes.

Excess inventory: If the inventory is not rationalized, if your sales department does not have the same reasonable expectations for what they sell as your operations group, or if there are things like positive purchase-price-variance incentives for the purchasing department in place, you will probably have excess inventory. Excess inventory tends to be "just in case" hedge inventory or "economic order quantity" volume-related inventory. In either case, the cost extends far beyond unit price to the need to warehouse it, carry it on the books, count it and handle it unnecessarily, borrow to finance it, throw it away when it has been properly aged in the warehouse and is considered a candidate for "excess and obsolete" reserves, etc. "Excess" and "inventory" are not words that go well together.

Waiting time: Just as the doldrums can take the wind out of a sailing ship, waiting time in a factory, the angst-inducing silence of not producing anything, destroys momentum, and causes premature career-aging to the management staff. Waiting for inventory to be brought from a prior operation, waiting for tooling or dies to arrive from the tool crib for completion of a machine changeover, waiting for information from the computer or a print from the print room before beginning production, etc., indicate unlinked or unreliable processes and inefficient factory layouts. "Watching the wash" or "waiting for the tea kettle to heat"—a worker stands idly by while a machine cycles for a significant period of time—is a waste of the operator's time and abilities. In Lean, material, equipment, tools, and information should be in place to eliminate the need for waiting time.

Transportation: If the required materials are not available or "actionable" at point of use, there is probably a physical equipment or plant layout problem, resulting in transportation waste. Most transportation problems can be significantly reduced simply by rationalizing the flow, establishing point of use for materials, laying out the work cell accordingly, and training the personnel who service the cell how to present picked materials. Rationalizing flows into cells does not mean huge investments in redundant material-moving equipment or elaborate conveyor systems. There are many low-cost options for setting up flows in cells with kaizen-driven planning and some creative thinking.

Excess motion: Any nonproductive activity by man or machine can be considered excess motion. A worker tracking down an engineer or supervisor for directions or clarification on how to make something, searching for tools or papers due to poor housekeeping and orderliness, inconsistent or missing work directions for making production, seeking out purchasing authorization signatures on routine buys, a drill fixture that drills out "air" in its cycling because of incorrect programing, etc., are all examples of excess motion.

Defects: A nonconforming part should be the most obvious form of waste. A bigger form of waste is not finding the defect until the final inspection. Although a defect can happen even in Lean processes, the one-piece flow of a Lean process tries to make the process itself as foolproof as possible. The use of templates, mechanical stops, visual displays of what is and is not acceptable, assigning operator responsibility for quality, and defined production processes with standard work to take variability out of the production process are some of the ways Lean tries to combat the problem of defects.

Overprocessing: Doing more than the customer is willing to pay for is overprocessing. Overprocessing can occur in either product or process. In a product, the use of 14 gauge sheet steel where 16 gauge will do the job and satisfy customer needs is a waste of material, as well as both machine and tool life. Using solid castings where less substantial castings will function and meet customer strength and safety requirements is overprocessing. Spending inordinate amounts of time trying to analyze which MRP-planned orders to release to the shop is overprocessing. Issuing new prints for unchanging parts with each shop order is overprocessing. Double checking computer on-hands to make sure they are correct before releasing a shop order is overprocessing. Stringent work rules and overly structured job descriptions, without due cause, can result in overprocessing.

Other textbooks speak of yet more wastes, such as "underutilized people." We could add to this list the waste of "lost opportunity" for not implementing Lean methods and utilizing Lean tools. You get the point. Anything to do with people, material, space, time, and effort that consumes resources or attention and creates no value needs to be eliminated. This is why a company needs to get beyond endlessly doing 5S (housekeeping) kaizens and plant-wide training and get a model total-value flow established that will serve as a benchmark to start process improvement and level-loaded production. The level-loaded cell is where the contagion for the "Lean epiphany" starts and where the Lean converts are to be found; hence, the purpose of this book.

As you read this book, there are several things you will need to think about as you start Lean. You will need to identify the "Lean champions" who will drive the activity and who will most readily understand the concepts. These could be some of your best employees—hourly, supervisory, or management. Everyone in your factory will have the names of these potential Lean champions on their lips. Get these people involved in the initial kaizens, and then use these people as mentors to seed the other kaizen teams going forward. In addition to champions, you will also need to find a supervisor or manager who will be relentless in not allowing any backsliding on the gains from the kaizens and who will help establish the day-to-day rhythm of the work cell. This supervisor should also be on the initial team. Once the one working model total-value flow is set up and functioning, it becomes the learning lab to give practical instruction to everyone else.

In the next chapter, we will discuss picking a product as a candidate, determining production unit of measure, and showing how a total-value-flow map works (a flowchart with documented inputs and outputs and activity classifications as discussed above). After we pick the product line, you do the 5S to prepare the area, and form the first kaizen team. Now plug in the Lean champions you have been thinking about, and we are ready to start rationalizing inventory and level loading the cell.

Chapter 2

A Different Way of Thinking

You should be thinking about who your "champions" will be and who will be the firm, yet reasonable, manager holding the line on kaizen improvements in the soon-to-be established production cell. As we go along in this chapter, we will posit more things for you to keep in mind as you read. Your answers to these questions will be crucial to the success of your Lean startup. We will address each "keep-in-minder" at length in following chapters, but how you answer these questions will determine how quickly you can get started on Lean, heijunka-driven cells.

Now is the time to think about product candidates that lend themselves to becoming the "learning lab" for the company by becoming the first production cell scheduled by a heijunka board. You should look for an easy win to build confidence, to gain momentum, and to get more support moving forward across the plant. In addition, think about locating the cell in a highly visible area to market the "coming, new way of doing business" to the whole organization.

Once the product-line candidates are presented for cells, we will do total-value flow mapping to point out how best to set up the cell. This process of setting up a cell can be relatively obvious or relatively messy. We will consider both possibilities.

First of all, when you are thinking about setting up a production cell, which will become the Lean cell incubator for your company, you need to make sure you select a product line that has significant enough product volume to operate on a relatively consistent schedule. You do not have to start with *the* main product line of your plant. This book is not about putting your factory at risk with one roll of the dice. On the contrary, a low-volume and infrequently made product is probably the wrong product to be a candidate. Remember, you want to learn from the cell, and you also want to see what measureable impact Lean has on your operation.

The ideal product-line candidate for the production cell will be a product that has its own unique, dedicated machines to support the manufacturing process and does not share these assets with other products. If (our example is for a metal product; if you have a nonmetal product, mentally substitute your product flow for the one following) you have a product that goes from raw material to a shear to a punch press to a bending press to a welding unit to a coating/painting operation to assembly to packaging to shipping, all on dedicated product-line equipment, this lends itself well to a cell candidate. If your product candidate is not made on dedicated equipment—that is, equipment is shared across many product lines (probably more the norm than exception), continue reading.

In the real, non-Lean, manufacturing world, many product flows are dependent upon a feeder machine such as a high-capacity turret press, centralized press department, or centralized injection molding machine that makes parts for many different product lines, or a centralized paint shop that paints all finished production parts. This use of shared equipment is not a fatal flaw for setting up a production cell. When you establish the product cell, you will just have to make rules and accommodations for these feeder machines to service the production cell. (Another thing to keep in mind: if you are in the process of capital equipment purchasing decisions as you read this book, we would urge you to get your cell up and running before you make any final decisions on equipment. Once you understand the Lean concepts, there might be smaller-scale options to large "feeder" machines, which could result in lower total costs and faster throughput.)

When you finally decide on the production cell and the flow, you can accommodate any manufacturing operation not in the cell by using techniques such as "in" and "out" lanes at the shared operation, using kanban cards with "when to run" rules in lieu of shop orders at non-cell machines, etc. This is called the "Curtain Effect" from the cell. These variations on demand-triggered signals, using FIFO (first in first out) at the "monument" or shared work center, will help to allow the shared operation to function as it normally does, yet, at the same time, give visual indicators of work awaiting that is needed to keep the cell running.

Lean can accommodate almost any set of circumstances in setting up a cell. When we finally get to the total-value flow mapping exercise, the above will become clearer. For now, keep thinking about which product line

would lend itself best to dedicated, or mostly dedicated, equipment. We will come back to shared assets and visual indicators in Chapters 5 and 14.

In the ideal world, the production unit of throughput—the unit you want to measure for productivity in the cell—is normally a finished, shippable product. That is, the ideal cell produces a product that is a finished-goods stocking item. If your factory flow is set up so that your potential cell supplies products to other finishing cells, your production unit of throughput might be different from a cell supplying "units" to finished goods. A feeder cell's production unit of throughput might be "pounds" or "feet" or "weldments" rather than each "can of food" or "reel of wire" or "metal cabinet." Keep in mind, in the ideal Lean world, the cell starts with raw materials and produces a stockable finished item. In the real world, Lean can accommodate all types of intermediate flows.

Some managers get worried when the time to start up the cell ultimately arrives. Since "Murphy's Law" is resident in most factories, the specter arises of lagging shipments or disabled operations due to prolonged attempts to get the cell up and running. If your product-line candidate could be a cause of customer revolt at the rise of shortages or lengthening of lead time, this gets you to another subject to think about: inventory build before the cell is established. Normally, Lean is not associated with the terms "inventory build," but, having lived in the real world long enough, we want our Lean conversions to go as painlessly as possible. One of the golden rules of a first kaizen is do not interrupt flow to the customer.

If you do not have alternate machinery to make things on or do not have enough inventory on hand to get you by for three or four days, while the cell starts up and works through the learning curve, you may have to build some buffer inventory. You must continue to satisfy your customer as you get Lean, and shipments must continue to go out as scheduled. Contacting your raw material suppliers or determining where to put the temporary inventory is something you can begin to think about after your product line is chosen and your inventory is rationalized (discussed in detail in Chapter 3).

If you have large inventories of raw materials (as most companies converting to Lean do), you probably have enough of a buffer to get you by during the startup period. The irony of this is, the fabrication areas begging for improvement sometimes are scrambling to make enough finished inventory, but other areas, probably less critical to overall flow, have excessive inventory. This is the nature of typical bottleneck operations. Beware: one of the common misunderstandings of Lean is that it is a *no* inventory system. It is not. It requires inventory. A better way to say this is that it is a "minimal inventory system." The goal is to stock as little inventory as possible without impacting the customer today and to continue to improve the process and reduce inventory as your systems improve going forward. It's a journey.

Part of the inventory "rationalization" for Lean is a calculation for finished goods required (for both internal and external customers). This will be discussed in Chapter 3. If you are worried, once you calculate your rationalized inventory, build your inventory to a reasonable level over and above the calculated levels. This will be a one-time build, and you need only build inventory for the hedge time as you learn to run your cell. Most total-value flows start up and function rather smoothly after two or three days of learning curve, and the rationalized inventory should suffice. Keep in mind, the cell will be set up with inventory rationalized and the work standardized and documented, and you will be producing at some rate, even while going through the learning curve.

There will be another issue with inventory and its effects on the income statement and balance sheet as you move forward in the Lean process. If you are on the standard cost system, you will be using up your inventory and not buying as much replacement inventory, as you work through your excess inventories. As you work through the inventory, your cash flow will improve, but your income statement may look worse and reflect higher costs due to absence of line items for new raw material purchases to offset revenues. Note that *this is a temporary hit* on inventory and income statements, until the old inventory works out of the system. If you are not aware of this, your executives may be having apoplectic fits, when they first hear the "good news" on how the Lean conversion is going.

This brings you to another thing you will have to think about: getting the accounting and sales/marketing departments on board. Both departments will be crucial to the Lean success, because they deal with two critical items in any company, the dollars and the customers.

The orientation to the upcoming Lean events and change in philosophy can be done upfront, even before the production cell is established. Generally speaking, accounting managers worry the most as a company undergoes a Lean conversion (rightly so, as they deal with the dollars, the lifeblood), but they tend to be the greatest proponents after the Lean conversion is up and running. Lean accountants love the fact that with an actual cost system they can know monthly and quarterly results within hours after a period close.

Lean is not just a manufacturing–productivity–improvement process; it is a substantial operational and accounting change for your company. As you go

Lean, you will be shifting from standard cost accounting to an actual-period cost system. There are several excellent books that detail the accounting changes you will experience as you move forward in Lean. Start getting your accounting department, especially your chief financial officer (CFO), to read some of the current literature or attend some Lean accounting seminars. In our bibliography, we list several excellent publications. We would also recommend that your CFO or accounting manager seek out other Lean companies in your area and try to befriend a peer in the Leaned company. This will help him or her learn how life will change under Lean, and it will also provide an excellent sounding board for questions and "how to" scenarios.

When you are sending your CFO off for instruction in Lean, you may also want to take a look at who will be doing your internal communications (and training) about Lean. In some companies, the communication personnel in the marketing department may be "turf war" rivals to the human resources department. The internal branding of Lean requires a cooperative and unified effort. Also, for strategic communications to be successful, whoever does the communications must have a thorough grounding in employee relations. The strategy-driven organization must create an internal brand that treats the employee as a "priority customer." The goal is to get employee buy-in, involvement, and acceptance. Message is key when changing a culture.

As your company rolls out the Lean implementation, do not neglect the sales and marketing people. Sales people, in particular, become as pathetic as beaten puppies when they feel neglected. As the rumor mill and uninformed opinion picks up titbits about Lean, most sales people tend to get upset about the possibility of reduced inventories. "You cannot sell from an empty cart." Reduced inventory from a factory that currently has problems expediting "hot" orders and offers insufferable customer lead times as it is— that is a recipe for disaster. A salesperson, whose pay normally has little to do with inventory levels, does not see an abundance of inventory as an evil. These ever optimistic souls see a floor to ceiling stack of inventory as an opportunity for ready sales and commission checks.

The sales force must have enough information on Lean to be able to articulate its benefits for both the customer and the company. They must understand that Lean inventory rationalization covers the majority of historical shipments. Lean is calculated to cover normal day-in and day-out demands from normal customers, but abnormal demands are treated differently.

The larger, abnormal demands (an "LTO"—limited time offer—in this book and addressed in Chapters 5 and 14) normally ship at lead time. Having said this, the sales department also has the option to strip out all on-hand inventory to satisfy one large demand, but when it does so, all other incoming "normal" customer orders will then be at lead time. This is a sales choice under Lean. We are not sure why any company would want to punish a day-to-day customer this way, but sales controls the finished goods inventory. Normally, the idea of LTOs becomes a non-issue with Lean, given the shrinking lead times. Typically, from our experience, most lead times, in a company vigorously pursuing Lean, end up one-tenth to one-twentieth of what they were before Lean. Typical companies see this within one to three years. This will be evident to the sales force once the total-value flow and inventory kanbans kick into gear.

Sales must understand the advantages the reduced inventories and substantially reduced lead times enabled by the rationalized inventory bring to the customer. The rationalized inventory acknowledges historical demand patterns, and a safety factor is normally built into the equation. If you can ship at the 85th percentile of historical shipment quantities for each day of lead time it takes to replenish the product to inventory (typical way to look at safety factor which is discussed in this book), you are probably covering most demands you will encounter on a day-by-day basis. LTO orders are, by definition, abnormal demands—some companies simply call them abnormal demands for high volume stock items, and there is a cost in inventory, space, material handling, excess and obsolescence risk, etc., for holding inventory to cover the possibility of outlier abnormal demands. High customer shipment service levels that cover most order shipment possibilities come with a high cost. In today's financial environment, cash flow from rapidly turning inventory—and not high quantity, slow-turning inventory levels—are what will keep a company afloat.

With Lean, expectations are set with the customer, and there should be fewer surprises on deliveries. Generally, from our experience, on-time delivery, in most startup production cells, will begin to improve immediately. Depending on how vigorously and intelligently a company plans and supports a continuous improvement schedule, it could be possible to be regularly in the 95 percent to 98 percent shipping "on-time, complete" performance category within one to three years after start up. Normally, scheduling will not cause an order to go late. Since production signals are released to the production cell at the last possible moment, the scheduler will know exactly what orders are in queue. Late orders usually will result from a quality problem, late vendor delivery, or a machine reliability or maintenance issue.

If an order will be late or sales makes a decision to move one customer order ahead of a previously scheduled customer order, the affected customers can be identified and called proactively and told their "new" dates for shipment. No one wants to get the dreaded "where's my order" call from a past-due, pissed-off customer who had made arrangements with his end user customers based on information (and repeated assurances) that everything was moving along on time with your production schedule. From a customer perspective, communications on shipment status of orders should improve exponentially. On an hourly basis in the production cell, the scheduler or sales person should know the progress of the order. Progress is obvious, visible, and timely.

Unless a customer needs inventory all at once to consolidate for "container loads" for a ship or train or some such thing, the idea of LTOs will probably not be a problem. Practically speaking, most customers not shipping container loads probably cannot use all shipped LTO inventory at once. In one of the ironies of manufacturing, your factory, due to chronically late shipments or unreliable lead times, may be the cause of your customer's abnormally high order demands. They may be doing this to pressure you—knowing that you cannot deliver on time and threatening your company to eat part or all of the freight costs on the late shipment. If you achieve a track record of reliable shipping 98 percent of the time of complete orders made in a fraction of the lead times you currently have, your customer's ordering pattern may completely change.

Once confidence builds in your company as a supplier, you can work toward becoming a preferred provider. Predictable, short lead time, quality shipments can cement an ongoing, mutually beneficial relationship. Customers will be able to reduce their inventories—and space and obsolescence risk and handling, etc.—as your company excels at shipping what the customer ordered on time. Lean, by constantly being focused on taking waste and cost out of the product, will probably help you become the competitively priced supplier. By sharing inventory information, you may be able to seamlessly replenish their inventory via kanban signals. At a more advanced stage, your shipping department may even become a value-added profit center by private labeling and shipping kanban controlled stock as a "pass through" directly to the end-user.

The bottom line is this: your sales department must get on board and understand the Lean transformation to understand the potential value it also has to the customer. Your sales force should be in a position to lead a tour of current and potential customers and to explain how the processes work and potential benefits that can be mutually exploited. Internally, chronic merit badge handouts for successful, heroic expediting and "hot" stickers on every order that is released to the shop must cease. Within sales, efforts to sell one-off oddballs with unproven, alleged high margins trumpeted throughout the factory should not be the focus. They are wasteful and ruinous to a company.

As operations cleans up their bad habits and installs Lean, sales should be concentrating on filling the newly freed-up capacity with new volume of your core products. If emphasis is on new product development, freed manpower can staff these new production areas. Incremental sale gains come at the cost of materials alone. Your manpower is already in place due to your productivity gains. Lean can and should become a sales point for your marketing and sales departments. Sales must lead the way to partnership with the customers, armed with knowledge of both sides' mutual interests in Lean.

In times of market slowdowns, Lean can lead to considerations of "insourcing" to reduce material and product costs. Like adding new product lines in growth, making component parts you formerly bought may come at the cost of materials only. Worst case, in economic downturns, Lean may allow your company to minimize the number of temporary employees, reduce overtime, or forego backfilling employees in times of attrition.

As a reader who bought this book with plans to implement Lean in your factory or division, the assumption is that your executives and upper management staff are supportive of your plans. If this is not the case, you will have problems—both political and operational—as you try to move forward. If your president or CEO expresses little interest in the Lean implementation, how are you going to get "buy-in" from other department executives or management peers? Even worse, how will you handle the "nay sayers" and the "fifth column" types without the authority or power to do so?

You need to have this discussion with your upper management. Your CEO or president needs to be the one who leads the charge for change. You need your CEO or president to discuss strategy and implications of that strategy with the management in the factory or division. The management staff, in turn, need to communicate the change to their workers. Everyone needs to be on board. If the company is large enough to have an HR person or a communications person, that person will be a critical player in creating strategic communications for the internal audience. In smaller companies, the marketing manager may be responsible for internal communications, while the financial manager may double as HR, risk management, etc.

If people want to be on board but lack understanding of the task ahead, they should be given education, in whatever form and timeframe makes sense, on the tenets of Lean and the startup plans in the company or division. If people are having a hard time appreciating Lean and are in critical-path roles, they should be reassigned or moved to a noncritical role. The point is not to terminate people. The point is to mobilize and utilize people and encourage them to contribute to the success of the Lean conversion. Lean, in its essence, is a philosophy of manufacturing and a business strategy, and it is picked apart and selectively implemented at its peril. If employees want no buy-in or persist in protracted, damaging, vocal resistance to change, there is one rule: if no buy-in, they go "bye-bye."

In our experiences, both as managers and consultants, most companies that have successfully converted to Lean are more than willing to share experiences with companies starting out on the Lean conversion. When we worked for companies, we opened our factories to visitors for "show and tell" explanations on Lean. We sometimes allowed personnel from non-Lean companies to participate in kaizen events at our factories. It was an easy way for us, as the "teaching" company, to fill out kaizen teams with manpower, and it also gave non-Lean companies a learning opportunity for key personnel. This might be a strategy for your company: work with other Lean companies to mutual advantage. You will have to get a determination on insurance and liability issues up front, but, if these can be resolved, it is an excellent way to get employees, your champions, to learn. A search on the Internet, some networking with local production and inventory associations or manufacturing engineering groups or accounting associations, or contacts with your local business or chamber of commerce roundtables should get you contacts. Seeking out these Lean companies, making inquiries, and networking can be started now.

The final thing to think about by way of preparation is the concept of "takt time" and who will be responsible for gathering data required to see what your cell will need to produce to meet customer demand. Takt time is one of the core concepts in Lean and also the key concept that drives the heijunka scheduling of your newly created production cell.

One of the easiest ways to comprehend the term is to think of it as the rhythm of production that is needed to meet the customer demand in any given period. It is different from the cycle times your standard-cost accounting department or industrial engineer can cite for any given part. A cycle time, as you know it, may have nothing to do with meeting the customer requirement for that part. In Lean, the customer sets the required production rate or takt time.

For example, at its simplest, if you sell 500 units of product A per week, in a one-shift operation, you will need to make 100 units per day. To refine this further, only actual, planned "up time available" is divided by customer demand. This means that any planned maintenance down time or planned operator absence must be taken into account.

Applying this to the above example, let us assume that your 8-hour workday, minus lunch and breaks, is actually 7 hours and 10 minutes of production time. For most companies, when production time is really studied, they often find less work time available than they think they have. Waiting time, housekeeping problems, and process waste will see to this. Assuming a 7-hour and 10-minute day (430 minutes), the takt time becomes 430 minutes ÷ 100 units required per day, the takt time requires a production rhythm of producing 1 unit every 4.3 minutes or every 258 seconds. Within the cell, the activities of the various machines and work are coordinated (line balanced) so that they can produce 1 unit every 4.3 minutes. (Usually, in Lean, takt time is most commonly denominated in seconds, not minutes, to eliminate conversions: in this case, a product would have to be produced every 4.3 minutes or 258 seconds.) This is the market-driven production.

Who, in your organization, is in the best position to analyze your product demands and do the calculations to determine daily demand? It will require some analytical skills, good judgment, product knowledge, and access to databases from which to derive data. If your materials manager or product manager is new and does not have a "feel" yet, consider who in the organization does. This will be the key to inventory rationalization and reducing lead times.

In most companies, it would probably fall to the materials manager (or the function surrogate) to do the number-crunching analysis and come up with the data. In other companies, it might fall to both the materials manager and the marketing/sales manager to derive the numbers. (We have included spreadsheets and worksheet examples of what data to review in the rationalization process.) Once the numbers are established and the production cell starts up, it will be incumbent upon the sales/marketing team to update product shipment data and, based on their experienced knowledge or departmental planning, to recommend changes to the operations team in the inventory rationalization. Making the changes to the kanban cards, which drive the heijunkas, remains the responsibility of the operations/materials department. Takt time is what will drive productivity every day in the cell.

In the next chapter, we will discuss rationalizing inventories and determining candidates that are "stock-able" and those that are "made to order."

We will also touch upon methods of product classifications to keep sales/ marketing and operations personnel in sync with shipment and lead time expectations. Sample spreadsheets and worksheets will be included to help analyze the demand patterns of sold items. We will also begin to talk about how Lean inventories can be used as a sales tool to strengthen both customer and vendor ties.

Chapter 3

Rationalizing the Inventory

Since you have chosen the product line with which you want to begin the Lean process, the next two actions involve rationalizing the inventory and doing a "before" and "after" total-value-flow mapping exercise. Although these two actions can be done concurrently, because inventory analysis can take more time and the same key personnel may be involved in both activities, it may make sense to treat the inventory rationalization first.

Inventory, the readily visible manifestation of cash flow (read, "lifeblood") in a company, is normally a controversial topic in companies converting to Lean. The sales force will be the first to "sound the alarm" about the possibility of reduced inventories. The concerns will be twofold: (1) fear for a reduced level of customer service from a factory that already has problems expediting orders, and (2) the well-traveled sales bromide that "you can't sell from an empty wagon." The operations group, in a similar vein, will worry about future beatings from sales and management if inventories are reduced, and operations fails to deliver on significantly improved lead-time promises from the newly created cells. In the middle of this is the plant manager or anointed Lean champion, who is charged with transforming the factory. What is to be done? Let's discuss the relationships of inventory to various departments within a Lean company.

One of the common misconceptions about "Lean" is that it is almost exclusively an inventory and operations "system" with minimal involvement from other departments in the company. In some of the poorer implementations we have seen, operations gets the responsibility to implement "the system" as best they can, by their own efforts, while sales, marketing, engineering, and accounting chronicle and score all the shortcomings of the operations group's efforts. That's why it's a good idea to pick a high-volume, but secondary, product line to be the template production cell to prove out concepts and on which to learn.

Involve all departments in the establishment of the cell and the setup of the processes. This will reduce the amount of resistance and pave the way for company-wide implementation. Above all, you want your first product cell to be a success, a learning lab that becomes a cultural change agent. If you are going to have a successful company-wide Lean program, thinking needs to change. All departments will need to be aware of the cost of inventory and associated waste and what their responsibilities are regarding inventory.

If you are to be a successful Lean company, the marketing department or product manager will truly need to become the eyes, ears, and voice of the customer. Working with information from design engineering, the sales department, and the customer's application engineers, marketers or product-line managers will need to articulate customer requirements and coordinate the translation of these requirements into sellable product lines with reasonable expectations for both customer and factory. The "calculated enlightenment" of the marketing department or product-line manager must become the loyal opposition to the unbridled and undisciplined enthusiasm of the company's sales department.

The sales department needs to think in terms of total company profitability when it comes to sales. Too often, raw materials are bought and the ensuing fabricated inventory is stocked on the assumption that the sales group needs to have a readily available, full, product line in stock to ensure successful sales. This is wasteful of your lifeblood cash flow, and it reduces your sales force to the role of order takers and not salespeople. If the product is not in stock, sales will put pressure on expediting any type of order, regardless of margin implications and other waiting customer orders, to get the product on hand "at risk of losing the customer." The resulting expediting comes with many hidden costs. In fact, expediting becomes *the source* of many forms of waste in the factory. It enforces the truism that any salesperson can sell if margins are no barrier, and he or she "just gives the stuff away." Lean inventories will have to become part of the Lean sales strategy with their customers (more on this later).

The engineering departments, both design and applications, also have a role in Lean: to work with the operations department to design for manufacturability to the customer's specifications, with reduced process waste. In many companies, the engineering departments work almost independently of the operations departments. The engineering department designs something, creates the print specifications, and then "throws it over the wall" to manufacturing to figure out how to make it. The result, too often, is almost impossibly tight turning radii for machines, needlessly difficult tolerances in design specs, exotic fasteners, another "non-standard," single product die or casting, and safety coefficients for materials far exceeding any customer product application standards. The biggest waste comes with ill-advised product designs, which were derived from internal sales specifications with little customer-application engineering contact. These languish on the inventory shelves until they are aged properly, and then, they are thrown out in the annual "excess and obsolete" calculation at fiscal-year end.

The point of the above paragraphs is that Lean is a company-wide undertaking and responsibility for inventory is everyone's concern. The cost of inventory affects all departments. The metrics of Lean (to be discussed in Chapter 16) should reinforce this, and any management bonus payout scheme should take this into account. Although we will discuss metrics more in depth in Chapter 16, the following will offer insights on what the metrics should be: inventory turns should be the joint goal for operations and sales; reducing scrap on the production floor should be a joint goal for both engineering and operations; insuring sustainable margins on product lines should be a joint goal for marketing, sales, engineering, operations, and accounting. The days when the purchasing manager is paid a bonus on achieving a favorable purchase-price variance objective, or the salespeople are rewarded strictly on sales volume regardless of inventory build or margin erosion, or the purchasing agent exclusively is responsible for reducing material costs by beating up vendors on price, or the foremen are evaluated on asset utilization as an end in itself and not in the context of serving real customer demand have ended.

When it comes to inventory, the demand patterns for shipped end items normally tend to fit statistically into a bell-shaped curve. This can be a good starting point for analyzing your inventory and what you should and should not stock. Usually a relatively small number of end items make up the core items that are shipped on a regular basis. The greater numbers of end items ship less frequently or, in some cases, are limited to one or two shipments per year. Reviewing the ranked usage of the sold end items is a good beginning point for starting the rationalization of the inventory. (More on this and related topics in Chapter 4.)

Figure 3.1 with accompanying commentary gives some insights and prompts questions your group should be asking when trying to determine

Line no.	End item number	Volume in cases	# of cust	# of ords	Ord interval in days	Unit valuation	Extended sales dollars	Cum dollars	As %age of total sales	Mode ord qty	Mean ord qty	High ord qty	Low ord qty	Single ord qty <10
1	1081	21054	1	69	3.5	$ 50.34	$ 1,059,858	$ 1,059,858	18%	324	305	504	72	0
2	1076	20907	1	98	2.4	$ 47.82	$ 999,773	$ 2,059,631	35%	252	213	468	9	1
3	2021	14029	6	85	2.8	$ 40.43	$ 567,192	$ 2,626,824	45%	5	169	1056	1	42
4	1120	7093	1	151	1.6	$ 48.95	$ 347,202	$ 2,974,026	50%	36	47	138	5	3
5	1204	5415	1	33	7.3	$ 57.89	$ 313,474	$ 3,287,500	56%	144	164	240	81	0
6	1103	5798	1	31	7.7	$ 50.34	$ 291,871	$ 3,579,372	61%	108	193	396	72	0
7	8817	5346	3	109	2.2	$ 39.41	$ 210,686	$ 3,790,057	64%	48	51	128	4	2
8	8223	4462	12	113	2.1	$ 36.65	$ 163,532	$ 3,953,590	67%	10	39	281	2	14
9	3052	4600	5	130	1.8	$ 30.96	$ 142,416	$ 4,096,006	69%	36	12	108	1	13
10	2023	2480	4	83	2.9	$ 40.81	$ 101,209	$ 4,197,215	71%	30	31	114	1	15
11	8224	2439	11	106	2.3	$ 41.03	$ 100,072	$ 4,297,287	73%	10	23	114	1	30
12	3051	3085	4	81	3.0	$ 30.96	$ 95,512	$ 4,392,798	74%	48	40	144	4	17
13	60050	1290	4	108	2.2	$ 67.50	$ 87,075	$ 4,479,873	76%	5	12	81	1	73
14	1202	2491	8	78	3.1	$ 27.84	$ 69,349	$ 4,549,223	77%	20	32	180	1	14
15	1491	1306	7	37	6.5	$ 52.05	$ 67,977	$ 4,617,200	78%	24	35	96	2	2
16	3053	2077	5	90	2.7	$ 32.52	$ 67,544	$ 4,684,744	79%	32	23	64	4	26
17	4231	1764	2	11	21.8	$ 36.75	$ 64,827	$ 4,749,571	80%		221	310	194	0
18	60054	1214	1	7	34.3	$ 52.83	$ 64,136	$ 4,813,707	82%	197	173	244	1	1
19	60052	1031	2	19	12.6	$ 62.10	$ 64,025	$ 4,877,732	83%	81	62	108	27	0
20	60000	2007	1	118	2.0	$ 30.69	$ 61,595	$ 4,939,327	84%	20	17	100	2	40
21	8265	931	1	16	15.0	$ 54.70	$ 50,926	$ 4,990,252	85%	63	58	100	1	1
22	60051	731	4	80	3.0	$ 67.50	$ 49,343	$ 5,039,595	85%	2	9	108	1	66
23	3050	1464	2	46	5.2	$ 30.96	$ 45,325	$ 5,084,920	86%	45	32	45	2	14
24	1113	900	13	65	3.7	$ 46.39	$ 41,751	$ 5,126,671	87%	4	14	66	1	35
25	1097	859	17	116	2.1	$ 48.19	$ 41,395	$ 5,168,067	88%	2	7	60	1	76
26	8867	602	1	9	26.7	$ 56.30	$ 33,893	$ 5,201,959	88%	36	67	168	1	1
27	8222	773	12	79	3.0	$ 43.40	$ 33,548	$ 5,235,507	89%	5	10	48	1	48
28	9834	519	1	8	30.0	$ 55.24	$ 28,670	$ 5,264,177	89%		75	97	53	0
29	2132	754	1	14	17.1	$ 38.00	$ 28,652	$ 5,292,829	90%	37	54	85	27	0
72	4613	55	1	2	120.0	$ 89.15	$ 4,903	$ 5,885,633	99%		28	30	25	0
73	4614	56	1	2	120.0	$ 83.33	$ 4,666	$ 5,890,300	99%	55	55	55	55	0
74	4616	124	1	1	240.0	$ 34.10	$ 4,228	$ 5,894,528	99%	124	124	124	124	0
75	4629	84	1	1	240.0	$ 46.02	$ 3,866	$ 5,898,394	99%	84	84	84	84	0
76	1101	76	3	14	17.1	$ 47.62	$ 3,619	$ 5,902,013	100%	3	5	30	1	12
77	4645	78	1	1	240.0	$ 46.09	$ 3,595	$ 5,905,608	100%	78	78	78	78	0
78	4648	70	1	1	240.0	$ 50.50	$ 3,535	$ 5,909,143	100%	70	70	70	70	0
79	4649	75	1	1	240.0	$ 46.76	$ 3,507	$ 5,912,650	100%	75	75	75	75	0
80	60057	89	1	1	240.0	$ 39.34	$ 3,501	$ 5,916,151	100%	89	89	89	89	0
81	4652	70	1	1	240.0	$ 49.43	$ 3,460	$ 5,919,612	100%	70	70	70	70	0
82	4658	50	1	1	240.0	$ 68.13	$ 3,407	$ 5,923,018	100%	50	50	50	50	0
							$ 5,923,018							

Figure 3.1 Product family "X" sales data for sales year ending 12/31.

what products should be stocked on kanban, what products should have "pacing" part number items stocked to allow for quicker delivery, and which products should be sold at full lead time without any stocking of inventory.

Materials, sales, and marketing (or the product manager) should meet to decide inventory-stocking classifications. It must be noted that when the group meets, it is not a democracy when it comes to the final decision. All departments must give input and have their voices heard, but marketing or the product manager, charged with the strategic importance of the product lines, gets the deciding vote.

There are many ways to review inventories and shipment histories to determine what should and should not be in stock. If you do not have reliable historical data, you may have to improvise. There may also be part numbers that do not neatly fit into shipment patterns, which you may decide to stock. For example, if you use specialized computer chips or arrays or specialty items like rare earth magnets, and these critical items are single sourced, you may have to get into the monopolistic vendor source's queue. Transoceanic container load parameters and lead times also figure into inventory calculations.

In Figure 3.1, we have ranked all product family "X" end-item part numbers by extended value of shipments by part number. This is the product family you are thinking about for your first total-value-flow and production cell. When you rank the part numbers this way, you can see the cumulative value and percentage of total sales readily. You will notice that a very small number of part numbers will quickly become the majority of all end-item part numbers sold. In our example, 82 end-item part numbers make up our table. When the reader gets to the part number 60050, the thirteenth on the list, he or she will note that the ranked part numbers have already reached the 75th percent level of cumulative value for shipped end-item part numbers within the product family. This means that the balance of the 69 end-item part numbers represent only 24 percent of the total sales volume for this product family. This may be a valuable starting point for determining what you should stock.

Referring to the same table data, let's do some further thinking "out loud." There are questions you must ask before you finalize your list of stocking candidates.

The first question that must be asked is: Are any of the volume-leading, end-item part numbers being phased out or replaced by newer part numbers? If so, is the cut-over immediate? If not, what are the projected volumes for the old number being phased out and the newer replacement part number?

The next question is: Are any of the shipments for end-item part numbers for customers you no longer have? Or, were the shipments "one-time" and non-repeating shipments to address specific customer demands (e.g., your customer opened a new warehouse, or your customer had a specific, abnormal demand for container-load quantities for a particular customer, etc.)?

When you add other delimiters to the data, you may see the data in a different light. For example, if you look at part number 60000, you will notice that only one customer orders this part number, but the customer has ordered it 118 times. The average order quantity is 17, and the mode order quantity is 20. In this case, if your lead time to produce the product is greater than 2 days, you may want to consider putting this part number in stock. (*Note*: When you are reviewing part number history, "mode" and "mean" give more considered information than the use of "median;" median tends to mask real activity by its blending aspect.)

Order interval (days between orders) may also give a specific view of historical shipments. If you see a particular customer ordering large volumes on an erratic basis, be aware his ordering pattern may change as your lead time improves. This might be a customer relations breakthrough for your sales department. In another case, if a customer always gives order releases significantly in advance of the projected ship dates and your lead times to produce in the cell are less than his desired lead time, it might be pointless to stock his end-item part numbers. This might be another sales opportunity to sell Lean to this specific customer.

The sales-history reviewers can also look at order quantities "greater than" or "less than" for insights. It is always good to be aware of "highs," "lows," or "zero demand periods" to discern any pattern. Some companies review means and their relationships to standard deviations to see how "well-behaved" certain part numbers are. (The lower the standard deviation to mean ratio, the better, e.g., a standard deviation of 2.6 shows high volatility to mean, i.e., a value of 0.6 shows low volatility in shipments to the mean.) Ultimately, your team decides what works for your company.

Unless you are in one of the most advanced Lean companies, most Lean inventories work on the assumption that regularly shipped, high-volume end items need to be available from stock, lower-volume end items less frequently shipped need to have reasonable lead times, and custom or exceedingly high-volume single order "outlier" quantities will have full lead-time implications. What makes up these various class definitions will be the joint decision of the marketing or product manager, the materials group, and the sales department. Actual demand data, or, in the case of new products, the sales forecast, will be the basis for making these decisions. (Once the total-value flow is up and running, it will be necessary to periodically review and adjust inventory levels and create new cards based on changes in demand patterns.) You should be aware that as a plus of rationalizing the inventory, all lead times will usually reduce significantly and customer service (as measured by on-time shipment performance) should significantly improve over time.

The resultant decisions defining what to stock and what not to stock need clarification by assignment of understandable names. For the purposes of this book and within your company, going forward, refer to the stratification of inventory by the following terms:

1. *Kanban* (a Japanese word indicating a replacement signal for inventory, usually in the form of a printed card used in conjunction with a "heijunka" or scheduling board) for stocked end and component items or stocked raw materials
2. *MTO* for "made to order" with some lead-time implications
3. *Custom* for non-stock end item with full lead-time implications
4. *LTO* for "limited time offer" which is an end item with an unusually high demand and lead-time implications based on quantities ordered

End-item part numbers involved in the various classifications will be marked by coding within whatever inventory/sales system your company uses. This keeps sales, operations, and information to the customer in sync on what shipment expectations are. Let me elaborate on each classification.

(Important distinction you need to understand: even though we talk more narrowly of kanban classification as referring specifically to "stocked" part numbers—either end-item, shippable part numbers or key component or raw material part numbers, the term kanban can be used to refer generally to the cards slotted on the heijunka boards to schedule production. All production scheduled in a Lean factory is done by scheduling kanbans. These kanban cards can be for "stock" or MTO or LTO or custom. This gets back to the basic definition of a kanban as a "signal." Everything being scheduled in a factory is done by some type of kanban or signal. It will get clearer as we go along.)

Some people with only a cursory knowledge of Lean are surprised to learn that a level of inventory is stocked in a Lean company. These same people seem to think that when an order is received in the factory, the vendors are beaten up to ship the raw material inventory "just in time" to the factory to make the product and then the factory ships the order to a customer. All the benefits of Lean accrue to the buyer and the vendor gets little by way of return. Both of these assumptions are wrong. Lean is not a zero inventory system; it is a minimal-inventory system in which each company will have its own minimal level based on their constraints. Vendors also derive benefits from a client company's rationalization of their inventories.

In your Lean startup company, inventory is stocked for several reasons. First of all, there is a need to uncouple your factory, by way of buffer inventory, from the "wild swings of the direct marketplace." If this is not done, every order is a crisis and an expedite nightmare. Minimal inventory serves as a smoothing bulwark in order to plan greater needs and availability of inventory, to negotiate with vendors on a non-frenetic basis concerning inventory, and to have some stable means of communicating production needs and expectations from production planning to the production cell, the warehouse, and the inside sales departments. Stocked inventory also serves, as we said above in the discussion of classification schemes, to help clarify shipment expectations among the sales and operations departments and the customer.

Kanban or, stocked inventory, can be one of two types. It can be an end-item part number (commonly referred to as an "SKU") kept on-hand, whose stocking levels are based on historical data and which ships immediately to a customer. It can also be a component or raw-material part number that goes into the stocked end item, or it is a critical component (due to pacing item lead time) part number stocked to reduce overall product delivery lead times for MTO orders. Where the finished-goods stocking levels and part numbers are determined by reviewing sales shipment data, at the component level, the inventory levels are also determined by reviewing usage data history, multiplied by the "where used" engineering bill of materials information. For custom orders requiring non-stocked (non-kanban) part numbers, confirmation from the vendors on lead times is required per occurrence of order.

The kanban population of stocked items is fixed by information printed on the kanban card. Once kanban populations are fixed, the quantity remains the same until the next inventory review. Inventory reviews for cell startups are done initially at three to six months, and the reviewers are members from the marketing department or the product manager, sales, and materials group. At that time, stocked levels are tweaked as needed and new kanban cards printed reflecting the new stocking levels. Normally, these early reviews, if the rationalization was done well, represent affirmations that things are going along reasonably well and that "tweaks" and not wholesale changes to the kanban cards are required.

The reviews focus on newly available demand data for the months encompassed in the shipping history since the first kanban cards were printed. The product review with marketing, sales, and materials departments focuses on demand changes at the shipped end-item level. The marketing department or product manager can also discuss specific needs for product launches or special marketing programs targeting specific products. Based on this information and time frame of expected change, the materials group may have options on what they do with the kanban cards. Actual kanban card changes, however, should be done only when it is absolutely necessary to do so. Inventory is captive cash flow. The materials group will be responsible for bringing the component kanbans in line with stocked end-item inventory levels and inventory classifications.

Before we go any further in the discussion of kanbans, one point needs to be clarified. Lean uses both stock kanban cards and "non-stock" kanban cards. As we said above, the kanbans are merely the signal to produce something. The database coding of the end-item part numbers, the manufactured components, and the purchased components, and the order classifications will determine whether the existing, circulating kanbans are sufficient to cover the order to be scheduled or whether the production control department will have to print other, "non-stock," one-use kanbans.

Stock kanban cards will be for stocked end items, stocked manufactured components or assemblies, or stocked purchased assemblies or raw materials. Purchased parts and manufactured parts "not stocked" will also require a one-time use kanban card to be printed as needed per order. All production orders scheduled in the cell, both at the end-item level and the component or raw-material level, will be governed by kanban cards. In summary, for both manufactured end items and component or purchased raw materials, you will have cards for stocked part numbers, high-volume, abnormal demand (LTO) part numbers, or non-stocked manufactured or purchased component or raw material (custom or ordered each time).

Every company starting out with kanban signals and heijunka boards should have physical kanban cards. You may read in literature that the ultimate goal is to get rid of kanban cards and have electronic signals or right-sized conveyances and containers replace the kanban cards. In this scenario, when the production cell is presented with an electronic kanban signal or physical right-sized empty container that serves as a signal, they simply make parts, and kanban cards become superfluous to the whole process. Whether or not you ultimately have kanban cards, you still have to understand the kanban as signal and have a rationalized inventory to support that signal. Start with kanban cards.

Depending on your company's creativity and knowledge of Lean, there will be many options for managing inventory and scheduling production down the road. For the purposes of this book, companies starting out in Lean need the discipline and learning curve experience that kanban cards represent. People need to be trained in Lean ways, and kanban cards can be an instrumental and very visual tool toward that end.

Following are examples of various types of kanban cards. Note the information on the cards, how the information is organized, and the depth of detail offered to the workers (Figures 3.2 and 3.3).

The format for kanban-card information tends to be the same for all types of cards, whether stock or non-stock. Usually there are two common formats with three segments for the information presented: a section for vendor or internal supplier information, a section for part number information controlled by the kanban card, and a section detailing disposition for part created on the kanban card. The sections can be arranged left to right or top to bottom. Either way will work. It will depend on how you create your kanban-card print program.

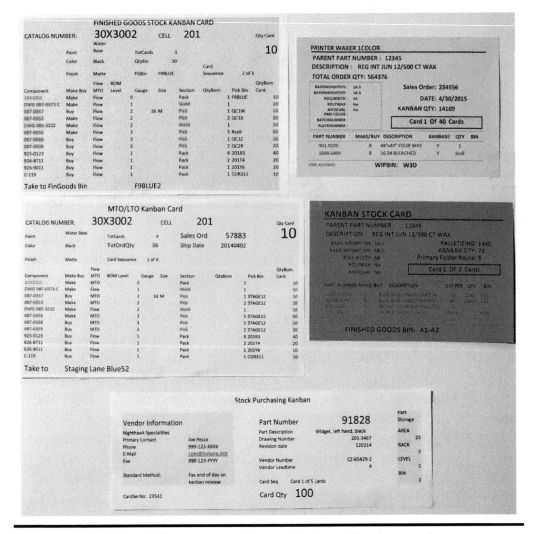

Figure 3.2 Illustrates different types, sizes, and colors of kanban cards.

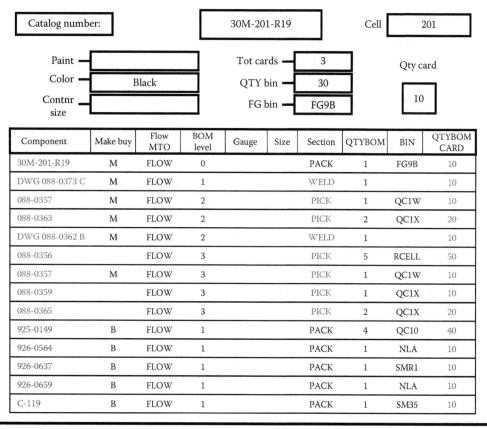

Catalog number:			30M-201-R19			Cell		201

Paint —
Color — Black
Contnr size —

Tot cards — 3
QTY bin — 30
FG bin — FG9B

Qty card

10

Component	Make buy	Flow MTO	BOM level	Gauge	Size	Section	QTYBOM	BIN	QTYBOM CARD
30M-201-R19	M	FLOW	0			PACK	1	FG9B	10
DWG 088-0373 C	M	FLOW	1			WELD	1		10
088-0357	M	FLOW	2			PICK	1	QC1W	10
088-0363	M	FLOW	2			PICK	2	QC1X	20
DWG 088-0362 B	M	FLOW	2			WELD	1		10
088-0356		FLOW	3			PICK	5	RCELL	50
088-0357	M	FLOW	3			PICK	1	QC1W	10
088-0359		FLOW	3			PICK	1	QC1X	10
088-0365		FLOW	3			PICK	2	QC1X	20
925-0149	B	FLOW	1			PACK	4	QC10	40
926-0564	B	FLOW	1			PACK	1	NLA	10
926-0637	B	FLOW	1			PACK	1	SMR1	10
926-0659	B	FLOW	1			PACK	1	NLA	10
C-119	B	FLOW	1			PACK	1	SM35	10

Figure 3.3   Illustrates an assembly stock kanban card.

Kanban cards can vary in color (which can be a meaningful visual signal), but they all tend to be uniform in dimensions within a classification. As the kanbans are reusable until they are changed via a review process, it is recommended that they be laminated (inexpensive, minimal-mil, plasticized coating) to eliminate the need for constant reprinting of paper card stock. One-time-use kanbans for make-to-order and custom parts and products do not need to be laminated.

There are other information fields that you should note on the cards. How they figure into the use of the cards to actually schedule the cell will be discussed later in depth. For now, notice the following information given on the cards: (1) each card gives the quantity to be produced per card, (2) each card has information for total number of cards and total quantity of production controlled by the cards, (3) the purchasing agent has all vendor information available on the card to purchase, (4) the warehouse picker has information available for quantity to be picked, bin locations from which picked, and cell to where parts should be delivered, and (5) information is available to the material mover to take finished product to either a bin or a shipping or further processing lane. As needed, particular information is supplied to the operator to assist in the manufacture of the part number.

All this information probably either already resides in a typical manufacturing requirements planning (MRP) system in the engineering or inventory modules. If MRP-system information is lacking, an Excel file–driven database can easily allow linking or adding information to any downloaded system database information. Your database will need to have fields covering all the information that appears on the kanban cards. If complete information resides only in an Excel file, other user departments will need to have access to the information via a read-only intranet access. Sales and accounting, in particular, will need to understand end-item classifications and what constitutes an LTO.

Almost counterintuitively in a computer-oriented work world, the forms and the defined process cause the kanban–heijunka process to function in a very understandable, low-tech way: human involvement replaces sophisticated, high-tech computer algorithms for scheduling the cells. After establishing cells, most companies turn off or simply ignore the MRP-scheduling shop floor-dispatch list-labor reporting portion of their existing software system for the new cells.

The forms and defined process also help to "democratize" operations knowledge and allow for interchangeability of people and cross-training. There is no computer "black box" that runs your factory schedule. Actual judgment, defined processes, and inventory rules replace the mystery of what the scheduler person does. No longer will the factory come to its knees when the one "key" person goes on vacation or the computer "is down." Instead, many multi-trained and capable employees will step forth to fill the talent and knowledge gap, and manufacturing can occur as long as your machines work.

Once you understand how the cards are used, the printed cards and a scheduling board (heijunka board in the Lean texts) will be all you will need to begin running your cell. The basic inventory, bill of material, engineering, accounting, and sales modules probably already exist in your current system, and you should be able to use them to populate information into your Excel-Access database files to create the kanban cards. We will discuss system requirements in more detail as we move along in the book.

In the next chapter, we will get into the details of inventory rationalization and suggestions for setting inventory levels.

Chapter 4

Kanban Signals

Rationalizing your inventory does many things: (1) improves your business unit's cash flow, (2) reduces total inventory costs, (3) eliminates the traditional wastes associated with nonrationalized inventory—constant expediting, cycle counting, cost of multiday fiscal inventories (and lost production time) to reset financial records, financial surprises of inventory change, exposure to excess and obsolete charges, expanding mezzanines or rental space to house inventory, unnecessary handling, etc., (4) sets internal and external expectations for shipments for sales, operations, and customers, (5) allows the sales department to establish a longer-term relationship with customers based on substantial improvement in on-time delivery and mutual benefits of reduced inventories, and (6) allows the purchasing department to develop more substantive and mutually beneficial relationships with vendors. Your company, your customers, and your vendors all benefit.

Of all the reasons for rationalizing your inventory, the setting of internal and external expectations on deliveries among sales, operations, and customers probably goes the farthest to improve quality of life for all concerned. Once an element of predictability is introduced into the process, the frantic phone calls, curses, and management heavy-handedness due to missed shipment dates are minimized. Facts—not unsubstantiated accusations or endless mulling of the "who shot John" questions—based on metrics and documented causes start to rule the day. As you fix processes, problems tend not to repeat, and life becomes better each day.

In factories where inventories are not rationalized, you can see evidence of problems on a cursory tour of the machining, processing, and assembly work centers. In one visited factory, there were flame decals on work orders. When there were competing time requirements on the same factory resources for other work orders, the "hotter" work orders had two flames. At a point in time, all work orders at the machines had flame decals on them, and on-time performance was not improving, while expediting costs were going through the roof.

In other non-Lean factories, on a quick walkthrough, you will see skids or totes of parts in the work center areas awaiting processing time. How the orders are run, in whatever sequence, is usually left up to the judgment of the foreman of the area. The foreman, accustomed to being beaten up in monthly management meetings for productivity and utilization percentages, consolidates like orders and runs them to keep productivity and utilization percentages up. The "other" parts, which are more troublesome—either due to long setup times or the troublesome nature of the part—sit until an expediter tells the foreman there is a crisis. So much for any thought of flow.

The classifications of orders (identified in the computer by coding associated with end-item part number) by the names of "kanban" (stocked), "MTO" (made to order), and "custom" help set the expectations, and there is a policy and philosophy of manufacturing behind the names to support it. Quantities ordered of the stocked, kanban part number determine whether or not it is considered to be an LTO ("limited-time offer"—exceptionally high-order quantity of a normally stocked and shipped part number). What defines an "LTO" can be as simple as a rule that an order quantity equal to or exceeding 150 percent of a single kanban card quantity is considered an abnormal demand. This limit should be defined for the sales department.

Order shipment history, order shipment quantities, and order shipment intervals are keys to setting the inventory levels. The resulting inventory classifications, reflected in the end-item part numbers making up the shipment data, are agreed to by the marketing, sales, and materials departments. Safety stock is built into the equation as needed. The Lean process involving heijunkas (scheduling boards) and kanban cards (authorization signals to manufacture or buy) ensures that the kanban cards circulate and inventory is routinely replenished.

The types of kanban cards printed—stock, MTO, LTO, and custom—are based on the assumption that you need to consistently service your loyal customers who support your business. By looking at individual order quantities and intervals between orders, you stand a better chance of serving the customers who support your business day to day. By using the various classifications, a safety mechanism is in place so that one exceptional-quantity order from a customer (an LTO) will not wipe out the normal stock levels established to support shipping-history demand patterns.

Having said all the above, sales, and not manufacturing or production control, decides which customer gets the parts coming out of the cells. It is understood that production's internal customer is the sales department. If parts are diverted from a loyal customer, sales will have the information upfront to communicate to the loyal customer the ensuing lead time for any future shipments. By setting expectations on shipments, communications improve.

In order to get to the part number classifications, you will have to do an analysis and ranking of your end-item, part number shipment data. When you use shipment history data, use shipment data that are representative of your current business. If the current-period data are not representative, use quarterly or semiannual data that are representative, and then annualize the numbers. Take out discontinued part numbers. Be cognizant of seasonality and trends. If there is a seasonality date for inventory buildup, make note of that and add it into the calculation conversation. If you had a significant one-time order, an outlier, which will never repeat, take it out of the data. If one-time orders from many customer sources are common in your business, leave them in the data. The spreadsheet in Figure 4.1 is an example of how to organize and review the data.

In most companies, the materials manager or production and inventory control manager is the obvious person to do the initial number crunching. This person can do the first draft on shipment history data, organize the data for review, and then present the final information to the sales and marketing departments for final decision making. Remember that the decision for inventory should be a three-way agreement with sales, marketing, and the materials department. Once the finished-goods part numbers are chosen for stock kanbans and the balance are designated as MTO or custom, the burden of work for coding and printing the cards is up to the materials manager or the production and inventory control manager.

The effort you put into analyzing the initial data for the kanban startup quantities will be rewarded. Since you will have to review stock quantities and new demand patterns periodically, getting good data to start the process off will mean that subsequent reviews should be tweaks rather than a complete "redo." Since cards will have to be reprinted for inventory changes by part number for status changes, this will also ensure that you are not printing and laminating a complete inventory deck every time you have a review. Having said this, keep in mind that customers and customer patterns

Kanban ABC analysis of product family "X"

A   Equals kanbaned finished goods part numbers
B   Pacing component part number to be kanbaned to meet 3-day order to shipping lead time
C   Items in red to be phased out within next 6 months
C   Balance of part numbers in family not highlighted will be MTO with quoted lead time

End-item part number	Qty of units sold	Sales price per unit	Extended sales dollars	Cum dollars of sales	Dollar value as a percent of total sales dollars	# of cust	# of ords	Frequency of ords in average days interval between ords	Mode	Mean	Std dev	High	Low	# of ords <10 shpg qty	85%ile service level qty	95% service level qty	Kanban qty	# of Kanban cards	LTO Qty level
5144	647	$ 34.40	$ 22,257	$ 22,257	12%	8	43	5.6	5	15.0	16.3	60	2	23	31	41	20	2	30
5143	465	$ 35.68	$ 16,591	$ 38,848	22%	7	30	8.0	10	15.5	14.1	50	1	11	30	38	20	2	30
9148	1058	$ 14.95	$ 15,817	$ 54,665	30%	3	42	5.7	30	25.2	22.3	129	5	8	48	61	30	2	45
5147	181	$ 83.25	$ 15,068	$ 69,733	39%	4	30	8.0	2	6.0	6.1	25	1	22	12	16	10	2	15
5151	402	$ 34.40	$ 13,829	$ 83,562	47%	6	45	5.3	10	8.9	5.9	30	1	21	15	18	15	2	23
9147	1063	$ 12.05	$ 12,809	$ 96,371	54%	4	51	4.7	10	20.8	22.1	144	1	9	43	56	30	2	45
5168	17	$ 32.85	$ 558	$ 96,930	54%	2	4	60.0	5	4.3	1.0	5	3	4	5	6			
5169	28	$ 36.50	$ 1,022	$ 97,952	55%	3	13	18.5	1	2.2	1.5	5	1	13	4	5			
9160	48	$ 16.15	$ 775	$ 98,727	55%	3	16	15.0	1	3.0	3.9	15	1	14	7	9			
4169	15	$ 87.50	$ 1,313	$ 100,039	56%		8	30.0	2	1.9	0.4	2	1	8	2	2			
4176	209	$ 41.00	$ 8,569	$ 108,608	61%	3	21	11.4	1	10.0	12.1	50	1	12	22	29			
5145	62	$ 42.40	$ 2,629	$ 111,237	62%	5	20	12.0	2	3.1	3.0	12	1	18	6	8			
5146	12	$ 41.86	$ 502	$ 111,740	62%	2	7	34.3	1	1.7	1.1	4		7	3	3			
5142	129	$ 26.00	$ 3,354	$ 115,094	64%	4	14	17.1	10	9.2	5.3	15	1	4	15	18			
9141	534	$ 14.95	$ 7,983	$ 123,077	69%	3	31	7.7	10	17.2	13.5	75	5	5	31	39			
5141	41	$ 88.25	$ 3,618	$ 126,695	71%	5	17	14.1	1	2.4	2.2	6	1	17	5	6			
4189	4	$ 36.76	$ 147	$ 126,842	71%	2	2	120.0	2	2.0	0.0	2	2	2	2	2			
5140	103	$ 83.25	$ 8,575	$ 135,417	75%	5	30	8	1	3.4	2.7	12	1	28	6	8			
5140	512	$ 13.75	$ 7,040	$ 142,457	79%	5	40	6.0	10	12.8	9.6	45	2	14	22	28			
4192	23	$ 64.71	$ 1,488	$ 143,945	80%	2	16	15.0	2	1.4	0.5	2	1	16	2	2			
4195	10	$ 59.67	$ 597	$ 144,542	81%	1	1	240.0	10	10.0	0.0	10	10	1	10	10			
4197	41	$ 27.76	$ 1,138	$ 145,680	81%	2	23	10.4	1	1.8	1.9	3	1	22	4	5			
4199	21	$ 38.70	$ 813	$ 146,493	82%	1	16	15.0	1	1.3	0.5	2	1	16	2	2			
9153	159	$ 14.95	$ 2,377	$ 148,870	83%	1	16	15.0	10	9.9	4.5	20	2	4	14	17			
5153	24	$ 88.25	$ 2,118	$ 150,988	84%	4	18	13.3	1	1.3	0.6	3	1	18	2	2			
5154	54	$ 36.43	$ 1,967	$ 152,955	85%	2	7	34.3	10	7.7	3.5	10	1	3	11	13			
5152	552	$ 12.05	$ 6,652	$ 159,607	89%	2	24	10.0	10	23.0	19.3	71	1	4	42	54			
5152	22	$ 83.25	$ 1,832	$ 161,438	90%	4	12	20.0	1	1.8	1.6	6	1	12	3	4			
5149	123	$ 24.45	$ 3,007	$ 164,446	92%	3	27	8.9	5	4.6	2.5	10	1	25	7	9			
5150	210		$ -	$ 164,446	92%	4	29	8.3	10	7.2	6.8	24	1	19	14	18			
5148	123	$ 87.38	$ 10,748	$ 175,193	98%	4	22	10.9	1	5.6	8.7	33	1	18	14	19			
9192	245	$ 17.61	$ 4,314	$ 179,508	100%	3	24	10.0	11	10.2	6.1	33	1	7	16	20			
			$ 179,508																

Figure 4.1   Kanban ABC analysis of product line A.

will change forcing your business to change; hence, your kanban cards will change. Order data must be periodically reviewed.

There are several scenarios that we would caution against. First of all, do not let your computer system drive your inventory policy and part number selections. Some of the MRP-type programs have built-in algorithms that calculate economic order quantities, period-of-supply quantities, or supply a standard deviation based on mean usage data to determine stocking quantities. Without the necessary human review to go with the data scrubbing, you could be ordering or stocking inventory that is not needed.

First and foremost, the whole inventory process should be understandable to the people who will be formulating the cards. For this same reason, we do not advocate having a statistician determine inventory quantities. The people you have in house doing the same job now should be able to derive the data. If you get too insistent on getting the "right" numbers, you can, after a protracted period of time, end up being "precisely incorrect" rather than "approximately correct." Your markets change. Your inventory will follow your markets. You do not want to get into "paralysis by analysis" and never get started with your cell. You can always make things more complicated as you advance in experience—if this is needed. Most companies will not need this level of sophistication once the total-value flows are established. The fact is that you will not probably have a statistician who understands Croston method or Poisson model distributions as an inventory or production control clerk. The people who do the job every day should have a basic knowledge of how the numbers are derived and have the ability to understand underlying assumptions. Strive for an uncomplicated, but effective, use of statistics.

On the above-referenced spreadsheet, you will see end-item part numbers with demand data showing, in descending order: sales generated by part number, percentage of total sales represented, mean usage, mode usage, standard deviation, highest order quantity, number of order quantities less than ten, number of orders shipped, number of distinct customers, and average-days intervals between orders. This should give the reviewing personnel enough information to determine what is kanban, what is MTO, and what is custom.

What may not be showing on the presented historical data are new products that have not yet taken wing or new product introductions. When taking final votes on what to designate as kanban, the marketing department's or product manager's vote should trump sales in the case of ties. While sales may have enthusiasm and optimism, the marketing person or product manager should have the facts and plans for the slow or new part numbers.

The materials department offers input to the review, but marketing gets the conclusive vote.

Since the "80/20" rule probably applies in most companies, the decision may be nothing more than drawing a line under the last descending part number (either in dollar-volume or unit-volume sort) that warrants kanban (stocking) status. If this does not make sense, list the end-item part numbers that should be stocked. The only caveat is that inventory is cash flow, and some of the lower volume part numbers probably will not need to be stocked. If a part number has many zero demand periods, it is probably MTO. If the demand pattern shows erratic shipment intervals or standard deviations much greater than the mean demand, they should probably be MTO. Be aware that seasonal or trend data may be skewed, and the marketing department or product manager may have to supply judgment in lieu of demand data. Keep in mind that all end-item part numbers will benefit from the reduced lead times and increased productivity that will result from the created total-value flow. As we mentioned above, in a startup Lean conversion, lead times, given an on-going and vigorous kaizen schedule, may reduce to one-tenth to one-twentieth of starting values within the first three years.

Once the list is agreed to, the preparation of the final numbers and calculation of any safety stock will become the responsibility of the materials manager or production control person. By using a bell curve sigma or safety factor times the mean shipment value, the safety stock can be established as a service level—after taking total-value-flow lead time into account. As a general rule, if you are unsure of the safety stock or service level factor, it is perfectly acceptable to err on the high side. If this gives you added comfort as you start with the Lean total-value flow, know that you will have to review and reset numbers as needed three to six months after start up. Just keep in mind that inventory is money.

Setting safety stock or service level tends to be a sticking point for companies trying to rationalize their inventory. There is no *one* correct answer for this issue. We think it works best for someone familiar with your inventory to review the data given on the spreadsheets and then make a decision. Key components to review are mean usage, median value, mode value, interval of orders, zero period usage, minimums for purchase or manufacture, and replenishment lead time.

We would urge against "black box" answers; part of the rationalization of inventory is to make the thought process of how the inventory values were derived available to external and internal sales and marketing personnel, to allow them to make intelligent decisions when talking to customers. You will have to have the person most familiar with your inventory (probably the materials manager or production and inventory control manager) pick a starting point. We would suggest a considered service level by end-item part number. The only "across the board" solutions might apply to part numbers within a classification—if this makes sense. If in doubt, we would recommend the inventory person discuss any questions with the marketing or product manager person.

If you used a service-level approach to inventory, it may be more understandable to the people who deal with the customers. For example, you set your service level at 85 percent (mean usage times standard deviation factor at 85 percent of bell curve), and your lead time is three days to replenish your stock; this would probably be safe and a good choice (i.e., one day of stock at eighty-fifth percentile value for each day of actual production lead time). The mean or mode values for shipment history probably best represent what an individual order quantity will be. Most probably, you will not get normal orders flowing in at the eighty-fifth percentile level on three successive orders. You also have a built-in inventory-buffering mechanism in the LTO classification, which is treated separately with its own lead time.

You have seen examples of shipment data for all products within a product family. You may also follow this method to look at the dollar-ranked, specific-product part number shipment history to set the kanban level. Sort the data by shipment quantity (and ascending dollars) and see what the order quantity is at the eighty-fifth percentile point in the ranked sales. Use this value per day of lead time to establish your kanban population. If this is easier than a standard deviation factor, use this. Both will get you in the ball park and started with the kanban process (Figure 4.2).

Your sales department may be the lone holdout against the inventory and service-level plan. Salespeople always get nervous with reduced inventory plans. What they need to keep in mind is threefold: (1) as productivity increases with Lean, lead times normally go down significantly (from our experience, a 90–95 percent improvement in total lead time), (2) over time, on-time delivery should regularly hover above the 95 percent on-time delivery to promised date, and (3) communication to the customer on order status questions can be made immediately. Your sales department will need to become sellers of "Lean" as well as the product, and this will be discussed later in Chapter 16.

In most companies, the LTO level is set at 125–150 percent of a single kanban card quantity. The selected number in units becomes a data field value visible to sales. If the order quantity is equal to or exceeds the LTO

	End-item part number	Shipped quantity	Shipment date	Invoiced dollars	Cumulative sales dollars	Cumulative percentage of total sales volume
1	60001	200	10112014	3600		One-time outlier: Exclude from calculation
2	60001	2	7032014	$ 52	$ 52	1%
3	60001	3	8162014	$ 78	$ 130	1%
4	60001	5	6292014	$ 130	$ 260	3%
5	60001	8	1082014	$ 200	$ 460	5%
6	60001	8	9222014	$ 200	$ 660	6%
7	60001	9	10282014	$ 225	$ 885	9%
8	60001	9	1012014	$ 225	$ 1,110	11%
9	60001	10	8142014	$ 250	$ 1,360	13%
10	60001	10	2052014	$ 250	$ 1,610	16%
11	60001	10	9202014	$ 250	$ 1,860	18%
12	60001	11	6172014	$ 275	$ 2,135	21%
13	60001	12	8132014	$ 300	$ 2,435	24%
14	60001	12	10202014	$ 300	$ 2,735	27%
15	60001	12	11032014	$ 300	$ 3,035	30%
16	60001	13	12082014	$ 325	$ 3,360	33%
17	60001	13	1032014	$ 325	$ 3,685	36%
18	60001	13	4072014	$ 325	$ 4,010	39%
19	60001	13	5292014	$ 325	$ 4,335	43%
20	60001	13	7072014	$ 325	$ 4,660	46%
21	60001	13	11012014	$ 325	$ 4,985	49%
22	60001	13	12092014	$ 325	$ 5,310	52%
23	60001	13	1052014	$ 325	$ 5,635	55%
24	60001	13	3162014	$ 325	$ 5,960	59%
25	60001	14	12292014	$ 350	$ 6,310	62%
26	60001	15	4232014	$ 315	$ 6,625	65%
27	60001	15	8122014	$ 315	$ 6,940	68%
28	60001	15	12282014	$ 315	$ 7,255	71%
29	60001	15	5182014	$ 300	$ 7,555	74%
30	60001	15	8012014	$ 300	$ 7,855	77%
31	60001	15	10302014	$ 300	$ 8,155	80%
32	60001	15	11232014	$ 300	$ 8,455	83%
33	60001	17	3022014	$ 323	$ 8,778	86%
34	60001	17	7282014	$ 323	$ 9,101	89%
35	60001	18	11092014	$ 342	$ 9,443	93%
36	60001	19	12042014	$ 361	$ 9,804	96%
37	60001	21	3032014	$ 378	$ 10,182	100%

Kanban card multiple could be set at 15 for each day of replenishment to stock lead time

Figure 4.2 Dollar-ranked, part number-specific shipment data for determining kanban service level.

value, the order is an LTO. If the order quantity is less than the LTO value, it can be shipped from stock. Since internal or external sales has information on incoming orders, this knowledge of the kanban card quantity and the LTO trigger quantity gives them some flexibility on how they want to deal with orders by looking at the demand pattern in process.

An added safety-cushion factor for service-level inventories involves making product in the most logical minimum or multiple, which minimizes waste. For example, if your service level results in a number of 87 pieces required for the total kanban population to service the replenishment lead time, but your product is made in twenties, the kanban quantity would probably be rounded up to a total population of five cards of 20 each. If you get 20 parts from a sheet of steel or 100 pounds from a batch or 25 parts from a drum of plastic pellets, this will factor into the kanban card quantity you establish. It would be against the principles of Lean to create waste in the process of making kanban card quantities.

When you review the examples of spreadsheets with typical data, you can begin to see the reasoning that goes into deriving end-item, part number kanban population. Know up front that there is no single right answer. Know up front, also, that you will have to periodically review end-item demand patterns and revise cards. You always, also, have the ability to change and reprint a single kanban end-item part number if you have significantly erred in your calculation. The key is to start with a number and perfect it as you go and get more experience with your total-value flow.

Once the final numbers are derived and dollar values approved, all end-item part numbers in the computer database need to be coded to reflect whether end-item part number is kanban (stocked) or MTO or custom. If you have a computer system, there should be available fields in the various modules that are user defined or unused reference fields that can be used. Code every part number accordingly: "K" for kanban, "M" for MTO, and "C" for custom. The field you select should be one that can be linked and sorted in any database or report writing applications. Specifically, you will need to be able to download coded bills of materials in the bill of material file, and the code should also be available for viewing to the order entry and sales departments, accounting, and scheduling. The coding will become the basis for setting expectations for lead times and shipment commitments among materials, manufacturing, marketing or product management, and inside and outside sales. This coding will also print out and define all kanban cards used in scheduling the factory. Accounting will use the coding designations to determine inventory numbers for period-end closings.

With this chapter, you are now to the point where you know how to derive what end-item part numbers will be stocked (kanban) and what will be MTO, custom, and obsolete. In the following chapters, we will discuss deriving dependent part numbers and kanban quantities, and what your policy should be for both purchased and manufactured replacement of inventory.

Chapter 5

Deriving Dependent Demand for Kanban

By now, you should have determined what your kanban quantities, with any added quantity as safety stock or service level, are for the parent-level part numbers. The information you used to determine your end-item part number kanban candidates—system end-item part number, part number description, unit of measure, lead time to produce, statistical information (mean, mode, median, standard deviation, number of shipments, interval of shipments), shipment multiple, shipment minimum—if your computer system is typical, should be extractable from your computer's database. You will also have coded every end-item part number with a classification coding, for example, "K" for kanban, "M" for made to order (MTO), "C" for custom, and "O" for obsolete.

With your end-item part numbers coded in your computer system in a field that can be sorted to reflect kanban, MTO, custom, or obsolete classifications, it is now time to derive the dependent demand corresponding codings and kanban quantities. There needs to be a linkage between the parent-level quantity stocking and the corresponding dependent-component quantity stocking, or your kanban replenishment system will not work.

There are many ways you can establish the data files necessary to print kanban cards. If you have an MRP-type system that can be extensively modified and ample programmers on staff, you can change code in your present system, with the hope that you can begin your Lean journey before you retire. We would caution against this. Modifying computer systems is always expensive, and it comes with a mental anguish factor or a reliability price when compatibility with updates or "Rube Goldberg" programing code intervenes. In most companies, buying or updating computer systems becomes an end in itself, and everyone seems to be working for the information technology manager rather than shipping product.

As long as you can have fields in the computer system to identify coding and you can retrieve the information into any spreadsheet application, you will not need to have an elaborate computer system to run a kanban–heijunka scheduling board. For our purposes in this book, we have created a system based on Microsoft Access, Excel spreadsheet, and VBA programing language for Graphical User Interface. If you own Microsoft business office suite, you probably have all the tools we are using in this book to create the kanban files and programs.

Most typical MRP systems have modules for bills of material, inventory, accounting, part master, sales entry and order shipment, purchasing and vendor master, etc. If you have such a typical MRP-type, modular computer system, you can probably, using a standard report writer function, download key information and link data by parent-level part number and end-item classification codes. These linked part number and product classifications make up the start to your kanban database, which will be used to make all cards to be used for kanban signals and for slotting on your scheduling (heijunka) board. (You will not need the MRP module portion of your system once the kanban–heijunka is up and running.) Selecting the parent-level end-item part number coding, download all bills of material and related data—dependent component part number, quantity per, procurement or production lead time, procurement or purchase multiple and minimum, vendor standard packaging, standard weight of packaging, etc.—into an Excel spreadsheet.

Once you have captured all the parent-level kanban bills of materials, code all the dependent-component part numbers with "K," just like the parent-level part number, to indicate kanban or stock. This will insure that the parent part number and dependent child part numbers are linked on kanban. Code the dependent demand for the non-kanban part numbers with the same coding as the end-item part number—either "M" (MTO), "C" (custom), or "O" (obsolete). This may require dependent part number sorts while maintaining parent-level relationship link. Note that "kanban" coding for dependent demand part numbers takes precedence over any other classification coding for multiple whereused (both kanban and non-kanban) part numbers.

The coding you do in your kanban database file should correspond to the coding in the part master or inventory module of any computer system you are using to run your business. This will be needed in the future for subsequent downloads needed in the review process; it will save you from "reinventing the wheel" each time you download. In most systems, there are enough "user defined" fields to allow for adding data peculiar to a kanban system. If you do not find enough blank "user defined fields," you may have to get creative with any alphanumeric fields you are not using in your computer (e.g., "commodity code," "product code," "harmonizing coding," etc.).

Now we are ready to derive the quantities that go on the kanban cards. If you do not have all the information detailed above, download what you can get from your computer system. Some fields may have to reside and be maintained in the Excel spreadsheets by the kanban administrator, but the data could be made available and viewable to all users on network-wide intranet in a read-only format. Once the kanban end-item part numbers are agreed to, making kanban cards or inputting or making changes to the kanban database will be limited to the kanban administrator, or designated materials or production control personnel.

Since the same dependent part numbers will have many parents (i.e., other "where used" locations in other bills of materials—some of which you coded as kanban and some as not)—it will be necessary to determine the aggregate demand from the downloaded kanban parent-level bills of materials. This aggregate quantity will be used in a subsequent calculation finalizing kanban population for dependent-demand part numbers. To this sum must be added (if necessary, as explained in following paragraphs) an aggregate number for non-kanban end-item part number usage (Figure 5.1).

Planning bill part number: Production cell 202 (variable height accessories)

End-item part number	Description	Quantity per equals total kanban card population for parent level	Kanban coding
5413	Impeller model A163	43	K
5722	Impeller model B163	86	K
6522	Impeller model C163	76	K
4587	Blower model D263	66	K
6251	Blower model D264	51	K
4987	Blower model D265	60	K

Planning bill blow-down aggregates and identifies all dependent kanban demand

Figure 5.1 A planning bill used to aggregate dependent demand for kanban.

When you are going through the exercise to determine aggregate demand, as you did in analyzing your parent-level data, you will need to take out any demand from discontinued product, add in a value for any replacement part number, and take out outlier demand from one-time, large and non-repeating orders. Discontinued product can be coded by "O" for obsolete. Once done, review remaining data to see if it is probably representative of "other" non-kanban demand.

Once you have this number, you will need to decide if this should be added to the aggregate quantity from the kanbans of the parent level. If you have low-value items—traditionally coded as "C" items in ABC inventory classifications—do not worry about these. Hardware, labels, plastic bags, tape, glues, skids, etc. will probably not be a problem to kanban, due to vendor minimums when ordering these types of items and total low value in the overall scope of things. Your bigger concern will be the non-kanban "A" and "B" part usage at the parent level (Figure 5.2).

If non-kanban demand for these A and B items represents 20 percent or less of total usage as expressed in aggregate demand of kanban-dependent demand (applying "80/20" rule), disregard any need to add a factor for dependent demand; your service level and minimums/multiples should normally cover fluctuations. If kanban, parent-level, end-item usage makes up a small portion of total demand for dependent demand, you will have to review other non-kanban, end-item usage and make a determination of what to add to aggregate value to determine part-total kanban population. If, for example, your kanban-coded parents use only 40 percent of total demand for a particular part number, we would suggest you annualize the remaining 60 percent and add only the lead time replenishment's worth as aggregate to the kanban population for that particular "A" or "B" item.

As you will hear us say many times in the course of reading this book, there is no *one*, absolute answer to how you set up your inventory. The important thing is to have the key personnel involved with all aspects of product production get together with sales to discuss the issue. Pick a starting point, after giving it your best collective judgment. For the most part, your choices will probably be fine to start off. If there is a particular problem or two that arises, deal with the particulars and leave the balance of the kanban part numbers and quantities alone for the short term. As you will hear us also say many times in the book, never allow sales to set inventory levels if this can be avoided—the deciding vote should always go to the marketing person who has strategic responsibility for the marketing plan and who is the closest representation to the customer.

Determining kanban information for part numbers with both kanban and non-kanban parent demand history.

Dependent demand part number	Make or buy	Parent level where used part number	System coding of parent-level part number	Historical demand for fiscal year ended	Total demand on kanban	Anticipated demand with forecast adjust	Total number of orders	Average order quantity	Average interval between orders in days	Lead time to replenish to stock	Vendor std pkg minimum or multiple	Kanban card quantity	Number of kanban cards
2011212MD	Buy	1073	C	0		0	0	0	0				
		1087	C	0		0	0	0	0				
		1093	M	412		412	5	82	48				
		1097	M	871		871	13	67	18				
		1100	M	12		12	1	12	240				
		1101	M	76		76	1	76	240				
		1107	C	0		0	0	0	0				
		1108	M	37		37	2	19	120				
		1111	M	538		538	15	36	16				
		1112	M	623		623	13	48	18				
		1169	C	0		0	0	0	0				
		1189	C	0		0	0	0	0				
		1204	M	1314		1314	21	63	11				
		5415	K	5415	5415	5415	34	159	7				
		2021	K	16720	16720	16720	43	389	6				
		3051	M	3085		3085	21	147	11				
		5123	M	0		0	0	0	0				
		8222	M	773		773	8	97	30				
		60004	O	0		0	0	0	0				
		60064	O	0		0	0	0	0				
		60065	O	0		0	0	0	0				
		72050.0004	M	5346		5346	32	167	8				
		72080.0023	M	931		931	9	103	27				
				36153	22135	36153	218	166	1	3	250	250	3
2011215DCM	Make	1120	C	7092	0	7092	23	308	10	5	NA	NA	
2011512M	Buy	1094	O	0		0	0	0	0				
		1208	M	120		120	2	60	120				
		1507	M	24		24	1	24	240				
		2022	M	287		287	8	36	30				
		2051	C	0		0	0	0	0				
		3050	K	1464	1464	1464	21	70	11				
		72080.0031	M	754		754	10	75	24				
				2649	1464	2649	42	63	6	10	100	100	2

Note: For this exercise, assume parent-level part number bill of material uses one per of dependent demand part number.

Figure 5.2 Method for combining kanban and non-kanban usage for determining kanban card population for dependent part number.

When the subject of lead time is used in this book, the usage always refers to a typical or normal lead time. It is never the worst possible case or the best possible case. It is the delivery time from vendor notification to point of readiness for use in your factory that would occur in eight or nine out of 10 orders. We have known many buyers who will pad lead times, because they do not have confidence in their vendors to deliver on published lead times. Instead of being beaten due to the fact of a late order, they pad the lead time to insure delivery. What everyone must keep in mind is that *lead time is money.* We do not advocate an "error on the high side" rule for lead times. There is a cost to inflated lead times. The lead times from the buyers must be typical or normal reflections of shipments from vendors. If you do not know your typical lead times, pull 20 purchase orders with delivery receipts and calculate actual lead times from date of origin to date of receipt. If the vendors are unreliable, buyers should also be looking into the reasons, and, possibly, looking for new vendors.

There are other points on lead times to be made before we leave the topic. If there is an internal lead time due to quarantine or testing of materials purchased before release to the factory, this must be added to quoted vendor lead time. Likewise, if there is an external lead time due to ocean-transit time or typical, five-day, freight-consolidation-point delay at the coast, this must be added to whatever lead time it takes your vendor to actually make the product and ship to the boat or consolidation point. We are talking replenishment lead time—how long is the time interval from the notification to your vendor to the point of delivery and availability for manufacture at your factory? Again, we are looking at typical or normal lead times.

You will finish determining the kanban population for dependent-demand part numbers by adding the kanban aggregate quantity (from all the kanban "where used") to the "other" demand from non-kanban part level bills of materials. This sum becomes the total kanban quantity, which will be translated into kanban cards by part number. The kanban population calculated in the spreadsheet at the end-item part number level (resultant kanban part number population times safety factor or service level) added to any non-kanban adder becomes the quantity subject to kanban card control for that part number. This gives you the dependent-demand population required during the replenishment lead time for all parent parts. You do not have to add any further safety stock or safety factor to this aggregate kanban demand number. Now, from this kanban total population, you will determine number of kanban cards and kanban-card quantity for each dependent part number. The kanban quantity multiple will be the same on each card, and the total number of the cards times the multiple quantity will add up to the total kanban population. '

When you set quantities for either internally produced dependent part numbers or externally procured purchased items, the method you use to set reorder quantities will be different from standard ordering formulae in MRP-type software programs. Most of these MRP-type programs offer period of supply, economic order quantity (EOQ), or across-the-board order point options for replenishments. What is inherent in this type of thinking is emphasis on purchased, individual, piece-part price, and not total inventory costs. Do not concentrate your efforts on piece-part price to the exclusion of viewing the potential savings of rationalized inventory and total inventory costs. (*Note*: "Make" kanbans will be discussed at length in Chapter 14 when setups and changeovers are discussed at length.)

Going forward, as a general rule, for all items you purchase or make internally, the quantity you procure will be the quantity on the kanban card that represents replenishment lead time for that particular part number. For part numbers that are not on kanban, your purchasing or manufacturing policy will be to purchase them lot-for-lot (procured in a one-to-one relationship with parent requirement). There will be some items that will be the exceptions due to exceptionally long lead-time queues (e.g., bearings or integrated circuit chips) or truly unique, single sourced items (e.g., rare earth magnets). Your experienced buyer should have these exceptions on the tip of his tongue.

When you have a purchasing policy incorporating the concept of "total cost" of inventory, you get different results than one driven simply by piece-part cost. It may be counterintuitive that producing only what you need or purchasing only what you need will benefit both you and your vendor and ultimately result in lower overall costs. Vendors all too often are seen simply as necessary evils where competitively bidding parts pits vendor against vendor. Too many horror stories are written about vendors becoming the whipping boys in one-sided transactions, and any mutual loyalty or beneficial relationship is non-existent when supplying Lean manufacturers. This may be true in some cases, but, if done correctly, Lean will benefit your vendor as much as your factory. This is what you should strive for: bringing vendors into your business as collaborators and as long-term, value-added suppliers.

When your emphasis is on unit piece-part cost, there are many unobvious other costs you fail to take into account. You misunderstand these hidden costs at your peril: the absolute, in any business, is that "cash flow is king."

Inventory costs have put many companies out of business due to drying up of cash. Let us review the benefits of purchasing on a "total inventory" cost basis.

In some companies, the management by objective (MBO) incentive for the purchasing department is to reduce purchase price by a percentage per year without tying purchases to the concept of total inventory and purchasing costs. What will happen in this situation is that the wily purchasing agent will negotiate lower unit prices for higher volume purchasing. What results is that the purchasing department meets their objectives, and the company's cash flow takes a hit. Reducing product cost should be the objective of many departments, not simply purchasing, and it should encompass better design engineering, input and recommendations from your suppliers, customer involvement in the design process where possible, and purchasing policies that favor both your company and your suppliers.

When viewing inventory merely as a snapshot, the inventory in the typical non-Lean company turns four to six times per year. As soon as the company becomes Lean, if its shipments remain steady on a year-to-year basis, most companies should see an increase in inventory turns by a factor of two to four within the first two years of Lean. Once you have a trained cadre of workers and they understand Lean principles intuitively, the workers, by their creativity, will find ways to reduce inventories.

Think of the space you have now to house your inventory. Some companies have to expand storage areas by purchasing mezzanines, renting additional warehouse space, renting temporary semitrailers for storage, buying additional forklifts or pallet jacks, racking, or expanding into would-be production areas. These capital improvements can be expensive. At the heart of this type of expansion is pure waste—the waste of inventory. With increased inventory turns, the space requirement will shrink by a considerable factor.

If your company does not have the luxury of adding or renting space or equipment, the housekeeping takes a hit. Clutter and disorganization work at loggerheads with the "Pygmalion effect" of a clean and well-organized company. Employees react to their environment—if it is dirty, dark, cluttered, and undisciplined, employees will probably also take on these attributes. This is why 5S (cleanliness and organization of Lean) goes hand in hand with inventory rationalization: sort through and get rid of clutter and the unnecessary, and set in order what remains.

Once inventories are rationalized, inventory space is defined and storage locations are fixed. If you are making typical progress, inventory space will probably be 50 percent less than your starting warehousing space.

The biggest problem you will have starting out will be the quarantine of excess and obsolete inventory, which must be used up first before starting with the kanban-controlled reorders of part numbers. We will discuss this aspect when we talk about placing kanban cards on stock.

With rationalized inventories, defined and visual inventory indicators, and set inventory locations, the need for cycle counting will go away. You will know the total number of part numbers and their values in stock. If your lead times are close to correct, at any given time as your kanban cards circulate, you should have approximately one half of your kanban population on hand. Since you are counting kanban cards and not parts, counting for physical to book inventories should take one-tenth the time of a full-blown annual inventory. This also means that formerly "down" days for counting can now stay in production at the factory manager's choice. Since the work-in-process inventory is controlled by kanban card and a maximum of only two jobs are probably at the production cell at any given time, during factory shutdown counts, the production departments can usually go back to work within hours of starting the count.

From an accounting perspective, some auditors, after test counts in established Lean systems, may simply accept the kanban population valuation at one-half value, knowing that the plus or minus percentages of variation are probably not material to overall inventory valuation. Best case, you may avoid interim inventory counts to reset records other than at your audited fiscal year-end inventory. An added bonus is that elaborate calculations and explanations for auditors for potential excess and obsolete reserves will be minimized. After a few years of inventory "right sizing," you should not have much, if any, excess and obsolete issue.

One of the big, potential benefits of "total cost" inventory buying is a better and longer-term relationship with vendors. If vendors are not judged solely by being the lowest price vendor, and they are judged as potential value-added, longer-term collaborators, this can be a great benefit to both the vendor and your company. The benefits usually dramatically exceed any piece-part price savings.

One of the best ways a vendor can help your company is by providing technological expertise to supplement knowledge your engineers may lack. It may be a total waste of time and duplication of efforts for your engineering staff to address problems that may better reside in the core of expertise your vendor has to offer. If you actually have a long-term relationship with a supplier, you can begin to take advantage of this help. Your vendor probably has access to a wide assortment of experts—metallurgists, lab scientists, stress and wear analysts, material coating and sealing experts, flavoring experts, staff nutritionists, seal and ring specialists, biohazard analysts, etc., which only a long-term relationship can help make available to your company.

By working with vendors on quantities you purchase, you may also reduce costs on product in indirect ways through collaboration with the vendor. The vendor may sell his product in a specified multiple; if this multiple works for you, the kanban-card quantity can become a multiple of this standard packaging. This will save your vendor picking time, and it should be a cost avoidance item for negotiation. If there is no acceptable multiple or minimum (it must be reasonably close to calculated kanban card need), you go with the number you calculated to support your kanban card.

Packaging is also a big item to review with your vendor. Eliminating disposal packaging and using permanent packaging that constantly recycles between your company and the vendor, can also become a point of cost avoidance for negotiation. A hidden cost for many companies is the charge for waste pick-up and hauling. Working with your vendors, you may eliminate this expense by permanent kanban-sized containers that go back and forth between your companies. Obtaining or making the one-time containers is a small cost for the overall gain of eliminating disposal waste. Rationalized inventories with standard kanban quantities allow this to work.

If you have long-term relationships with suppliers, you can also minimize paperwork processing costs for both you and your vendor. Instead of individual purchase orders for every purchase, put monthly or quarterly or longer pricing agreements in place. The faxing, scanning, or e-mailing of the kanban replenishment authorization serves in lieu of an individual purchase order. The packing list accompanying the parts back to the company matches to the kanban card, and it is signed off by the receiving department. This the buyer can match to outgoing authorizations as procedure requires. Since kanban quantities are used as the ordered quantity, and only shipments having this quantity are accepted, using permanent containers fitted for kanban quantities eliminates the need to count or weigh receipts on either the receiving or shipping end. This is another cost avoidance negotiation point. In Chapter 15 discussing the receiving function, we will cover how to handle purchasing kanban cards.

Another point of negotiation with your vendor is the elimination of constant expediting of product. If your inventory is rationalized and you follow the rules for MTOs and custom orders, there should be little, if any, expediting needed. If you do expedite with a vendor, it now becomes a matter of mutual agreement and not daily, unrelenting mayhem. Expediting is as disruptive to your vendor as it is to your company. Nothing erodes margins quicker than premiums for shipped materials and endless emergency-driven overtime for expedites. Once you get your production cells running, vendor–company relations will improve. This is also a point of negotiation as a cost avoidance to both sides.

We have spent a lot of time discussing vendors and pricing, but the point in all the preceding discussion is twofold: (1) pitting vendor against vendor and competitively bidding every purchase order is not a symbiotic, mutually beneficial relationship, and (2) emphasis on unit piece price and not total inventory cost is wasteful. Many companies cannot get past piece-part price sticking points. Piece-part price should be discussed in the context of a long-term relationship where both parties work with each other on the elimination of waste. When you are really on your way with the Lean process, you can even exchange personnel with your vendor to work on productivity improvement and waste elimination kaizen events. In Lean, life is more than beating a vendor for a piece-part price reduction.

By definition, non-kanban, end-item part numbers are subject to lead times for promised orders (MTO), and they statistically do not make up the volume of your customer business. You may, however, want to consider putting critical lead-time-dependent part numbers for selected MTO end-item part numbers on kanban, if lead times for the end-item parent part number would be prohibitively unacceptable from the customer without stocking the part. This is perfectly acceptable. This would probably apply to very few items in your inventory, and every purchasing agent will have them on the tip of their tongue: castings from Brazil, paper stocks from Asia, integrated chips from Malaysia, industrial ceramics from Korea, rare earth magnets from China, etc. Quantities should be equal to demand for reorder lead times in these cases (where possible). Like most inventory stocking decisions, the situation should always be discussed with marketing/product manager and the sales department.

One final thing about vendors and sourcing: if you have unreliable vendors, you will have problems. When we have gone on visits to qualify potential vendors, there have always been things we looked for: orderliness, factory cleanliness, metrics, lighting, and attitudes of personnel working there. We have also always looked for indications that the vendor was truly "Lean." A Lean vendor opened up options that would otherwise be closed with non-Lean vendors. Lead time and related inventory levels were always in the forefront of our minds. All things being equal, we would choose a Lean vendor over a non-Lean vendor.

As a buying company, we also wanted our vendors as close to us as serviceably possible. Time is money. We did not like buying overseas, unless it was the last resort. Again, pricing may be cheap, but there is a cost to inventory when you are faced with six- to eight-week ocean-transit times. Unless you have volume that makes daily or weekly receipts possible, receiving your quarterly shipment of product (evidenced in one or more ocean-going "container" loads) can really kill the rhythm in a factory. Most factories are not set up to be able to expand and contract as inventory levels fill up and empty out of the building. Pulling manpower to handle, count, and locate the inventory is another level of complication.

A story. One of the clients we worked with bought unfinished wire mattresses in China. After receiving the bare-wire-formed mattresses, the client company finished them into specialty mattresses for niche clients. The client's business was small, but growing, and the company ordered mattresses in quarterly shipments. When the containers arrived, usually two or three ocean-going containers in one shipment, his factory was upside down for weeks, until he could "burn off" some of the excess, which was placed in aisles, walkways, etc. His reason for buying from China was price. He could also not find domestic sources. Well, to make a long story short, we helped him find a domestic "Lean" supplier of wire products that had the technical ability to adapt to make his mattresses. His company ended up with a Lean supplier who shipped twice per week from 170 miles away to his factory. This is a classic case of what a long-term relationship with a vendor will do. Both made money, and both secured the "takeaways" they wanted in the deal. Even though the unit cost was higher per mattress, the local supplier was less expensive when viewed through the lens of "total inventory costs."

When we discuss setting up the total-value flow, we will talk about how to integrate the kanban cards into day-to-day operations, how to start the card process, and how to set up inventory locations and bins. At that time, we will also talk about how everything integrates with selected modules on any existing MRP system you might have. For now, you have enough information to get someone working on creating the kanban card file, and, while that is taking place, we will turn to the idea of creating the total-value flow where the cards and heijunka board will be used.

Chapter 6

Documenting the Current State in a Process Map

Everyone has probably heard the aphorism that "if you don't know where you are going, any road will get you there." Unfortunately, many companies, with a patchwork of methods and competing, unregulated and non-rationalized, out-of-control processes, tend to go full speed ahead down these waste highways. With this chapter, we discuss the idea of process mapping to create a "future state" from a documented "current state." The "current-state process map" depicts your company's methods and processes as they are used in day-to-day business now. Once you know everything that goes into your current state, you will then critically review information presented and create an idealized "future-state process map." This will be the new, enlightened roadmap for your company's future.

The mapping exercise is a form of "hands-on" flowcharting with visuals added to help better analyze what you are looking at and understand how activities are connected. With this concept of process mapping, we will revise the above aphorism to "before you know where you want to take your company, you need to have some idea of how you got to where you are." This encapsulates one of the key tenets for being able to improve in Lean methods and philosophy: document reality. Every kaizen productivity improvement event or process map mandates that current reality must be documented to gain a clear understanding of the starting condition or starting processes. In the course of process mapping the right road for your company, we also identify and eliminate as much waste as possible from the future state.

The process mapping we will use will be different in detail from other process mapping exercises you can read about in various Lean books. Some of these alternative methods are more detailed and attempt to capture cycle and setup times, distances materials move, inventory levels at a particular point, and time metrics replete with their own set of icons for the actual mapping—in both the "current-state" map and the "future-state" map. It tends to be more of a strategic tool by which the whole process can be documented and mapped for focused activities.

In contrast, the process map we employ in this chapter will be a view from a slightly different perspective. Our focus in the process mapping is more tactical and definitely geared with a bias toward action. Kaizens, continuous improvement events, are the natural byproducts of our method. We are looking to get to a level-loaded, heijunka- and kanban-driven production line as soon as possible. This is our goal. We want a successful start to Lean activity, which can serve as a teaching tool and model to rapidly expand the lessons learned into your factory as soon as possible.

This tactical approach will consist of two stages. It starts by primarily concentrating on defining actions with accompanying paperwork, in a flow that begins with a customer order and ends with the product shipping to the customer. From these defined actions, you will be able to see the waste in the process that you will wish to eliminate from your future state. Then, once you have a future state concept, the office or factory floor becomes your reference point for setting up your metrics, measurements, and implementing your improvements. This slightly different focus is in line with our intent in this book to get companies up and running with kanbans and heijunkas as soon as possible. Your company will fill in the metrics, do necessary line balancing, and establish production goals after you decide on the actions in your future state.

If you are going to have a good process map session resulting in the best possible information to create the best possible future state, you will need to set some rules that everyone must follow. You will need to set aside dedicated time to perform the mapping that documents current reality and establishes the future flow, get a focused individual with good group dynamics ability to lead the group, and involve the right people in the process.

For doing a proper job with the process mapping, you should plan, as a company, for setting aside three workdays to do the exercise. Some companies have simpler flows and can do both the current-state and the future-state mapping exercises in less than three days. Having said all that, this is the roadmap to change your company, and you need to dedicate whatever time is needed to make sure you get a successful conclusion.

Normally the days would be allocated as follows: one day to map out the current state; one day to map out the future state; and the last day to discuss and set up the implementation plan and prioritize other good collateral ideas which come out of the process map exercise. The ideal way to do this would be to set aside three consecutive, whole days, but, we recognize, some smaller or tightly managed companies cannot afford to have key personnel away from their primary jobs that long, at the same time. It has been our experience that half-day blocks of time work (minimum of four-hour blocks), but anything less than this will probably be counterproductive.

The time for the process mapping should be considered "dedicated time," and personnel should avoid conducting regular business during this time. Unless there is a compelling reason, mute the iPhones, Droids, and iPads, and make a rule to forbid checking messages except at defined breaks. Set up communication/break periods for conducting business and catching up on and answering the electronic messages. After breaks, mandate all personnel return to the meeting *on time* and fully prepared to concentrate on the process mapping.

People need to be available and fully participating in the discussions the whole time the group is meeting. Sometimes, the disinterested perspective of a team member "onlooker," who has company and product knowledge, but who is not intimately involved in the details of a particular portion of the flow not their own, can offer insightful observations or poignant questions. The discussion leader must make sure all personnel are able to voice comments without bias or ridicule from other members. Group dynamics and discussion are at the heart of process mapping success.

Concerning the individuals who make up the core group doing the process mapping, key individuals from involved departments—such as a member from the sales/marketing, production/inventory control, operations, information technology, engineering, and accounting departments—would be a good, diverse team to participate in the activity. People selected should be knowledgeable and have some responsibility for day-to-day operations for their particular department. You normally would not choose a group exclusively made up of "big picture"–type executives. The chemistry of the personnel chosen should be a fit. While not necessarily the best of buddies, they should have basic mutual respect for each other and be good listeners.

The person to lead the team and orchestrate the activity should be the person or leader charged with the Lean implementation in your company. Ideally, this person should be well read on basic Lean concepts, even if he or she is short on actual experience in implementing Lean. Since group dynamics often push discussions off track, this person must be able to keep the group focused on the process maps at hand. This ability to listen, to create a constructive atmosphere, think analytically, guide discussion, and to ensure all participants are involved is crucial.

When some of the basic concepts underlying the current process are examined, the leader of the group may face challenges revolving around territorial or defensive team members. Pride of authorship, a "this is the way we have always done it" attitude or long-standing departmental rivalries can arise. Sometimes a member, long in years and historically looked upon in the company as the "go to" person for answers, will now have to keep an open mind and work objectively and in concert with the other members of the team. The group leader must be able to deal with and guide the team through these troubled waters. The basic rule must be made clear from the get-go: check egos and vulnerabilities and intimidation and practices beyond scrutiny at the door. This is an opportunity to "reinvent" your company. What a gift to be able to do this for and with your employees.

Although the process mapping team has dedicated members, the key rule for process mapping is: the person who actually does the job, though not a member of the team, is called into the meeting when discussing his or her part of the current-state process map. The group leader, following the Socratic method of pointed questioning, should draw out the essence of the current-state activity.

When you first start the process map, as an overview, the group leader should walk the team through the actual flow in the actual areas where the actions occur. This will allow the team to see the physical surroundings and equipment involved in the processes. For purposes of this overview and giving context to the process map, department supervisors in the specific areas can briefly explain the flow from receipt to hand-off of the order. Team members should be making notes of the flow.

When the actual flow is being created by the team and points of confusion arise from the person describing the activity in question, if still unclear, walk the flow again—this time with the actual personnel who do the jobs giving the explanations. Use the "Three Actual Rule": go to the actual place where the process is being performed; talk to the actual people involved in the process and get real facts; and observe and chart the actual process.

The cardinal rule is: the people who do the job on a daily basis are the "experts." Always talk to the actual people who do the job. This applies to both office and the factory.

The current state should never be derived from operations manuals or existing flowcharts. Above all, never have the departmental manager or engineering supervisor explain how things are done or show you system answers when you get down to the details of actually filling in the process maps. Too often, this information does not reflect how things are really done. It has been our experience that even busy department managers too often do not know the actual details that go into their workers' jobs. Routings and bills of material may not always be updated, and workers, choosing the path of least resistance, may develop practices of batching work so they do things once or twice per day rather than in real-time sequence per the procedures manual.

When you are ready to begin the current-state process map, there will be certain necessities and supplies that you will need to get. The first necessity is to secure a room with substantial wall space uninterrupted by windows, so that you have room to hang the butcher's paper (also known as Kraft packaging paper or "brown" paper), upon which the maps will be created. Most companies require a room with a minimum of 15 or 20 linear feet of space to create the current-state process map. (One of the worst process current-state maps we were ever associated with was 30 feet long!) Ideally, you should have a second wall in the same room with slightly less uninterrupted space to create the future-state process map. When you are creating the future state, it is highly desirable to be able to look at the physical copy of the current state your team created. Part of the success of creating the future-state process map is seeing the actual waste you are eliminating. This can be a motivating "ah-ha" moment for all participants and an affirmation of what "Lean" can do for a company.

Besides a minimum of 50 linear feet of three-foot-wide butcher's paper, you will also need tape to suspend the paper on the wall. If you are using a conference room, there are excellent painter tapes that act like masking tapes to hold the paper to the wall, but they do not tear off paint or varnish when the tapes are removed and maps are taken down. Since the butcher's paper will become very heavy during the course of creating the current-state process map, apply the tape liberally to hold the paper to the wall.

Other items you will need for your process maps are multicolored pads of Post-it (or equivalent) notes (many office supply stores have six or eight different colors of pads in one bundle), multicolored, broad point markers to write on the Post-it notes, Scotch tape, stapler, and a 30-foot tape measure or comparable measuring wheel. It is also a good idea to have a flipchart or "meeting-type" tripod with two pads of paper available for the team to "think out loud" on paper or document other questions or suggestions that you might want to review later during the future-state process map. (We discourage grease boards unless the writings and drawings can be captured easily.) We explain how all these things will be used as we walk through the process of creating the current- and future-state maps.

For your purposes, to get your heijunka and kanban card system going as rapidly as possible, the current-state process map will begin with the scenario and question that a customer has just contacted your company via e-mail, telephone, or fax to place an order: What actions happen next? Starting with the answers to these questions, the group will follow the flow through all the current activities that result in the shipment of the order from your dock. Keep in mind, also, that although you are doing a process map exercise centered around the time and activities originating in customer order receipt and ending with product manufactured and shipped, process mapping can be used in any office or factory flow. This is a good tool for breaking down complex processes to eliminate waste. We will discuss more about this as we go through the book (Figure 6.1).

Use one color of the Post-it notes to identify a particular department's role in the activity. Going forward with the map, always use that color to represent that particular department's involvement wherever it reappears in the flow. Place the Post-it squares, containing the written essence of actions performed by that particular department, consecutively and side by side to define all that department's actions, until the process is handed off to the next department. Make sure the squares for a particular department always remain on the same horizontal level on the butcher's paper. If there is a hand-off to a subsequent department, place the new, unique color of notes for that particular department directly below and to the right of the last note of the hand-off department. If the department already has been involved in the process, the note should be placed on their already established line and on a vertical axis to the right of the handing off department's last note. Time always marches to the right.

If the process comes to a decision point (i.e., the process at that point can go to different departments for different actions), turn the current color note to stand on a point in a diamond shape to indicate that a question exists. The note will have a "?" written in the square. Each leg of the alternative process should be documented and a note written and placed on the

Figure 6.1 A completed current-state process map.

separate levels of the butcher's paper. You may have to rearrange some pre-viously-posted notes to different horizontal lines. After the alternative routes are captured, the action returns to the main flow and the department having the next activity. The current-state process map continues along following this method until the process is fully captured on the butcher's paper.

The role of the team leader is crucial in overseeing the proper filling out of the Post-it notes and the placement on the butcher's paper. This team leader is also the one person charged with asking the questions: *Who* did it or is involved? *What* are they doing? *When* do they do it? *Where* do they do it? *How* do they do it? *Why* do they do it? If team members are unclear about the process or feel other questions are needed, they also have a right to ask questions. If things are still confusing, persist until the group gets answers. All the notes describing the activity of the department should contain (ide-ally, start with) action verbs. The team leader can also assign roles to team members to keep them mentally in the effort: one writes the notes, one places the note on the butcher's paper, one person tapes the note, etc.

As the team goes along defining the process of the current state, the team leader must not allow the group to "improve upon" the process of the current state in the current-state process map. Sometimes, as the notes are placed on the butcher's paper, the redundancy of effort or unnecessary action or wasted efforts will become obvious to all the members. It is common to have the urge to fix the process. Instead, capture ideas with "cloud bursts" above the process step to note the opportunity, using the color for that particular department activity for the cloud bursts.

When cloud bursts arise in the course of creating the current-state process map, sometimes, team members can become defensive, if the defect cited lands too close to home turf. The team leader must be vigilant, if this type of behavior even hints of rearing its head. Reiterate to the team members that the exercise is not a version of assigning "pin the tail on the donkey" culpability, and processes singled out as needing review or improvement are not indictments of departments or individuals. Problems are usually attributable to broken processes. Your team's future state brainstorming will address process issues.

The point of the current-state process map is to discover exactly what the reality of the flow is now. Everyone should understand that the current-state process map is not an indictment of existing personnel or policies; it is simply documenting reality. Do not incorporate any changes into the current-state map that conflict with the discovery process as told by the people doing the job. The future-state process map will incorporate improvements and waste eliminations.

The team leader must also drill down to the essence of the actions as they are described. Failure to ask the right questions or enough questions may lead to incomplete information showing up on the current-state process map. Normally, this will be caught downstream in the process map exercise, but it is easier to do it correctly the first time.

To elucidate the point, let us look at a typical response one might get in determining the content of the notes in process of being placed on the process map. Suppose the answer in response to how orders are received from customers is "Inside sales department receives phone calls and e-mails, and collects faxes sent to the receptionist." At a cursory level, this sounds like it has all the components for an answer. For our purposes, this is not a crisp enough answer. Consider the following.

First of all, two different departments appear to be involved with this receipt of customer orders. For this reason, at a minimum, there should be two different colors of Post-it notes used on the butcher's paper, for the two processes of different origin: one for the inside sales department directly receiving e-mails and telephone calls and another for the receptionist receiving faxes. Second, there is still much detail to be flushed out. Looking only at the receptionist's role in retrieving faxes from customers, there are many more questions to be asked: Where is the fax?, At her desk? Fifty feet away and shared with the accounting department? Does she walk to the accounting department to retrieve the faxes? When does she check for faxes? At break times? Once per day at end of day? Whenever she gets time? Does she have any other responsibilities with the faxes? Sort quotes from sales orders? Check for existing customer account numbers? Sort and route new customers to an inside sales manager? Only route dollar amounts over "x" dollars to an inside sales manager? Initiate "Dun and Bradstreet" (D&B) credit check requests with the accounting department on all new customers? Initiate D&B credit check requests only on orders over x dollars? etc. We hope this makes our point clear that the team leader must ensure that the questioning drills down to the process detail. Whatever substantive and sequential actions are discovered in the questioning must be documented and placed on the butcher's paper.

After the team has driven to the details of the action in the process, fill out the notes and place on the butcher's paper. Directly under the note at the bottom of the butcher's paper, attach copies of all reports, daily reports, papers, "screen prints," forms, etc., used in conjunction with that particular action. If you need a computer screen, form, report, template, or any other electronic or paper item to complete the step in the process, it should be documented and attached to the current-state process map. If you are dealing with computer screens, print the screen. If you are using forms or paper reports, take a sample page or Xerox a copy and staple to the bottom of the butcher's paper directly under the department utilizing the screen or form. As you create your future state, you will have to evaluate the need for the form or screen presented.

There should be enough information on the attached screen print or printed matter example to state what the purpose of the form or screen is. If you only intermittently refer to a screen or printed matter, document on the form and place on the butcher's paper. If this intermittent use is the result of a question in the process, make sure the process notes reflect this decision tree.

Before we leave the current state, there is one more task that needs to happen. You should gather the appropriate metrics that correspond to the documented current-state process map. While the team is meeting to document reality and create the future-state map, some appropriate persons, not on the team, should be charged with gathering whatever metrics are available for the current state. Some suggestions would be: on-time delivery percentage to acknowledged date to customer, on-time delivery to requested date from customer, inventory turns, published lead times to customers, expediting costs for typical period, unplanned downtime in work centers, scrap and salvage costs, expedited freight costs, etc. You probably already have company-specific metrics you use for your painful monthly or quarterly management meetings. This will become your baseline that you will measure your Lean progress against.

At this point in your Lean journey, you have accomplished two major goals: (1) determined kanban quantities and rationalized your inventory for your targeted product line, and (2) selected and empowered the first transformative team to document the current-state process map of your company. Now you are ready in the next chapter to create the future-state process map for your future-state Lean company. Before you get to this exciting next chapter, one more minor goal needs to be achieved: using Scotch tape, place a small square of tape on each note to secure the note to the butcher's paper to augment the adhesive on the back of the notes. Given the rough contact surface of the butcher's paper and dry conditions in the meeting room, if you do not do this, you may find all your notes have fallen to the floor overnight. Now you are ready for the next chapter.

Chapter 7

Creating the Future State Process Map

At this point in your company's nascent Lean journey, as your group begins day two, the team has successfully completed putting together the current-state process map. Ideally, it is hanging in view on one of the walls of your meeting room. If you remembered to reinforce, via Scotch tape, the Post-it notes denoting the process on the Kraft packaging or butcher's paper, everything is in the place where the group put it. On a facing wall, there should be a second canvas of blank, hanging butcher's paper awaiting the notes that will be placed on it to create the future-state process map. This should be an exciting and long-awaited day: this is the first day of the rest of its life for your fledgling Lean company.

For the purposes of creating the future-state process map, we will follow a specific process. The first step will be a review of each of the activities posted on the current-state map to determine whether it is a value-added process or not. Once the current state's posted notes have been discussed and judged, the adjacent, blank butcher's paper will begin to be populated by newly created notes and a new process map will start to emerge. Along the way, we will discuss the role of the computer in your new process, the method for obtaining data for reporting and metrics, the process for incorporating the heijunka–kanban concept into the flow, and what are reasonable gains to expect from the first attempt to turn a current state into a future state. Since you are not expected to know how this will work, at the point in the process where this all comes together, we will fill in the necessary knowledge of how the linkage works. This point will begin when the sales order is ready to be scheduled and a ship date is to be given to the customer by production control personnel.

Since the members of your team probably have varying levels of under-standing of what is waste and what is value-added content, the future-state discussion should always start with a review of the types of waste alluded to earlier in this book. By default, if all possible waste has been removed from the process, the remaining actions should be value added. Another way to consider what is waste and what is value added is to answer this question: If I were a customer buying this product and I reviewed your process, would I be willing to pay you (or expect you) to do this particular action to produce the product for me? If the answer to this question is "yes," the action is prob-ably value added. Since the members of the team will be making judgments based on these concepts, time spent reviewing "value added" and the types of "waste" will be most beneficial. Keep in mind, for some members of the team, this may be some of their first in-depth exposures to Lean concepts and methods training.

The easiest and best way to review the categories of waste is to start with definitions. A follow-on activity to the definitions might be a pointed discus-sion of examples of specific wastes discussed. Since the group will review the current state systematically once the placement of the Post-it notes begins and the future-state process map starts to take form, there is no need to scrutinize the current-state butcher paper for examples. Team members, following prompts and questions from the discussion facilitator, should have enough examples from their work experience to fill in the definition content for each waste. The point of the review is that the various concepts of waste are understood by all team members.

Once the review of waste versus value added has been concluded, the group will next turn their eyes to the hanging, current-state process map. Starting with the first note posted, the group will reach a judgment whether the action notated is value added or "non-value added" or "non-value added but currently necessary." As you are reviewing each note, review the asso-ciated, attached forms and screen dumps. This can be achieved by simply marking a "V" (for value added) or "W" (for waste) or "NVN" (for non-value added but necessary) on the notes and associated forms or screens with a marker. Going note by note, follow this process all the way down the current-state process map. Stop at the point where the order is ready for scheduling.

If there is controversy and disagreement, allow enough time for all partic-ipants to make their argument. From experience with these types of events, the consensus of the diversely selected group, driven by insightful questioning, will normally arrive at the correct judgment. The following paragraphs may help in guiding the discussions to determine the note classifications. We will also include a brief discussion of the idea of "wasteful but currently necessary activity."

Just as the group facilitator needed to be cognizant of the need to ask questions to drive down to the core activity that was written on each of the posted notes, likewise, the facilitator must again be diligent to ask enough questions to determine where on the continuum scale of absolute waste to value-added activity the classification for the note in question resides. This is critical.

Operating in the background of this questioning are two stated goals: (1) to get the level-loaded, heijunka-driven total-value flow up and running as soon as possible; and (2) to eliminate waste from the process. Among these tasks is a potential conflict. This brings up the dilemma of the ideal versus the real—seems like we keep running into Plato on our Lean journey!

The dilemma is this: if you wait to get everything fixed and perfect before you start to create the total-value flow, the reality is, you will never start. You want to start now, so you will have to incorporate some wasteful but necessary activities into your future-state process map. How do you deal with these inconsistencies when you say your goal is to eliminate waste in your processes? The answer is: in your future-state process map, you will go after as much "low hanging fruit" (i.e., eliminate gross and obvious waste) as possible in your initial attempt at Lean. This is your compromise with an imperfect world. You have to pick a starting point. In the following paragraphs, we give you some examples of short-term compromises with waste.

Let us suppose for a minute that you are a metal fabricator, and your ideal future state is a cell that stamps, forms, welds, and assembles a finished weldment assembly. The ideal in Lean would be to have a self-contained cell where inexpensive, flexible, and dedicated equipment could make all similar weldment assemblies within the cell to replenish actual customer demands. For the purposes of this example, your company may not have the money budgeted to buy the equipment to set up the cell to be self-sufficient. Sending raw material to a centralized-function, excessive-setup-time stamping department in batches may be wasteful, but you may not have options to do otherwise until a following budget year. This is a "wasteful but necessary" situation until you can purchase right-sized equipment for your cell.

In spite of everything (in our theoretical example), you were still able to free up and move a suitable forming press, move a welder, and add assembly to the budding cell. Even though you still have to send material to the punch press department, you laid out your cell to be self-sufficient in terms of forming and welding and assembly, so you have still made a Lean gain in flow and productivity. Your initial efforts have gathered all the "low hanging fruit."

Another example of wasteful but necessary activity might revolve around the issue of time and attendance labor reporting. In some companies, because of how the payroll system works, employees must punch in and out of jobs in order to be paid. Many of these types of systems are residues from outdated, standard cost accounting practices. Employees must account for all direct labor and all indirect diverted labor in their workday. In your future Lean company, you will not need to do labor reporting by punching in and out of jobs. In a completely Lean company, the employees are paid from the time they punch in to start work to the time they punch out to go on break, go to lunch, or finish work (however your company defines payroll clock paid time).

In the short term, if your existing accounting system does not calculate employees' pay unless they continue to punch in and out of jobs, and if this is an integral part of your labor reporting system, until accounting can make the necessary system changes for the payroll reporting based on attendance, you may have to have the employees (or surrogate) do as they always have done—punch in and out of jobs, while ignoring the resultant efficiency and productivity data. This is an administrative example of wasteful but necessary activity. The future goal will be to eliminate this remnant of standard cost accounting.

Since our goal is to start Lean in the factory as soon as possible, we make the decision to accommodate a nonideal world knowing that Lean *is* continuous improvement and never ending. Elimination of waste becomes our perpetual goal. Our first attempt at Lean is our best start possible given the circumstances ... but, be it noted, the first step is not the end of the trip. This is why we tolerate the non-value added but currently necessary steps. Our goal is to *minimize* waste as much as possible in order to start. Our plan is to have a program in place to remediate the waste-causing situations through kaizen (continuous improvement) events. We will discuss the topic of continuous improvement more in depth as we move through the book.

As the team leader goes through the determinations of waste versus value added with the group, other key questions may help the group's decision become a little more sharply focused. Emphasis should be on why are you doing or collecting this? What is the purpose and who is the audience? Is it a requisite for the making of the product or a "nice to know or have"? What are the repercussions if we stop this activity? Are there other options for getting the same info? Are these activities for management reporting? What does your management do with the reporting? Is it required by your standard cost accounting system? Who specifically does what with the reports? Is the information critical to operations on a daily basis? Is it required for regulatory purposes? OSHA? Food and Drug Administration? An underwriting or insurance requirement? Is it part of the product testing or a product safety or safe work practice concern? Is it a customer-mandated and specific requirement? Is it a "political" or "management-self-defense" activity? Is it a redundant review process? Is a check put into place because the existing process is sketchy, undocumented by standard work instructions, or subjective to the point of being personality dependent? Is it something your company "has always done"? Is something required by an ISO or other certification-driven activity? Do forms drive the activity or reporting? Worse yet, does the computer system drive the policy and activity in your factory? By reflectively answering these types of questions, you will be able to decide whether the activity is wasteful or value adding.

As you go through your analysis, this is also the time to review the forms, reports, and screen inputs you have attached to the current-state process map. Review each document just like you reviewed each note. If it is waste associated with a wasteful activity, it should be eliminated. If it is value added or needed in the interim as wasteful but necessary, keep it in your future-state process map. Be aware that forms and reports and screen inputs can become ends in themselves that drive activity.

Continue reviewing the notes until you come to the point in the process where the sales order is sent to the production control department for a scheduled promise date to the customer. As you go through discussing the notes, you may have a group insight for longer-term improvements or alternatives that need to be researched after the process mapping exercise. Put a "cloud burst" above the note using the same color of note as the department in which the activity occurs. Make sure you put enough information on the note to remember the details of what the suggestion was. Avoid computer system fixes where possible (at least until you understand the role of the computer in the level-loading heijunka system). For Lean scheduling and inventory control, you will discover that computer systems are not as important to day-to-day operations as they are to MRP systems. Cloud bursts can be investigated later as a "to do" list growing out of the process mapping exercise.

The future-state process map will begin with the same question that powered activities on the current state: "A customer just telephoned, e-mailed, or faxed an order to your company—what happens next?" Begin creating the future-state process map by writing activities and posting the notes from the current-state map that will be part of the future-state map. (*Note*: Write new notes for the future-state process map—do not reuse notes from current-state map.) Use the same colors for the original departments and follow the placement protocols. If you have added or changed process from the current-state mapping, describe the activity just as you did on the current-state notes.

Although you may have included wasteful but necessary coded notes, ideally, there should be no notes denoting "waste." I say "ideally," because, as beginners, this may not be the case. Do not get discouraged. As we said earlier, Lean is a journey governed by continuous improvement. If you cannot eliminate it on this future-state version, you might be able to eliminate it on the next iteration of the future state. Make improvements where you can. It is not an all-or-nothing effort. Do kaizens as relentlessly as your time and resources allow. Remember you will still be better off than where you began.

Computer systems should never drive policy. Computer systems should fit the appropriate role they most capably serve in a company. In a Lean company, when it comes to running a heijunka and kanban system, their role is to create cards and remain a depository of part number data. This is a stark contrast to MRP-type systems where computer algorithms determine inventory levels and give purchasing and manufactured-inventory reorder advice, create planned replenishment orders for schedulers to release, and track shop orders as they travel through the factory. We need to discuss the proper role the computer will play in our heijunka–kanban driven factory.

Many MRP-driven companies considering adopting Lean practices in their division or factory are operating under the assumption that they will have to get rid of their current MRP-type system and buy some "Lean" software in order to succeed with any Lean conversion. This is not necessarily the case. If the kanban cards and the heijunka scheduling boards are functioning properly, they stand alone and functionally replace the MRP order creation, order release, perpetual inventory tracking, and dispatch lists. If you have a functioning MRP system, that is modular in makeup, you should be able to blend in the heijunka scheduling methods almost seamlessly.

If you have a modular-type MRP system, you probably have modules for part master data, sales entry and customer data, inventory control, purchasing, bill of materials, shop floor control, picking and shipping, accounts receivable and payable, and some type of net-change MRP or regeneration MRP-type program. Most systems also have some report writing capability to allow you to download data. Most, also, have "user-defined" fields available for coding information.

Within most traditional MRP-type systems, though not necessarily standalone modules, there are checks and release points (e.g., purchasing receipts have optional switches routing newly purchased items into "inspection" for release before use, "work in process" rejects go into a quarantine "bucket" awaiting release, etc.) for insuring quality control policies are carried out. Underlying most MRP-type systems, there is an accounting framework that tracks variances and movements of materials, values inventories, and creates reports on labor reporting (e.g., measures productivity, utilization, and efficiency). Along with the modules of the preceding paragraph, these attributes make up most of the systems that are probably in use in most non-Lean companies.

If the system described in the preceding paragraphs is the system you have, especially if it is modular in mode, it can probably be adapted. If your company is smaller and everything is driven off Excel spreadsheets and you have your own homegrown scheduling methods, you will probably experience even less trauma with a change to a heijunka–kanban driven process. If your system is not modular, but integrated, you can still probably use the system to complement the kanban–heijunka process, but it will require your accounting department to become aware of what the changes are. In this latter case, the kanban-related part number coding will become absolutely critical, until your whole company is up and running on heijunkas. The heijunka portion of the business may have to be downloaded into Excel, and the Excel portion combined with the non-heijunka numbers from the business for your current accounting practices. Once your factory is totally on kanban, you will have one very simple, actual-cost, period accounting system.

This is the reason we stated earlier that, early on in your transformation to Lean process, your key finance and accounting personnel should seek out books and training in Lean accounting. (We have provided an excellent bibliography at the end of this book.) This is also a good reason to seek out other Lean companies to talk with about the transition issues. Seek out companies your key personnel can visit. (Your local business councils, chambers of commerce, societies of engineers, and local manufacturing associations are good starting points for networking. Many even have Lean subgroups for this very purpose.)

We like to point out where the key changes will typically take place with existing manufacturing systems. In a heijunka–kanban process, manual processes replace computer algorithms. The circulating kanban cards replace your MRP inventory-module, perpetual inventory record with a defined part number population based on replenishment lead time for the part. Parts coded "K" (for kanban) are only made or procured based on the pulling and turn-in of a kanban card. The kanban cards will all be scheduled through placement on the heijunka boards. The cards with their coding serve as a closed inventory system. Parts unique to the targeted product line and not on kanban, are coded as "C" (for custom), and bought or made on a per order basis. The pulled and turned-in kanban cards for the stocked kanbans, along with one-time kanbans for the custom parts, are either bought or made by means of the heijunka scheduling board system, which replaces the MRP-driven, planned-order to released-order calculations. Your other part numbers and products not involved in the Lean startup continue with their existing system until they can be changed over to Lean.

In addition, there are other changes that come with Lean implementation. Since Lean is not a standard cost system, productivity reporting is done by the operator and posted at the production cell as the work is accomplished, and not calculated by the accounting system in variances through labor reporting. The metrics for your utilization and productivity, as well as on-time performance, will be obvious to anyone walking through your factory. (More on this later.)

For your purchasing, you have negotiated pricing agreements and blanket purchase orders with release quantities from the vendor in multiples of kanban-card quantities processed to the vendor by the buyer. All parts you purchase, whether a stock kanban or a custom kanban, will be by kanban card and also scheduled by a heijunka board. You enter the blanket purchase orders into the system with designated pricing agreements. Daily release authorizations to the vendors, triggered by turned-in kanban cards, against the current pricing agreements will substitute for individual purchase orders. Parts will be received and checked against the packing lists per your normal operations.

Shipping is done through your computer modules to capture the system dates and informational record. Item part master, sales order entry and customer data activity, bills of materials, shipping, and receiving can probably all be adapted to blend well with the manual scheduling. Standard cost accounting systems will be replaced with actual cost, period based systems. The standard work and metrics for running the manual system will be posted and visible at the production total-value flow. For quality control, the operator becomes the key inspector in real time. Operators will report quality problems for all onlookers to see. The operator is helped by standard work documentation, "foolproof" manufacturing methods as much as possible, basic operator maintenance responsibilities, and the ability to stop production and resolve quality issues as they happen.

Since you will not be using the MRP module for scheduling or the shop floor module for tracking shop orders, you can choose to ignore them or shut off the modules. Your systems people will have to discuss any ramifications for this action. If your system is integrated far beyond just planning, releasing, and tracking orders, you may have to adapt as needed. Running MRP to support your Lean total-value-flow start or labor reporting to track orders through the shop is not required.

As far as the perpetual inventory goes, for all the parts coded as kanban or custom for your total-value flow, there is no need for receiving part numbers into the perpetual inventory or issuing part numbers to shop orders to satisfy any need for your Lean cell startup. Inventory levels for parts coded as kanban or custom that go through the cell are controlled by kanban cards, and real inventory resides in the fixed population prescribed by the kanban cards. (There is one caveat for this: if you have excess inventory for part numbers running through your total-value-flow startup, you will need to isolate it and use it up before you start using your kanban cards. For high-volume part numbers coded as "K" (stock kanban), this will probably be a short-term problem. If you have excessive "C" (custom) inventory, this will be a longer-term problem, and your accounting department will have to deal with it.)

Once excess inventory is gone and kanban cards circulate, the valuation for the stocked kanban is roughly one half the replenishment lead time valuation for the kanban quantity. Since your inventories should be substantially reduced, some auditors will accept a calculation—with appropriate test counts—in lieu of full inventory counts for Kanban-controlled inventories. For annual fiscal inventories, since quantities for cards are a set multiple, and only one card is pulled at a time until completely used up, fiscal inventory becomes primarily a matter of counting cards. For rationalized inventories, a plus or minus 5 percent swing in valuation may not be considered "material" by your auditors in the substantially reduced and fast turning inventories. (Your financial person should have this discussion with your auditors to determine their position and experiences on counting Lean inventories.)

System interfaces will have to be discussed with the appropriate, knowledgeable information technology staff in your company. Systems are not universally the same. There is variation in program designs and the default values you have selected to run your current system. The accounting department representatives should be in all relevant discussions. You will still have to do monthly and quarterly reporting to keep your shareholders and creditors happy. You will also need to talk with auditors to keep them apprized of your Lean plans. As long as your accounting staff is nimble enough to use spreadsheet programs to supplement your existing MRP-system programs, you should be able to get all the data you need for filing financial and balance sheet statements.

When you start up, someone will also raise the concern about running the Lean production cells in parallel with the MRP system until you see how things shake out. This idea would be strictly one of placating the MRP system—there would be no beneficial effect on the day-to-day functioning of the kanban–heijunka system. We would recommend against doing this. We would also argue against having the personnel involved in your total-value-flow startup be doubly distracted trying to manage two systems. Our suggestion is this: train hard, prepare and train your staff and all personnel who will touch the cards, hold managers accountable for their department's responsibilities, make sure accounting has the ability to get the numbers they need, and then start. Before you start, have several "walk throughs." On the second "walk through," have the people doing the actual activity explain to the assembled group what they are doing.

People in the company will need to be aware of the changes to the system when you discontinue the MRP and perpetual inventory record-keeping for the exclusively "K" and "C" coded part numbers being processed through your new total-value flow. Depending on how your current system operates and the default values selected, you could have strange looking data. For openers, if all kanban receipts to stock are not incremented in your system's perpetual inventory record and you have some type of backflush logic that automatically deducts bills of materials when orders ship, you will have a perpetual inventory that is constantly building negative on-hand and dollar valuation numbers. Or, if people are looking in the MRP shop floor system to see when an order is scheduled to be run, they will not find it on a dispatch list—it will still be only a "planned order" awaiting release in the MRP module. These are only some of the strange data situations you might encounter when you go live and choose to ignore the MRP portion of your system.

If you feel you know enough now to insert the kanban–heijunka portion into your future-state process map, do so. Finish off the process map to the point where the part ships from stock. If you do not feel confident to fill out the notes yet, read the next chapter, where we will discuss in more detail a typical flow for kanban cards and the use of the heijunka boards. At whatever point you understand enough to finish the future-state process map, do so and make sure you save it. You will need the future-state process map to help create and document the standard work instructions, which will drive your total-value flow.

Chapter 8

Understanding Kanban–
Heijunka Card-Flow Process

The kanban card is the agent that drives the level-loaded production cell. (Level loaded is a method of scheduling, whether for single or mixed product, loaded at takt time.) When it is placed on the heijunka (scheduling board) for a given date and time, it becomes the authorization to produce or replenish that particular kanban part number at that particular time. When it is residing on the part numbers it represents in its defined bin or stock location, nothing happens with the card, nor is there any need to produce or procure anything. No need to replenish is created until the part number is picked or shipped and the card is turned in to the scheduler. Only when the card circulates is any production activity set in process. When the kanban cards are placed on the heijunka board following defined scheduling rules, these become the level-loaded schedule for the shop. For these reasons, the kanban cards control both inventory levels and shop schedules.

In the next two chapters, we will discuss, in depth, both the kanban cards and the heijunka-board scheduling process. We will flesh out more detail on the kanban cards—how to make the cards; explanation of information and source of information on the cards; how this information helps the foreman, scheduler, and stock picker; and rules for handling the kanban cards. For the heijunka boards, we will discuss how to make the heijunka boards (keep in mind, there are two different types—one for production scheduling and one for purchasing replenishments), where they should be placed, who is allowed to touch the boards, and how the schedules are to be determined and cards slotted. When you are through these chapters, you should have enough knowledge to return to your future-state process map (if you have not already finished it), incorporate the kanban–heijunka flow portion, and finish posting your notes for the complete process.

There are two classifications of kanban cards: manufacturing kanbans and purchasing kanbans. Within the two classifications are three subclassifications: a card can be a "stock" kanban; an "LTO" ("limited-time offer" for an abnormally high demand for an otherwise stock kanban part number); or a "custom" (think, one-time purchase, or make) kanban. Thus, you can have stock-manufactured kanbans, custom-manufactured kanbans, stock-purchased kanbans, custom-purchased kanbans, and abnormal-demand cards for either manufactured or purchased stock part numbers. All of the kanbans, regardless of subclassification, are put into action by slotting on a heijunka board. Custom kanbans and LTO kanbans, both manufacturing and purchasing, are created as one-time use cards when production control schedules the sales order they are linked to. Purchasing kanbans are only slotted on the purchasing heijunka, and the manufactured kanbans are only slotted on the manufacturing heijunka.

Kanban cards can be made from readily available paper stock materials. Since there is some durability required during the time of their use, we would recommend using something like index card stock (32 pound minimum) paper. Many sizes of cut index-card stock are available, or you can readily buy reams of higher pound-value paper that you can cut to your specific size. Some companies find it useful to use different colored paper stocks to differentiate stock kanbans from custom kanbans and manufactured kanbans from purchased kanbans. Lean factories tend to be visually oriented (more on this as we go through the book), and visual cueing is to be encouraged in Lean processes wherever it makes sense.

The size of the cards used with the typical kanban-card creation program is adjustable to your needs. Many of the standard-cut, index-sized cards are four-inch by six-inch or five-inch by seven-inch—a good size for the cards. If you do not use precut cards, size the card to get minimal waste from standard or legal size paper. Any size will work depending on how much information you need on the cards. Both the stock and the custom kanbans, for both manufacturing- and purchasing-part numbers, should be printed on this type of paper. One caveat: the kanban card size you choose should easily fit in the slotting boxes you purchase or make for your heijunka boards.

The stock kanbans only, whether manufacturing or purchasing, should, in addition, be laminated in readily available, three-mil, plastic sheet laminating pouches. (You will have to research which of the laminators and laminating pouch sizes will work best for your cards.) This normally eliminates the need to reprint stock-kanban cards due to normal wear and tear from constant recirculation. Custom and LTO kanbans, given that they are intended for one-time use, do not need to be laminated.

Kanban cards are divided into three parts. The left side of the card normally has the internal or external source information and specifications—"make from" raw material, vendor source and contact information, etc. The middle of the card contains information about the part number you are making or buying—part number, description, kanban quantities, etc. The right side of the card has disposition or shipping instructions or, if a stock kanban, final stock bin information. This is the most common format for card data and information. (At this point in your Lean education, it might make sense to review the example kanban cards in Chapter 3.)

The data that go into the card creation come from the database application—usually utilizing Excel and Access applications. This kanban database, in turn, consists of data that are both entered and maintained in your company's primary computer system and data that are entered and maintained in the kanban database. The downloads into the Excel spreadsheets, enabled by appropriate codings, which tie the information to the part number, make sure that information is maintained only once in the appropriate database. You do not want a system database where information has to be redundantly keyed. One person, with trained backup, should be assigned responsibility to maintain the kanban database, and this accountability normally resides with the scheduler who creates and issues the kanban cards. Your information technology personnel can do downloads from your main computer database as needed to refresh the kanban database. If your scheduler or production and inventory control manager is report-writer savvy, he or she may be able to download and do any necessary data linking from your main system directly into the kanban Excel database.

We have included typical information, in our examples, needed for functional kanban cards. If you wish to add information to print on the cards, there may be "user-defined fields" that could probably be adapted as needed. Keep in mind, the kanban card is used in conjunction with standard work and part number-related information (such as blueprints, tooling schedules, programing directives, etc.). These forms of documentation normally are physically or electronically kept in the production cell and maintained by the foreman and scheduler. In the typical MRP-type computer program, this kind of information usually came to the work center in the job packet created by the scheduler.

The current system you have for disseminating engineering change notifications (ECNs) or product change notices (PCNs) for products should be modified to have an acknowledgment sign-off requirement (electronic or written) by the kanban database administrator. If the part numbers affected have kanban codings ("K" or "C") for the part numbers, the administrator will have to make the appropriate changes to the database records and reprint cards as necessary. In the event of new products, input from the product manager will determine what codings will be used to add the part numbers to the database. For lack of historical usage patterns, the product manager, in the case of new products, will have to provide potential shipment numbers, which will go into the makeup of the kanban cards.

The ECN or PCN details the form, fit, junction, or technical change required in the part numbers involved and authorizes documentation revisions in bills of material, process sheets, drawings, standard practices, tooling and fixtures, programing, test fixturing or test procedures, dies and castings or molds, and schematics.

Besides the normal identification of the part numbers involved in the change, the notification used to communicate the ECN or PCN must now be altered to include actions required for kanban cards, kanban database, bins, and the value stream where product is made.

- Are the part numbers involved in stocked kanban? MTO? or custom?
- Will kanban database need to be updated or refreshed with correct coding for parent level part numbers?
- If existing kanban affected, will the kanban card quantity or number of kanban cards need revision?
- Will this change require LTO quantity coding revision at parent part number level?
- Will this change require part number coding revision to MTO from kanban at any level in the bills of material level?
- Will standard work, scheduling rules, or visuals—either in scheduling, purchasing, or the production cell—need revision, addition, or deletion?
- Will drawings or blueprints, test procedures or fixtures, process information such as program numbers or inspection protocol printed on kanban card need revision, addition, or deletion in the cell?
- If the container or conveyance is the kanban signal, do they need creation or revision?

■ If additional kanban part numbers are created, will parts be stocked at point of use, at supplying work center, or in warehouse designated bin? What is the bin address?

■ Etc., etc., etc.—the questions tailored to the specific needs of your kanban–heijunka system.

Responsible sign-offs will be required for kanban database updates, kanban card creation, and production cell standard work, drawing or program changes, etc.

As you are probably beginning to comprehend, the information on the kanban cards complements the point-of-use information and standard-work documentation resident in the production cell. The information should be self-contained—the operators or fabricators should have all the information they need to make the product. There should be no need to delay the start on any kanban product due to the need to retrieve information from the office or "hunt down" the expert in the shop for answers. By emphasizing standard work in the production activity, standard processes using kanban cards, and a quality-control-reinforcing manufacturing process, cross-training can begin. Never again will the plant descend into chaos as key people, with pieces of knowledge required to make the product, decide to go on vacation.

Who can touch the kanban cards, where kanban cards can reside, when kanbans are slotted on the heijunka boards, and how kanban cards flow are part of the defined process for using heijunkas. There are rules and information about kanbans, which must be communicated to all the personnel who will be touching kanbans. If kanbans come up missing, there can be problems. We will try to address all these issues in the next paragraphs.

Normally, the people who touch the kanbans are stock pickers, line stockers, receiving personnel, operators, buyers, and production control personnel. In most companies, the line stocker who delivers materials to the production cell is the same person who does the picking of the component material to satisfy the kanban card. As a general rule, responsibility for handling the kanban card should reside with the person who first touches the card—hand offs between pickers and line stockers, or receiving clerks and stock handlers should be minimized as much as possible. "Hand offs" generally result in adding waste to the process.

Anyone whose job does not require him to handle the kanban cards, should not touch the cards. No one other than the operator and his/her supervisors or production control personnel should be allowed to handle kanbans affecting the office scheduling heijunka and production cell takt board kanban card holders. Only the buyer and the receiving personnel should be allowed to take kanbans from the receiving heijunka boards. Even when authorized personnel temporarily remove a kanban card from a heijunka, it is a good idea to have "place holders" (a laminated strip of colored paper) available at the heijunkas to place into the slot from which the card was taken. This ensures the card is replaced in the original slot when returned to the heijunka. There should be policy in place that reinforces these guidelines. Given how crucial the slotted kanban cards are to creating the production schedule, any unknowledgeable person who re-slots the cards can cause mischief to scheduler-promised customer ship dates. Any person who knowingly and intentionally re-slots kanban cards to create scheduling mayhem should be dealt with according to your disciplinary policy.

The handling cycle usually starts when a stock picker breaks into the make- or purchased-kanban-card quantity (the multiple for that particular part number printed on the kanban card) either to satisfy a shipping order or to pick to satisfy an internal manufacturing order. If there is an existing partial-multiple quantity in the defined bin, it should be used completely before the next kanban card is pulled. Exhaust one kanban-card quantity multiple before moving on to the next kanban-card multiple. Only one card is pulled at a time, and the quantity is used completely before going on to pull the next kanban card.

Once the part is picked and the kanban-card multiple breached, the line stocker or picker places the kanban card into a posting box. The posting box is simply a slotted box, highly visible by signage and color, that is placed at obvious traffic points in the picking process. (Keep in mind that walking or driving a forklift hundreds of feet, tens to hundreds of times per day to a lone posting box is waste to be avoided. Have a reasonable number of posting boxes in proximity to where picking is occurring.) The posting box serves the same purpose as a mailbox. Think of the deposited kanbans as letters dropped into a mailbox, which the "mailman" (read, scheduler, or production control person) picks up at multiple times per day. Any kanban, manufactured or purchased, can be deposited into the same posting box.

The production control person or scheduler makes rounds of the factory floor and retrieves the kanbans multiple times per day and brings them to his work area next to the scheduling heijunka boards. If the production control person handles both purchasing and manufactured kanbans, he can either choose to slot the cards into a scheduling heijunka for reorder or slot the cards in an "unscheduled" or "future" marked heijunka box following specific reordering rules. If the scheduler does not handle purchasing kanbans, the cards are delivered to the marked purchasing inbox for kanbans.

Note that stopping points for cards should be visual, defined, physical locations. Buyers should not keep cards in desk drawers or vendor-named "hanging files" and schedulers should not keep cards in their back pants pockets or comingled with other papers in their desk "in" trays. If the scheduler or buyer had to leave suddenly, the trained backup should be able to pick up exactly where the last person left off. This aspect of "standard work" is part of the company discipline required by Lean methods and principles. Both buyers and schedulers should put cards they defer action on into the official "unscheduled" location for the cards.

The standard heijunka boards have at least a two-week, rolling window, columns labeled by weekday name only, for scheduling. If your company has weekend days as normally scheduled workdays, they should also be represented as part of the two-week, rolling windows with their own, individual boxes. The heijunka boards also contain boxes for "future" or "unscheduled" cards. The scheduler or buyer moves the "today is" indicator at the beginning of the day to pinpoint the beginning of the rolling, two-week window. Cards should be slotted on the boards in either a scheduled box, "future" box, or "unscheduled" box as soon as possible. In some cases, the scheduling or buying rules state that cards will be held until a specified number of cards, by particular part number, are accumulated. In other cases, cards are slotted on a card-for-card basis. These guidelines are spelled out on the scheduling or purchasing standard-work posted at the heijunka board or the kanban cards themselves.

If there is a need to accumulate purchasing kanban cards until a certain number are attained, there are many ways to keep track of cards. One of the easiest ways is to set up a visual reorder point for the accumulated cards, to see when the signal to purchase should be given (Figures 8.1 through 8.4).

When the time comes for manufacturing to make the part number on the kanban card slotted on the scheduling heijunka board (Figure 8.2), the scheduler will take the card to the production cell and place it in the hourly, heijunka-schedule boxes visually placed in the cell. In some cases, the hourly schedule boxes are placed on the same structure holding the takt sheet (Figure 8.4). If not, they need to be immediately adjacent to the takt-sheet holder. The scheduling boxes, along with the takt sheet, are visual indications of schedule adherence, and they also serve as a focus point for line stockers serving the total-value flow.

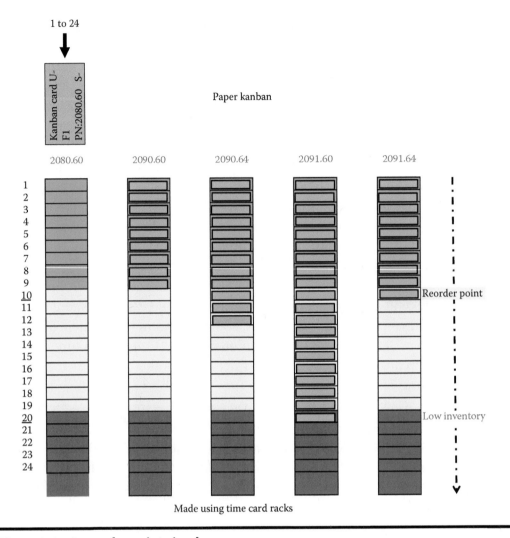

Figure 8.1   A reorder point visual.

When the scheduler takes the kanban cards to the production cell for manufacture, he or she does so following defined scheduling rules. The production cell is always loaded to required takt-time values (the production rate that is required—historically derived but modified to meet current sales plan). Posted standard work or instructions on the kanban cards give specific rules and guidelines on scheduling the cards. It is not critical to schedule every kanban card immediately. The scheduler knows what is in stock and what is in process, because the total population of the specific part number is known from information on the kanban card. If multiple cards exist for a part number (for our example, say there are six cards for a particular part number), and the scheduler only has one in hand, he or

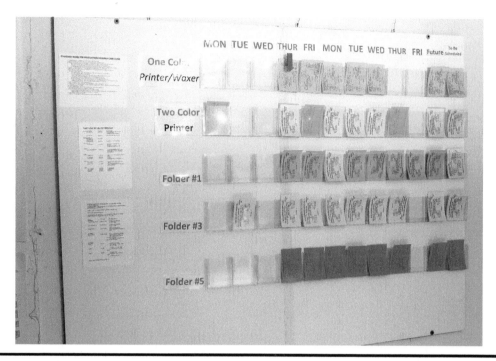

Figure 8.2   A typical scheduling heijunka board with posted standard work.

she has the option to schedule other, faster moving cards (for our example, say there are eight cards for a particular part number, and the scheduler is holding five of the eight in hand) ahead of the single, temporarily slower-moving card.

The posted standard work (Figure 8.3) and instructions on the kanban card are part of the defined process involved with using heijunka boards. The standard work and instructions should be clear and evident to anyone learning the scheduling function. These items not only ensure that the production cell is loaded properly, but they also facilitate easy transfer of knowledge, which in turn speeds cross-training of employees. Unlike MRP-type systems where employees need passwords and training on screen after screen to plan, approve, and release orders before they create the necessary shop packets, the scheduler needs to be able to read and understand a few simple, posted rules and understand card flow.

Some of the posted standard work will arise from the particular nature of your business, and some of the instructions will arise from how far along you are on the Lean journey. As you eliminate the "non-value added but necessary" steps in your process, the standard work will have to be rewritten to reflect this. As you eliminate "setup" waste or buy "right-sized" machines to optimize flows in the production cell, your standard work will

Scheduling standard work for print, wax, and fold cells

Takt unit of measure:

One color printer/waxer	Feet	Folder 1	Case
One color printer as waxer only	Feet	Folder 2	Case
Two color printer	Feet	Folder 3	Case
Waxer 5	Feet	Folder 5	Case
Waxer 6	Feet		

Work day for scheduling purposes:

All work cells are to be scheduled for $7\frac{1}{2}$ hours per shift and 2 shifts per day. Exception:
Waxers 5 and 6 and one color printer/waxer or one color printer as waxer only
are to be scheduled 8 hours per day times 2 shifts.

Cell	TAKT time	Restrictions/Other
Printers	(in feet per hour)	
One color as printer/waxer	30,000	No paper weight restrictions Can run 56" paper Can run "onionskin" paper
One color as waxer only	57,600	No paper weight restrictions Can run 56" paper
Two color printer	9,600	Preference for polycoat orders changeovers/set-ups are substantial (2 hours)
Waxers		
Waxers 5 and 6	44,000	Waxers 5 and 6 are interchangeable with one exception—waxer 5 does NOT run tissue (tissue equals any 10.75 basis weight paper). Reserve 20% of daily capacity on waxer 5 for pizza rounds.
Folders		
Folders 1 and 2	See table	Can NOT run 64" paper Can run tissue (10.75 basis weight) Can run 56" paper
Folder 3	See table	Can NOT run 56" ot 64" paper Can NOT run tissue (10.75 basis weight)
Folder 5	See table	Can run 64" paper Can NOT run tissue (10.75 basis weight) Can NOT run 56" paper

(Table is titled "folder standards by cell by paper weight")

Figure 8.3   Examples of posted standard work scheduling rules.

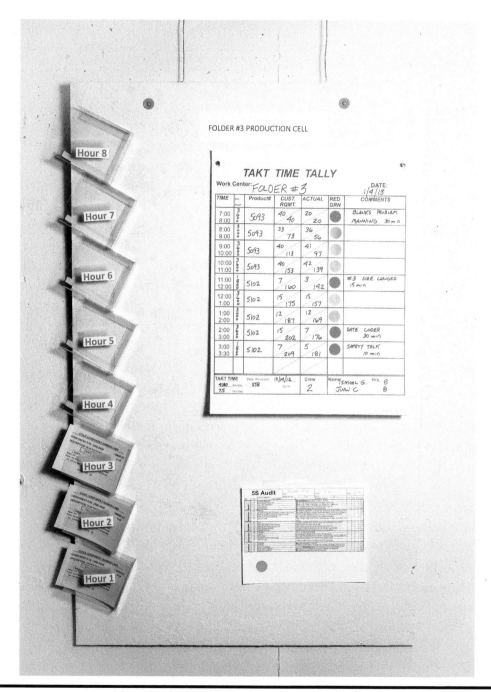

Figure 8.4   A production cell takt board with scheduling boxes.

have to reflect this. If the process changes, the standard work must change. Part of the housekeeping metric for the production cell is having proper documentation and standard work in the total-value flow.

An example of guidelines resulting from the particular nature of your business might be: if you are running a food line, you cannot follow one food, containing one monitored allergen to be processed in equipment shared with another food containing a different monitored allergen without purge and clean-up of the first allergen. Another example might be gauge or type of metal used—if you are machining a particular gauge of metal, you run, all things being equal, whatever cards you have for that particular gauge of metal consecutively. A further example might be, if you perform a major setup for one part number and a minor setup adjustment for a related part number, you run these parts successively. Keep in mind that some of these rules are due to the fact that your total-value flow may not have quick changeovers immediately, and, until you get to the equivalent of the "single-minute exchange of dies" advocated by Shigeo Shingo, the guidelines may be temporary compromises with the ideal of minimized waste in the setup.

The scheduler will take the cards to the production cell to be slotted into the hourly, heijunka-schedule boxes in a timely fashion to notify the line stocker and to the operator of jobs that are coming. If there are multiple shifts in the plant, there must be continuity on the part of the schedulers to load the first hours of the next shift. The line stocker will need to be able to pick parts and bring them to the production cell to meet the scheduled, kanban-card, hour-start time.

If for some reason, the schedule is disrupted by unforeseen events and the production cell suffers considerable down time, the takt-sheet production reporting notes this fact and the operator, foreman, and scheduler make any adjustments to the scheduling, as necessary. If orders committed to ship to customers are compromised, the foreman or scheduler needs to get this information to the inside sales department in order to notify the customer. This is real-time reporting in a Lean environment.

It is not advisable to put many days' worth of cards in the production cell at any one time. As a rule of thumb, we would recommend, unless your particular circumstances warrant, that no more than the next two jobs or four hours of production are posted in the production-cell hourly heijunkas. You want the flexibility in your schedule that Lean allows, and you also want your scheduler on the factory floor and aware of how the production cells are producing.

If an expediting request comes from a customer who wants his order moved up in the schedule, and the cards are still on the scheduling heijunka board, the scheduler simply rearranges the cards to accommodate the change. If the requested change will result in one customer order going late to the commit date because of another customer order, the sales department can make that decision and inform the "moved" customer that their order will be late. In the cases of expedites, the final decision of what moves and what stays resides with the sales department. In Lean, with minimal work in process, you know what affects what when expediting occurs: in MRP-type environments, the casualty customer's order is not always known.

The production cell should be scheduled to the required takt time. For example, if the production cell needs to make 80 units per hour, schedule the production cell for 80 units per hour. This takt value should be achievable, if your established production cell's physical makeup and level-loading assumptions are correct. If you schedule your production cell for 80 percent of what you need to produce per shift—leaving time for quality rework issues or "catch-up" time—you will soon be meeting 80 percent of the schedule 100 percent of the time. Scheduling less than takt values needed from the production cell is building waste into the schedule. Work overtime, if you can, to meet the schedule as needed, and monitor your committed lead times until you can meet the required takt times. The information you will receive on why you missed your hourly schedules will be important, in the long term, for driving your next productivity-improvement events.

Keep in mind that the operator in the production cell has the power to stop work or shut down the line once he or she is aware of a work or quality issue that will result in questionable parts. By establishing the takt time as the benchmark for production in the production cell, you are not forcing the operator to do the impossible task. The production cell arrangement and manpower assigned to meet the takt time were arrived at by concluding those values were what an average worker could achieve per hour, day in and day out, in normal circumstances. The production cell was not set up using only the fastest or smartest or "superstar" employees to set the standard. It should be achievable following the rules for slotting the kanban cards. In the final analysis, if the schedule is not met, the movement of the kanban cards by the scheduler is the admission of lengthening lead times and possible missed commitments for customer orders.

The information written on your takt boards by the operators as the reasons the schedule is being missed will guide you to where your next kaizen (continuous improvement) events need to be focused. In most production cell startups, the issue will be a quality control issue resulting in rejects (you need to foolproof your process as much as possible), or it will be a setup issue due to inordinate amounts of time to do the changeover. In either case, you will have valuable information to lead you to your next productivity improvement.

When the operator completes the kanban multiple, he or she has the responsibility to place the kanban securely on the completed parts for line stocker or material handler pickup. There are many standardized ways to attach cards—tie wraps, alligator or pressure clips, clear envelopes with adhesive on back, Velcro fasteners, etc. If the right-sized container is the kanban signal itself, this is the ideal solution.

The line stocker who brings parts to the production cell normally takes the completed parts away. This falls in line with the idea of avoiding unnecessary hand offs. The material is then moved to the final destination—either shipping lane, next cell incoming lane or assigned bin, or finished goods stock bin location. The kanban card remains affixed to the product until a picker picks the product and the multiple is breached, the card is deposited in the posting box, and the cycle begins again.

Purchased kanban cards function in the same way as the manufacturing cards. The buyer gets the deposited kanban cards from the inbox location, sorts them, and makes decisions whether to notify the vendor for a release, or she keeps the cards in a defined, "unscheduled" or "future" box at her desk. If the buyer notifies the vendor to release the next kanban quantity, she then takes the purchasing kanban card and slots it in the appropriate "date due" box on the purchasing heijunka board—counting forward the printed lead time on the card after disregarding the current day. This is the typical, agreed-to lead time representing the passage of time in days before that part is expected on the dock and ready for use from the vendor.

On the appointed day, the shipment should arrive from the vendor. At receipt, the receiving clerk checks the shipment to make sure it is for the kanban multiple printed on the purchasing kanban card and in the correct packaging multiple. If the sent quantity or packaging multiple is different from the kanban card multiple, the buyer must be notified to initiate corrective action with the vendor. (In some cases, there will be a "plus or minus," due to the type of product purchased; this variation should be defined in discussions with the vendor and notated on the purchasing kanban card.)

If the quantity sent by the vendor is correct and packaged in the correct multiple, the receiving person affixes the kanban to the parts and moves the parts to the destination printed on the kanban card—final stock bin or incoming lane or bin in a production cell. Parts are matched against accompanying packing list per standard receiving procedures, and receiving papers and other required documentation are forwarded to the accounts payable department per company policy. In the case of purchasing stock parts, the cycle begins again when the kanban-card multiple quantity is breached, and the cards are deposited in the posting box.

At the end of the receiving day, whatever kanban cards are left in the purchasing heijunka for that day are considered "late" orders. The buyer will then have to follow up with the vendor. At this point, the buyer shares information with the scheduler to determine if any committed orders are affected, and appropriate calls are made to the customers as needed.

In the next chapter, we will finish up our discussion of kanban cards and the heijunkas.

Chapter 9

Kanbans and Heijunkas

We discussed the materials used in making the kanban cards in the previous chapter, and now we should discuss suggestions for placing and fabricating the heijunkas. There are many ways to make these, and they should not be budget busters. We need something that is visual, functional, mobile, and inexpensive. When you are having your follow-up kaizen events to put the activities discussed in your future-state map into action, some creative members of the kaizen team charged with establishing the heijunka boards should be able to make these in one or two days.

If you ever visit a Lean factory with an active program of kaizen events (continuous improvement), you will notice that there seems to be an abundance of wood, corrugation, duct tape, PVC piping applications, acrylic or fiberglass sheet, and erector-set-type metals everywhere. The materials used have common attributes: they lend themselves to modular application, they are flexible, they are relatively cheap, and they are easily reconfigured and expandable. You will not see finely finished, high-cost, "permanent" solutions. Since the goal with continuous improvement is to eliminate more and more waste in the process, the materials used tend to reflect the acknowledgment of the "interim" nature in the pursuit of perfection.

One of the first questions you will have to answer when it comes to the heijunka boards is placement of the boards. The easiest one to resolve will probably be the receiving heijunka. It should be in the receiving department in a conspicuous, high-traffic, but non-disruptive, place. The receiving clerks will have to have access to the board as they retrieve and match up product received with appropriate kanban card. If all products must go through the adjacent quality control department before being released for use by the factory, the board should probably be directly outside the quality control area where released, approved quality product is moved.

The makeup of the receiving heijunka board can vary. In theory, you only need one row of boxes for slotting the cards to cover the rolling, two-week window, and the "futures" box. In practice, you may want to vary the number of rows, if it gives your process better visibility or ease of work in handling the cards. Like everything in Lean, you learn the theory and methods, and then you adapt to fit your company.

In some companies where one or two particular vendors (e.g., an injection molder who supplies all your plastic parts, or a particular food source that supplies all your flavorings, or a steel distribution house that delivers all metals, etc.) have daily deliveries with high volumes of receipts, you may want to add that vendor name with its own line of boxes for card slotting. If your company has high volumes of receipts from outside service providers like painters or platers, you might want to split out your painters and platers with their own row of boxes. If you start adding rows to your heijunka, how the cards get slotted and where to look for the cards should be obvious, with minimal training and posted standard work, for the employees who do the job. If it is not obvious how you know something is a flavoring or what is an outside process part, you probably do not need the extra row of boxes.

The size of the receiving heijunka should be equal to: the row label + (width of the boxes sized to fit your cards × the rolling two-week window in days) + the "futures" box. (*Note*: If your buyer prefers to keep the "futures"—unscheduled deliveries—cards in a defined bin in the office area, that is fine, as long as it is visible and covered in standard work.) In addition, there should be enough room on or immediately adjacent to the heijunka board to post the relevant standard work, the process flowchart, and any other required information for effective use of the board and slotting of the cards. There should also be enough room between the rows so that the cards can be slotted with ease, given the height of your slotted kanban cards.

When it comes to the placement of the scheduling heijunka, there are various possibilities depending on how your physical plant is laid out. Because hand offs are an indicator of waste of motion and effort, we would recommend that the scheduling function and scheduling heijunka be in as close proximity to the inside-sales takers as is possible. If this is possible, communications between the two departments should improve and ship-date commit questions should be readily resolved by reviewing the board—even while the customer remains on the phone. In some processes, the scheduler may be able to receive faxed and e-mailed sales-order releases from Lean customers and schedule them without the inside sales department touching the order. If the order takers are nowhere near the production facility, this layout may not work. If the scheduler cannot be situated by the inside sales people, he should be close to the production lines he serves.

The scheduling heijunka will generally have the same size requirements as the receiving heijunka. There will also be a need to leave room for posted standard work and scheduling rules, a process flowchart, and any other information or direction required for the scheduler to do his job. The only difference is that the scheduling heijunka will have an additional box for "unscheduled" kanban cards. They are "unscheduled" because they are "future" orders not due to start or they do not meet the rules for single-card processing. For this latter group, once the prerequisite numbers of cards (indicated on the particular part number kanban card) are received, the order can then be slotted into a workday box on the board. The "unscheduled" box is on the scheduling board to eliminate the problem of losing or misplacing cards—they have an assigned place if they are not scheduled. This, again, is part of the discipline and standardization of practice required for a successful Lean implementation.

The hourly schedule boxes at the production cell will be covered when we talk about what is needed to set up the production cell. These are far easier to set up. The boxes for kanban cards only cover the immediate time (usually in minutes or hours) for the scheduled periods in the defined work shifts. There are no "overtime" boxes, "futures" boxes, or "rework and repair" boxes, for obvious reasons.

The boxes at the buyer's work location should also be defined and visual by way of labels or markings. In some cases, the buyer will hold cards until the requisite number of kanban cards has been turned in to trigger the vendor activity. These should be placed in a labeled, "unscheduled" box. In some situations, there might be placed orders with lead times greater than the number of rolling, receiving-day boxes on the receiving heijunka; these can be notated with grease pen or Post-it note and kept in a "futures" box at the buyer's desk or at the receiving heijunka, as we previously discussed. In some cases, it makes sense to have specially marked boxes for the high-volume vendors who deliver daily at the buyer's location.

Bottom line, all kanban cards should be accounted for in defined and marked boxes. Kanban cards should never be allowed to accumulate in top-right desk drawers, in vendor-marked file folders, or in the buyer's rear pants pocket. It needs to be obvious, and the trained buyer backup should be able to find every kanban card without having to ask or telephone someone in the case of an absence. Here, again, this is part of the Lean discipline. These also become posted, metrics housekeeping grading points on daily walk-throughs.

All the heijunkas discussed can be economically created. The cheapest functional boards we have seen have been made from a four-foot by eight-foot sheet of corrugation (tri-wall), which was spray painted white and had commercially available, right-sized, white, brochure-type dispensing corrugation boxes, hot-glued to the tri-wall corrugation sheeting. All the labels were printed out from standard, bold, large font, computer programs. The heijunka was affixed to an interior wall by long dry-wall screws. All the standard work and accompanying flowcharts were posted immediately adjacent to the heijunka. In contrast, some of the more expensive heijunkas involved the use of a plywood or acrylic-sheeting backing and acrylic, clear, right-sized boxes affixed to the plywood or piece of plastic.

These first heijunkas will become focal points for your Lean efforts in the plant, so we can understand spending a little more to market and showcase the change your company is making. This will become one of your primary tools to "sell" Lean to the uninitiated employees or to any customers your newly informed sales force might want to bring through your plant. Keep in mind that our effort, as we said in the earliest chapters, in beginning Lean, is to create a success story that is visible, that all personnel in the company can learn from, and that future activities can be modeled after. Regardless of which way you go with materials, you can see that the final product is relatively inexpensive for what it will produce for your company.

Before we leave heijunkas, there is one point of clarification. You can put multiple product lines on one office-scheduling heijunka. It boils down to a matter of space and what you want to do. You do not need one heijunka board per product line—unless the manufacture of your product warrants it. If you have many fabrications and subassemblies that end up in one final-assembly production cell, it would make sense to schedule all the component parts and subassemblies for the final-assembly production cell, as well as the final-assembly production cell itself, on one, visual, all-controlling board. In this example, you would have rows for scheduled subassemblies, which tie into the final-assembly scheduling row.

If this is not the case, each row of unrelated product on the scheduling heijunka will operate independently, and each row can schedule a different, defined production cell. If you have multiple product lines for multiple production cells, make sure you leave room to add all the particular scheduling rules that apply to each product line. The point of the work rules, flowcharts, and posted standard work is to make sure whoever is scheduling has all the information he or she needs to schedule the cell.

The physical placement of the scheduler should also be where the equipment needed to operate the kanban–heijunka process will be located. The computer linked to the kanban database and card creation programs should be there along with a kanban card printer, laminator, cutting board (as needed), and related supplies. For the relatively inexpensive costs of printers, we would strongly recommend dedicated printers for the card printing. This will save "changeover time" and wasted toner and card stock, after adjustments that occur when printing the cards on a commonly shared printer.

The posted standard work and scheduling rules should be simple and clear. Flowcharts should cover in detail the entire process—from hand offs to the scheduler, to processing the cards from the scheduler to the production cell or receiving board. Where possible, use pictures—if they can contain the same information as words. Pictures can transcend language issues or help with reading comprehension. The postings have two goals: (1) to make sure the scheduling follows the defined process as seamlessly as possible, and (2) to allow for cross training of personnel.

One of the best ways to test your posted standard work is to bring someone not associated with the process, but who has some knowledge of what you are trying to do, in to review the standard work and flowchart. Questions on the standard work or the flowchart are indicators where clarification may be needed. Edit for required changes and repost as necessary.

As should be becoming very clear, the heijunkas and the whole scheduling process depend on the circulation of the kanban cards. It is also probably becoming very clear that lost kanban cards are a problem. Without a kanban card circulating to set off a series of replenishment events, nothing happens to that kanban-controlled part number. Parts are used up with no replacements forthcoming. Eventually, there is a surprise and an acute shortage with an accompanying expediting frenzy to replace the missing parts.

Until the workers charged with handling the cards fully understand the consequences of not following the process and using the defined points of placement for the cards, there will be lost cards from time to time. Most will be taken home in pant pockets or be lost on the floor due to methods for attaching to the part numbers they control. From experience, lost kanban cards have a small window of mayhem—once everyone is accustomed to the cards, they are rarely, if ever, lost. During startups of production cells, this will be more prevalent, but there are ways to mitigate the problem of lost cards.

First of all, there should be established rules about who creates and handles the cards. In day-to-day operations, the scheduler should be the only person to create kanban cards—stock, custom, and LTO. This rule applies to both manufactured and purchased kanbans. The scheduler (or someone in production or inventory control) should be assigned the responsibility to maintain the kanban database, which creates the cards. By having the scheduler create all kanbans, he or she can ensure the integrity of the customer order, committed ship date given to the sales department. For vacation coverage or other absence, specific backups should be designated and cross-trained—not only on card scheduling, but also on database maintenance.

Handling of the scheduled kanban cards should follow the defined process for the cards in that production cell. Normally, this would mean that only the line stocker, receiving clerk, buyer, and operator would have need to touch the cards. Plant personnel, including supervisors, should not be allowed to take cards from the heijunkas or "unscheduled" or "futures" boxes without the scheduler's or buyer's knowledge for fear of re-slotting the cards in the wrong time or day slot.

In some production-cell startups, it may make sense to establish an interim (two to three weeks in duration) kanban-card cycle count program as the personnel go through their learning stages. This could apply only to the extremely long-lead-time parts or high-dollar-value parts or critical, single-sourced items, or it could be kanban-card inventory wide. We would recommend this only as a short-term undertaking (wasteful but necessary in the interim) that should go away as soon as startup training and handling issues are resolved. Cycle counting, as a prolonged activity, is an admission of failed processes. In lieu of on-going cycle counting, do a kaizen (continuous improvement) event to pinpoint the problem and eliminate the wasteful conditions that allow for lost cards in the process. If you can avoid cycle counting cards, do.

If you have need to do a short-term cycle-count program, remember that the point is to count cards, not parts. This should substantially cut the time commitment for the counting activity. Do this as part of end-of-day activities. Although the kanban cards contain information about total number of cards for that particular part number and which number in the series that particular kanban card is, for example, for part number 123 having four kanban cards, the individual cards will indicate "card 1 of 4 cards"—it might be easier to assign serial numbers for each kanban card printed and cycle count by part number by serial number.

The cycle counter should make efforts to determine root cause for lost cards. These "root causes" will identify points in the process where something—education of handlers of cards, attachment of cards to parts, needs for more posting boxes or movement of existing posting boxes, bins not properly and visually marked, found "formerly missing" kanban cards, etc.— needs corrective action. Cure the problems through management action or schedule a kaizen event (continuous improvement) to handle more wide ranging problems with the lost cards. Lost cards should be reprinted only by the scheduler responsible for the kanban-card printing.

There are rules covering the standard work for use or application of kanban cards. These rules should serve as a basis of education for handling kanban cards, and the rules should be posted wherever cards are handled.

They are

1. There is *no* production without a kanban signal.
2. Do not accept or move any material without a kanban signal.
3. Rotate kanban stock: always pick top to bottom, left to right, and front to back.
4. A material handler or line stocker (for internally manufactured parts or purchased parts) moves a triggered kanban signal to nearest posting box.
5. No over or under production of kanban card quantity is allowed.
6. No over or under shipment by vendor of kanban card quantity is allowed.
7. No hand-written kanban cards are allowed.
8. One kanban card multiple must be used up completely before triggering next kanban card: multiple partials for same part numbers not allowed in bins.
9. Kanban cards can only be created, changed, or deleted by the materials group or responsible scheduler.

Kanbans need to be visually associated with the part numbers they control, and they need permanent bins or inventory home locations. Failure to follow these rules will probably account for most of the startup kanban-card problems.

There are many ways to attach kanban cards and locate inventories, so we will spend some time discussing both.

Kanbans need to have permanent bins or home inventory locations. Do not use random inventory bins. This permanent bin location is the one that will print out on the kanban card. Since the inventory will be "right sized" to the production needs, having dedicated inventory locations should not be a problem. This is a required activity for insuring the kanban-card-controlled inventory is set up properly to support the initial production cell. As the dedicated bin is established, excess inventory exceeding the kanban card population should be taken and put in an "excess" area for first use up.

When you set up your permanent bins, you should try to establish them so that there is as little dependance as possible on the need for "equipment" (moving ladder platforms, "walkie" or driven forklifts, picking "buckets," etc.) to pick or put away parts into their established locations. For smaller parts, if you limit the height of racks and shelving units to no more than five feet, this will generally eliminate the need for other equipment when picking or putting parts away. This eliminates the waste of "waiting" for material-handling equipment for stock handlers or line stockers.

Pay particular attention to conveyors and mezzanine-type structures; these two handling methods tend to be intermediate in nature and require double handling of inventory. In other words, they may be "waste" waiting to happen. Having said this, the bulky size or weight of your inventory or available square footage for storage may require using other equipment to handle and locate inventory. Keep in mind that the square-footage-availability problem will be improved as identified excess inventory is used up before starting on kanban cards.

In cases where forklifts or other handling devices are required for skid loads of bulky or heavy materials, it may be inevitable that you will need equipment to pick and move materials to the production cell. In those cases, it may also make sense to make one skid load of product equal to a kanban card's worth in quantity (if this is the normal supplier quantity). If you go this route, each spot in the rack should be a dedicated inventory bin for the picked skid's replacement. Do not use random inventory bins!

Defined bins can be allocated space on a shelving unit or rack, lines painted or taped on the factory floor, gravity-feed units, color-coded PVC tubes, or the conveyance itself (a cart or stackable tote that becomes the kanban signal), right-sized for the specific kanban card multiple. However you define a bin, it must be clearly marked and labeled. If I am new to your warehouse, and I am picking a part from "section A, row 2, shelf 3" (as printed out on the kanban card I have in my hand), there should be enough information posted by way of visuals to find the location.

There are many ways to set up effective visuals for inventory bins and locations. Color coding can be very effective when used as painted lines or colored tape on the floors. Suspended, tri-corner, laminated signs designating rows or sections are cheap, easily made, and viewable from any direction (assuming you adhere to five-foot height limitation on racks and shelves). Bin information affixed to stanchions is easily made and placed. Cones on the floor can identify addresses or identify where in stock rotation in the row to pick from. Pictures of types of products can complement any color indicators. You can color code the bin location on the printed card to match the color-coded location in the warehouse. The possibilities for creating visuals are limitless. This is a point where the collective imagination of your implementation teams to solve problems will dazzle you.

In the ideal world, there is one bin location for each part number, and it is at the point of use. Unfortunately, things are not always this neat in the real world. If you have multiple product lines that require the same part numbers, you may have to keep the reorder trigger for the supplier vendor or feeder cell in the warehouse and refill the production cell from the warehouse via transfer kanbans (kanbans between the cell point-of-use location and the warehouse location). If there is enough turnover volume and the various product lines use the same kanban multiple, you may be able to stock the inventory at point of use and eliminate the warehouse-location kanban. Common hardware and packaging supplies should always be the exception to this discussion. They should always be stocked in the production cell and controlled by kanban signal.

Generally, if you do not have a bunch of "wild hares" handling your materials, we would advocate stocking kanban-controlled part numbers at point of use. This eliminates the waste of double handling and unnecessary line stocker picking; but if you do not think you have the discipline to enforce the kanban handling rules cleanly from the beginning, leave the product in the warehouse bin for line stocker picking, educate all parties on the rules for handling the kanban cards, and then subsequently move the inventory to the cell when it is clear discipline in handling the cards has been established. This short-term strategy eliminates complicating the process while everyone is in learning mode. The movement of the inventory to the point of use could easily be addressed in a subsequent kaizen event.

The best inventory bin and kanban signal is the conveyance, right-sized for the kanban-quantity multiple, that moves from the point of use to the replenishing source. As you get your vendors and other internal production cells set up and gain some expertise in Lean, your goal should be to establish conveyance kanbans. This eliminates costly packaging materials and labor (and disposal costs) if fabricated correctly, provides easy visuals for counts, ensures consistency of kanban multiples, and helps with handling and quality of part issues.

There are many cheap and effective ways to affix kanban cards to the part numbers they represent. Probably the easiest is the use of clear (avoid the ones with the words "packing list" preprinted on them), thin-mil plastic, packing-list envelopes with adhesive on the back. You just peel the backing off these, put the card inside, and position and press into place in a designated and conspicuous area where it will be easily noticed. Affixed to the front of racking and shelving units, they also demarcate the bin where the kanban multiple resides. They are easily usable when attached to conveyances. As with everything in Lean, be consistent and try to standardize how you use whatever method you choose to affix the cards. If this is difficult to do due to variation of containers and parts, choose what works best and is most clearly understood.

If you do not use the packing-list envelopes, you can use other cheap and readily available items. Ziploc, food-storage bags come in all sizes and can be used suspended from metal rings or plastic ties, glued, or placed in secured alligator or binder clips. Bean bags or small plastic cones holding kanbans can be placed on top of parts. Stanchions can be used to hold clipped kanbans. A more expensive attachment material is Velcro. There are fold-back binder clips, regular binder clips, compression clips, "O" rings used to hold keys or curtains, bag clips, clip magnets, etc. The possibilities end with your paucity of imagination.

The point with the attachment method is to find one that functions and meets your budget—you will be surprised how creative members of a kaizen team can be when tasked to find ways to attach kanbans to the parts they represent. As previously mentioned, color visuals are very helpful. If you use something like stanchions or alligator clips tack welded or screwed to a weighted base, paint them to be seen. Choose a bright color that will not compromise fire or safety colors already in use.

There is always a question that arises as to when to pull the kanban card and process it for replenishment activity. The question is this: Do I pull and turn in the kanban when the first piece is picked? or when the last piece is picked? The correct answer is that it does not really matter as long as the trigger signal is turned in for processing, and the signal was calculated based on a relationship of typical demand to typical lead time. It is probably easier to train the material handlers and line stockers to trigger the card when the first piece of a card quantity is pulled. However you go, pick one method and make it the standard work for all triggering activity. If replenishments are consistently arriving with bins still full, watch out for the buyer-"padded" lead times; that is, the system replenishment lead time is listed as eight days, but the receipt always arrives on the third day. As we said earlier when discussing inventory, lead time is cash flow. Monitor for compliance and "reasons" at the end-of-shift walk-throughs.

When you have all your kanban cards printed and verified, and all your bin locations and attachment methods established, it is then time to match up your kanbans with the part numbers they represent. When your team is doing this, it is imperative to match inventory exactly with the kanban multiple printed on each card. When all is matched, the bin or inventory location should have no more quantity than the total kanban population for that particular part number (kanban multiple × number of kanban cards).

After the kanban-card matchup, whatever is left over should be taken and put in a separate "excess" area to be used up first—*before the regular kanban cards are activated.* The easiest way to do this is to shrink wrap the bins printed on the kanban cards and to post a message that excess must be used up first from temporary excess location "XXXX." During the startup phases, this is one item that must be checked during the daily, end of shift "walk-around."

We will discuss in depth the metrics that are used to monitor your performance with the heijunka boards and the handling of the cards when we finish discussion of establishing the total-value flow and balancing the workload. The end of shift walk-around with key players involved in the production cell startup is invaluable, and it will help you obtain a daily score on how well you are doing. The "walk-around" covers both the process activities and the housekeeping of the various areas.

In the meantime, if you are unable to finish setting up the inventory bins and the matching with the kanban cards within the kaizen week, make sure there is a plan for a follow-up "to do" list with assigned names responsible for the actions and agreed-to completion dates. Top management must stay on top of this list and support the responsible person as needed with manpower and whatever else is needed to get the job done. In some cases, this will require a second formal kaizen event. When you finish this portion, you are halfway to your goal of getting started with the kanban-driven, level-loaded heijunka board process.

Chapter 10

Continuous Improvement, the Kaizen Event

The very good Lean companies we have known have had a bias for creating change through the use of a kaizen event. The very bad Lean companies have been the ones in paralysis by analysis, content with 5S (housekeeping) exercises and endless "strategic" planning sessions—all the while waiting for a "Lean epiphany." The bottom line is: a company can do 5S (housekeeping) exercises and strategic planning until the cows come home, but until you actually do something disrupting the waste-invested status quo in a business or factory, you have not really started on your Lean journey. And ... if you really want to become Lean, you do more and more and more kaizen events. In this chapter, we will talk about how your company can translate the bias for action into "change" and productivity gains through the continuous improvement event—the kaizen.

Responsible for the success of the kaizen event is the kaizen team: six ordinary individuals with varying skill sets who come together over the course of one workweek and achieve extraordinary results in your company. They are not the individual superachievers or the "Six Sigma black belts" or "the brains" or "Lean gurus." They are your everyday workers, the experts at their own jobs, who, when they are trained in the kaizen process, use their powers of observation, rational deduction, and a sense of imagination to stand the *status quo* on its head.

When you are selecting people for your kaizen teams, you will want to set up cross-functional teams. You do not want all the team members from the same department. For example, if you are trying to solve an inventory problem, do not fill the team entirely with inventory department personnel. Or, if you are trying to solve an accounting issue, do not have all accounting personnel on the team. This will strip out critical people from the functioning department, and it will dampen the objectivity and process questioning that come from a person not associated with that particular department and that particular problem.

In general, here are rules to follow for setting up the kaizen team. Most teams will consist of five to six individuals—depending on scope of the issue to be tackled. The ideal team would consist of: (1) a representative from local management, (2) a person who works within the process being focused upon, (3) a person who works upstream from the process being focused upon, (4) a person who works downstream from the process being focused upon, (5) a "fresh set of eyes"-type person, and (6) a "problem solver"-type person.

The fresh set of eyes and problem solver people are typical of the complementary skills needed to provide dynamic to the team—let us emphasize they alone are not responsible for the "fresh outlook provided" or the "problem solved." When the inertia of starting up the kaizen event is past, group dynamics should start to take over and drive discussions in which all team members participate. The point is that the success of the team, like the success of any group undertaking, is dependent on having a good "chemistry." Any good manager we have ever known knows who these "fresh eyes" and problem solver types of workers are. You want the mix of product expertise and knowledge, imagination, and interrogation. The challenge with chemistry is to match people and time available to achieve the objectives of the kaizen event.

When you establish your kaizen team, you should make sure that all employees selected will be able to serve without distraction for the duration of the kaizen event. On most kaizen teams, the workers will be involved with the kaizen event for five full days. The kaizen event is designed to be high-intensity activity performed in a short period of time. Because momentum is such a vital part of kaizen team activity, it is best done in full workday chunks. Keep in mind that team members are not only identifying the problems during the kaizen week, but also implementing the solutions or conclusions within the same kaizen week.

Early kaizen team staffing is problematic. No department manager can spare anyone, all departments are way too busy, and the timing is absolutely wrong to have to cough up personnel. This is typical, and your company needs to work through this. Unlike factories of the past, today's realities rely on pools of temporary workers to supplement a small cadre of full time, very valuable, knowledgeable workers. Temporary employees ebb and flow with the peaking and ebbing of product demands. It is also typical that finding manpower to staff kaizen events becomes less an issue as you do more and more kaizen events and start to appreciate some of the benefits of resultant productivity gains.

If you don't have the resources to commit a team of employees five full days in a row, you could do the event in smaller doses. Because you need consistency or you lose momentum, you will need blocks (four hours minimum) of time for kaizen events. Full days are better than half days, but half days will work if no other alternatives are available. Kaizen events with one to two full days a week—not to exceed a three-week horizon—will work. Half days over two or three weeks will work.

Once the rhythm is lost with kaizen events, the concentration and sense of urgency also tend to go down the drain. The result is that your company is back to the "bold stroke" or paralysis-by-analysis point, waiting for the great Lean epiphany. Our only word of advice on kaizen events in blocks of time greater than one full week is to be relentless in getting the kaizen done in the protracted timeframe. If "there is never a good time" becomes the mantra, it will become self-fulfilling, and you will never finish any kaizen event.

One other point we will make on kaizen staffing is: if manpower is still an issue, seek out other companies trying to become Lean and, if trade secrets, insurance factors, and trust are not issues, propose to mutually share people to populate home and away kaizen events. Everyone wins with the experience and training, and manpower shortages can be somewhat abated. As long as you have key team members to maintain the knowledge and flow of your kaizen event, this should not hamper your efforts. Local president clubs, commerce associations, and engineering societies may be good sources to cultivate to determine interest in mutual Lean learning.

Preparation for the kaizen event—in both training and attention to machinery, manpower, and materials that might be needed—is crucial to the success of the actual kaizen event. It is up to the plant Lean-implementation director, with underpinning from plant upper management, to make sure the kaizen activity is publicized and support is given unequivocally to the team. Because of the short-term intensity of activity of the kaizen, someone with enough authority needs to stand by, in reserve, to cut through the politics, as needed, to make sure the kaizen team is properly supported. The "take a number" or "we'll get back to you" approaches need to be suspended during the kaizen event. Time is of the essence during the kaizen team's workweek.

The team members should be assembled a week before the event starts to receive training in basic Lean concepts and the basic kaizen process. The training should be specific to the type of kaizen event planned. If you are doing an office event, draw your waste examples and "value-added" discussions from the office environment. If it is a factory-floor event, let factory-floor issues and vocabulary drive the training discussion.

During the one- to two-hour orientation, the definitions and goals of "Lean manufacturing" should be discussed, and there should be a discussion of the various types of value-added, "wasteful, but necessary," and "waste" activities and examples. The kaizen activity should be explained in the context of a team activity where everyone has an opportunity and responsibility for helping to achieve the kaizen's objectives. The forms used in the kaizen event can help direct focus of the discussions (Figures 10.1 and 10.2).

Since production, for three to five days, could possibly be disrupted by the kaizen event, management must be aware to take the proper precautions to not jeopardize customer orders. Usually, working overtime in advance to build product for inventory solves this problem. If date coding or other process-specific events preclude inventory building, you will need to confer

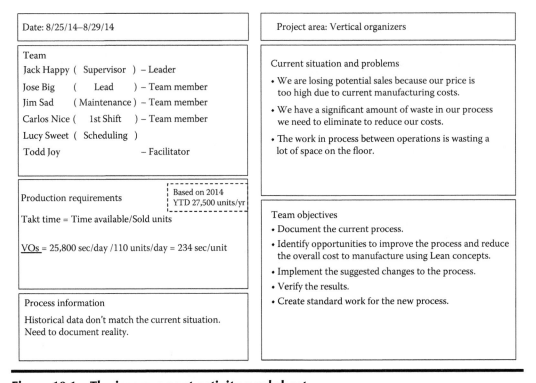

Figure 10.1   The improvement activity worksheet.

Kaizen event target sheet

Key measurement	Goal	Start	Mon	Tue	Wed	Thu	Fri	Percent change	Follow through
Space (sq ft)	50% ↓								
Part travel distance (ft)	90% ↓								
Crew size	Least waste way								
Cycle time (sec)	20% ↓								
Productivity (units/work hour)	25% ↑								
Inventory (WIP)	90% ↓								
Cell created	Up and running by wed								
5Ss	First 2								
Standard work	1 VO								
Visual control	1 SW 1 TT Visual cell brian guage								
Lead time (hrs)	90% ↓								

Figure 10.2   A blank target sheet.

with your internal experts to see how to free up assets for the days required in the kaizen event.

Depending on the objectives of the kaizen event (and implications, which should be obvious), prior arrangement may be needed to have certain trades or skills people available as needed to help in the progress of the kaizen. For example, if the team is looking to actually set up the production cell and plan on moving 60-ton presses to the newly forming cell, there may be a need to use proven equipment movers. Moving 60-ton presses is not something you would expect the team to do. You would need to have contracted with machine movers or have made arrangements for maintenance staff, skilled in these areas, to be available for specific days within the kaizen event to be on-site and available with their equipment.

Likewise, you would never expect a kaizen team player to do electrical work, if he or she is not qualified, nor would you put anyone in harm's way by an unsafe or illegal practice. Although there is some sense of "interim" for the efforts reached in a kaizen event, it becomes the permanent, worka-day world until the next kaizen event. The team should never skimp on recognized and needed safety measures (like failing to reinstall saw guards, failing to thoroughly ground electrical equipment, etc.), and skirting building codes (not properly collecting or filtering paint-booth byproduct) is sending the wrong message. Lean methods are not about cutting corners on employee safety or lessons in how to test the surprise building inspector's powers of observation.

If one of the kaizen event's activities is to build heijunka boards, you will need to have some idea of what materials you will want to use before you start the kaizen event. In some cases, if you use acrylic, clear plastic boxes, there might be a lead time involved in the quantities you will need for however many heijunka boards you plan on constructing. If you have a maintenance department, you probably have some plywood, stick lumber, glues, PVC pipe, hand tools, duct tape, some structural steel and aluminum, sheets of acrylic, and paint on hand. You will probably not have what will be required for the kaizen event. The conclusion is plan ahead—"waiting" time on a kaizen event is the height of Lean irony.

Over time, most active Lean companies will develop their capacity to support a vigorous kaizen schedule by creating a "McGyver" shop with all of the capability to make anything normally associated with kaizen needs—including fixtures, jigs, etc. Through the course of pursuing kaizen activities, the materials required to be kept on hand for the McGyver shop will become self-evident. It will be critical for allowing your kaizen team members to find clever solutions to seemingly unsolvable problems in a short period of time.

When the team is assembled at the start of the kaizen event, one of the first activities, led by the Lean-implementation director after prior review with the team leader, is to define the current state and problems the team will address on the kaizen. At this point, the group is simply made aware of the issues and problems; they are not told the solutions to implement. The solutions will be addressed in the form of objectives the team will try to reach during the kaizen. The team will also be given production and cell production requirements—usually stated in terms of takt time. This becomes the production rate that is needed (usually stated in seconds, minutes, or hours per part), and serves as a focal point for their efforts. Finally, team members are assigned specific roles within the kaizen event (more to come on this).

Besides objectives to be met during the kaizen event, there are also goals to be met for specific aspects of Lean activity. Performance to goals, and, in the process, reaching the objectives, becomes the metric for the kaizen event. These goals encompass establishing basic 5S (housekeeping) within the cell, reduction of space used, reduction of inventory, reduction of head-count, setup reduction time, creation of standard work, etc. The target-sheet form used has typical Lean expectations given as percentages—the team will contrast this with their final numbers at the end of the kaizen event. The kaizen ending numbers are quantifiable and measurable, and skeptics can calculate for themselves. Going forward in time, the results of the kaizen event are expected to be repeatable and become the new standard for the total-value flow. The results are normally "dollarizable."

Determining the proper "takt time" is crucial for the total-value flow or cell. In a nutshell, as we discussed previously, takt time is the quantity of like products going through a value steam (factored for new product intro-ductions from marketing and sales forecast plus historical data for existing products factored for budgeted sales-level increase or decrease) that you need to make on an annual basis translated into your total-value flow's mea-surable time production unit.

As a simplified review, if you sell 44,000 units per year historically, and your new products are expected to add 4000 units to an unchanged histori-cal sales figure, your takt time will be 48,000 units ÷ production cell's mea-surable time production unit. If you work one shift and 240 days per year, you will have to produce 200 units per day or 25 units per hour (assuming eight hours available for work) or one unit every 144 seconds. This is your takt time. The team will want to structure the production cell to meet this takt-time rate.

When you are determining takt time, you will also need to take into consideration the "mixed modeling" that goes through the production cell. Not all products have the same takt times. Not all products have the same cycle times. Not all the products have the same setup times. If all the vari-ous products are made on the same equipment in the newly established total-value flow or cell, this should not matter. Lean is very adept at allow-ing mixed-model manufacturing. The sum total of setup and run times for product A, B, C, etc., should equal what the cell needs to produce and the manpower required to support the volume.

For the scheduler, this should not pose a major problem. The posted standard work and scheduling rules should cover kanban-card equivalencies for level loading for mixed models. For the production cell, life goes on as usual, and they simply work to produce the kanban signals they are given. Since inventory is rationalized to support each product's takt-time needs, inventory availability for mixed models, even where they share the common usage of particular part numbers, should not be a problem. (See Chapter 14 for in-depth explanation for determining manufacturing kanban-card quantities.)

The kaizen week is divided into different types of activities. The first part of the event involves documenting reality, gathering data and facts, and establishing baselines for the week's goals. The next part involves analyzing the data and brainstorming possible solutions. In the third part, the team plans out and implements the agreed-upon strategy to reach the event's objectives. The fourth part involves compiling the metrics for the kaizen event and preparing for the kaizen presentation. The fifth part is the actual presentation of the results of the kaizen event to the management and fellow workers in the company. The sixth and most important part is the celebration of the team's achievements with a hearty round of applause in recognition of their efforts. For most employees, this will be the first time in their working lives they will have heard management commend them publicly for doing a good job.

We need to spend a few paragraphs talking about employees. The celebration aspect of the kaizen event is significant. You downplay it, and you send the wrong message to the workers who are there to help shape the profitable future of your business. The basic fact of human nature is that people want to be acknowledged for their successes. Ignore effort, and resentment or less than stellar efforts will follow in the future.

Team-member acknowledgment after kaizen success feeds continuing employee involvement and "buy in." Ignore the employees on the team or be indifferent to their concerted efforts, and you send the message that this was not a transformational activity—it was more akin to a good overtime effort or a successful annual fiscal inventory count. Remember, one of your goals of setting up a total-value flow is to establish an early success story and model for Lean training—it is also for inculcating the mind-set in employees that Lean *is* important and it *is* transformative and it *is* your future. It may be the vital difference in safeguarding jobs and maintaining profitability in a more competitive world.

When the team members are "reporting out" at the kaizen presentation wrap-up meeting (attended by management and exempts, or "company-wide," if practical), it is important that all members participate in the presentation. The team leader should briefly state the current state and the objectives of the kaizen event. He or she then should introduce each member and have them give a brief description of what they did and results of their efforts. If people are self-conscious or have a problem with language, have them hold or point out visuals or assist another person in the presentation. The point is not to make anyone stress out; it is to ensure they are acknowledged for their efforts and as members of the team.

After all the team members present their portion of involvement, the team leader should briefly review the metrics and point out gains over the documented starting positions. If it makes sense, the kaizen meeting can take place on the factory floor at the newly established production cell, and team members can walk everyone through the new process. If not, have it in the usual assembly place. All in all, the meeting should be relatively brief—no more than 30 minutes in duration. Each of the team members should be limited to a three to five minute maximum to discuss their involvement.

The presentation concludes with a discussion of any items left over from the kaizen event. This "to do" list details action items that could not be completed during the kaizen event and which are due to be completed within 10 or 15 days. The person responsible for ensuring the list gets completed is the team management representative. The Lean director must ensure that follow-up status reviews are scheduled to check completion dates are met.

The intent of the kaizen event is to get most, if not all, of the objectives completed by the end of the kaizen week. If you have a kaizen event, and most of the required activities are "follow-up" items on the 10- or 15-day "to do" list, you need to rethink your planning on kaizen objectives. Your kaizen scope bit off too much, you ran into unanticipated problems, or your team leader was ineffective. The team leader is key. He or she must make sure that everyone on the team is doing his or her share in a timely manner and that the team's needs are supported by the greater company. It is almost a truism to say that if a team member does not have enough work to do on the event or the opportunity to contribute to proposed solutions, they will have a bad experience and want to opt out of future kaizen events.

If your "to do" list shows someone forgot to order the acrylic boxes needed for the heijunka construction or you had to wait until the last day of the kaizen event to get a simple, required lumber delivery, these are unsatisfactory reasons to be on a follow-up list. If your kaizen turned up a special safety part that needed to be ordered and installed or a specialized outside service that needed to be contracted to finish the production cell, and both were unanticipated prior to the kaizen event, these are legitimate "to do" items. The point is the kaizen team leader must make sure the team reaches as many of the objectives of the kaizen as possible within the kaizen week.

One final point before we leave the employee portion of the chapter. Employee involvement is crucial to the success of kaizen events and Lean. You need to keep this in mind as you pursue productivity improvements.

As you successfully finish kaizen events, you will begin to free up plant personnel. What you do with these freed-up individuals needs some thought.

Some companies pursue Lean improvements strictly as headcount-reduction activities. Some see the downward financial spiral of their business as needing immediate and drastic actions. Headcount reduction is an immediate response. Most employees, market-tested, wary, and distrustful of company motives, can pick up on this immediately, and they begin to view Lean as the enemy and a cause of conflict. If your company is in "critical-care" stage, it may not matter. If you are looking to make an otherwise solid company more profitable for the longer term, you may have a problem if you get rid of personnel after each kaizen event.

The most successful Lean companies are the companies with an aggressive kaizen schedule. An aggressive company, for sake of definition, is one that has one to two kaizen events weekly. Teams are operating both in the office and in the factory areas. The personnel to staff these on-going teams are the result of prior kaizen efforts to free up manpower and improve productivity. In these companies, in the ideal world, improved market share and new product lines provide opportunity to redeploy freed-up employees. In some cases, normal attrition is allowed to take care of headcount reductions. In the meantime, the aggressive kaizen schedule results in overtime reduction, continued productivity improvement, and, in modern companies—something that may be very significant—the reduction of the number of temporary workers required to make product every day. As newly adopting Lean companies with just a few successful kaizen events under their belt know, attacking the "low-hanging fruit" can have significant and immediate payback.

Needless to say, we would recommend that you use the freed-up workers to aggressively pursue kaizen improvements, cross train to increase skill sets, and put the pressures on your more highly paid sales force to find more customers to grow the business. New, incremental business comes at the cost of materials—your staff and workers are already in place. The productivity gains could be in higher volumes on existing product lines, the additions of new product lines, or both. Further, focused kaizen events can make sure you can support the increased volumes your sales force finds. This approach becomes a "win-win-win" for factory workers, sales force, and factory management.

One of the other options Lean may give your company is the ability to "insource" during slower demand periods. If you have freed-up people due to production slowing, think about how to use them rather than getting rid of them. One of the companies we were associated with reduced their cost of materials from 40 percent to 28 percent by utilizing freed-up workers to make component parts "in-house" that were previously bought. For the cost of raw materials and open machining or fabricating time, you can lower your cost of materials with a freed-up and available workforce. Do not succumb to "imagination failure"—even a "no growth" model can make better use of freed-up labor.

We do not want to downplay the importance of standard work and defined process in allowing for cross-training of personnel to handle all jobs. Too often, especially in smaller companies or undocumented companies, if someone goes on vacation, the incumbent's established, normal process breaks down. The "fill-in" worker does the best he or she can with the brief orientation they receive, but it is inevitable that factory flow is put at risk. With the documentation that comes from the kaizen event, the standard work "democratizes" the knowledge to perform the job. "Democratization" ensures continuity in process and opens up possibilities for better manpower utilization and training.

If your company is unionized, you may have another complication to work through. Existing work rules and detailed job descriptions may cause problems initially with the flow of work on the kaizen team. If the team cannot plug in a power cord or use tool crib or maintenance tools to make things for the kaizen event without waiting for the appropriate labor and job grade worker, you will have a problem with the effectiveness of the team. You will need to have a discussion with the union before embarking on the kaizen activity.

Nowadays, both unions and management are aware of the effects of globalization. A vigorous and honest discussion of the methods and needs for successful Lean activities, the company's goals in pursuing Lean, a "no layoff due to kaizen improvement gains" policy, and the possibility of profit sharing resulting from meeting the company's financial and operational goals may result in reducing or eliminating the hindrance of endless, rigid job descriptions and job grades, curtail inventory-building "piece work" pay, and temper unreasonable seniority rules. This issue is one your company will have to work through, and it is not a focus of this book. Our point in mentioning it is that some Lean companies are unionized, and there are case studies of how management and unions were able to work together to implement Lean. One has only to look at the American and German auto makers who are profitable, highly unionized, and models of Lean practices and employee involvement in plant operations.

Keep in mind, as you start out on your Lean journey, many small incremental steps accomplished through kaizen activities will always triumph over the "bold stroke" or the "grand slam" approach. The latter approach can become a trap for many companies. They plan and plan to make the game-changing impact only to discover that they lost opportunities to make many smaller improvements, in aggregate representing greater productivity and financial gains, as time marched on. You need a strategy, but you also need to aggressively begin tactically. For "bold strokes," results almost always fall short of intended results. Every company has a bumper crop of low-hanging fruit waiting to be harvested. An active kaizen schedule focused on low-hanging fruit will significantly out-perform in dollar savings and productivity gains any grand slam strategy.

When you are planning the kaizen event, recognize your limits and go for a little more than you think you can accomplish, but not so much as to leave a large "to do" list as follow up. For example, if you are planning on setting up the total-value flow or cell, do not think that you can establish the heijunka boards, print out the kanban cards, train incumbents on how to use the boards, and set up metrics *while also* tackling setup reduction, trying to foolproof manufacturing methods, and creating operator preventative-maintenance processes in the cell. In this example, the topic of setup reduction may be four or five separate, subsequent kaizen events in itself. On the contrary, you should be able to establish heijunka boards, print out kanban cards, train incumbents on heijunka use, and establish metrics within one kaizen event.

Good Lean companies, as we have stated many times, need to develop a bias for action. The more Lean events you do, the quicker you will learn and gain the productivity and process advantage. The intangible will be the acquisition of the Lean mind-set. Good companies will know they are getting there when everyday employees start noticing and asking management what they plan on doing about the waste they see.

Elimination of as much waste as possible is always the ideal in Lean. Continuous improvement centered in the kaizen event is the process to eliminate the waste. Each resulting, new "current state" after a kaizen event is, by definition, an interim "current state" to be improved upon. The Lean journey is a continual trip that involves the imagination and analytical skill sets in solving the ever-present "what if" question.

In the next chapter, we will continue our discussion of the timeline of the kaizen event and specific activities on how to set up the total-value flow and begin the level loading.

Chapter 11

Beginning the Kaizen and Documenting Reality

If you want to get a clear idea of where you need to go, begin by getting a clear idea of where you have been. To paraphrase for Lean purposes: if you want to know how much your company needs to adopt Lean practices and methods, you need to know how much waste you currently have in your system. This is the starting point for your kaizen team in setting up your total-value flow or cell. This also brings up the starting point for all Lean kaizen events: document reality. Know your current state of operations.

Never, ever, take a short cut and bypass the documentation of reality portion of the kaizen event. The process itself is designed to discover data, information, and circumstances—formal or informal—which, for better or worse, are a part of your production cycle. When filling in the information and values for the current state, do not use existing operations manuals, process sheets, routing sheets, standard cost data, industrial-engineering time studies based on averages, or input from "experts who know," or those with pride of authorship or ownership of the process or product. Do not extract numbers from your rectum. (Everyone likes the percentage 85!) The information may or may not be correct, but there is a real probability that it is not. It is up to the kaizen team's documentation of reality to determine starting values for the kaizen event.

The only acceptable kaizen "prework" and information that you absolutely need to bring to the kaizen event ahead of time—if it is done during the kaizen event, it must be available by conclusion of the documentation of the current state—is the takt-time value for the total-value flow to be established. This value—expressed in product per seconds (normal measurement), minutes, hours, or shift—will be used to set the market expectation of production in the cell. When you begin brainstorming how to set up the production cell and balance the load, this is the baseline, measureable, throughput production value that you must meet to satisfy market demands. Normally, takt-time calculations must be done before the kaizen event—it does take time to properly derive the answers.

The roles of the team members during the kaizen event are somewhat malleable, but there are certain tasks that must be matched up with personality types and skill sets and assigned at the start of the kaizen event. One of the stated purposes of the kaizen, besides actually creating a load leveling, total-value flow or cell, is to begin the Lean transformation of your company with an undisputed success to showcase results and to serve as a Lean "learning lab." Therefore, you need to put some thought into the selection of the people on this first team. You do not need to stack the deck with your "best" people, but you do need to have the right mix of people to get the job done.

It does not matter what position they currently hold in the company, as they will be taking work direction from the kaizen-team leader and, as needed, the Lean-implementation director. Going forward, these people will become the "veterans" to individually populate and lead the new kaizen teams and provide the voice of experience for the newer "recruits." This ensures continuity of effort and practice on the kaizen teams.

Since the purpose of this book is to help get the first level-loaded production cell up and running, let us review prior discussions on personality types and augment suggestions for first total-value flow team member skills. You will need someone from your engineering department familiar with the process and the product. You will need someone from your materials group, preferably the person assigned to maintain the kanban database and make the cards. You will need one of your operators from the product area you are targeting for the total-value flow or cell. You will need a leader from some level of management or supervision. You will need someone with basic literacy and computer skills who can document, create standard work, flowchart as needed, and prepare PowerPoint presentations. You will need someone from the line-stocking or material-handling group.

You can also have any number of supervisors or executives on the team, but they must remember they function not as supervisors or executives, but as team members taking their work direction from the team leader. They need to come dressed and prepared to work and get their hands and clothes greasy and dirty. They are receiving work direction—not giving work direction. Group brainstorming and consensus will determine countermeasures needed to set up the future-state total-value flow. On a team, these people become "worker bees," just like everyone else.

If you have managers or executives on the team, you must be sure that your chosen team leader is not easily intimidated or deferential to the offices represented on the team. The goal is that the team follows the kaizen process, and all team members perform their assigned functions and participate with equal voice in the brainstorming of countermeasures. Having said all the above, however, teams must have a reasonable representation from the workers who do the actual work in the targeted area. The day-to-day workers are the true experts—they are not "vicarious" or "theoretical" experts.

These types of personalities and skill sets would be "ideal" candidates for the kaizen, but you will have to tailor for your specific needs and manpower availabilities. You can always pull people temporarily into the kaizen event for specific help. This frequently happens with maintenance and engineering people when particular, required actions or questions arise. They temporarily advise or assist in the task at hand or answer the technical questions, and then they go back to their work.

The one requisite you will need on the team will be someone with technical and product expertise. Your created, total-value flow or cell will be a technical or engineering entity, and you will have technical or engineering issues that need to be addressed. Keep in mind, the product or industrial engineer chosen does not have to be the team leader—he or she only needs to be open-minded enough to participate in the team's activity and protect the integrity and quality of the product. The questioning attitude, the open mind, the respect for fellow team members, the absence of negativity, and the mind-set that one does whatever is needed and required to help the team meet its goals and objectives are attributes not only for the engineering person selected but they also apply to all the other candidates chosen for the team.

As you read these paragraphs, you already know who the team members are. They are your solid employees with the questioning minds, who, while not necessarily your fastest or best workers, are the ones whose names pop up in every conversation about promotions and who are the informal leaders within their peer groups. Your team leader is the no-nonsense supervisor or manager who has the respect of his or her subordinates and, though firm, has the people skills to guide a team through a time-sensitive project. The leader does not have to be an engineer or technician as long as he or she knows how to question and when to draw in expertise as needed in the process. The resources of the company, as stated before, must be available to the kaizen team when requested.

We discussed the backgrounds and perspectives needed for team membership. Now we need to discuss the actual roles the employees will be playing on the team. The roles evolve somewhat as the kaizen event moves through the week. Generally, it follows the typical pattern we are about to describe.

The team leader's role is to make sure all team members understand the kaizen-activity worksheet with its goals and objectives for the kaizen event and the target-matrix sheet, which is the metric of improvement of all areas for the event. He or she also gives the team the role assignments and makes sure the team is supported with whatever it needs to get the mission completed. Leadership, doggedness, an organized approach to get work done, and people skills are very important for this role.

Although each employee is assigned a team role, the unwritten rule is that the team leader can move people as needed to serve the evolving objectives and goals of the team. It is like the army. Each soldier may be trained with a specific specialty such as cook or mechanic or truck driver, but, as needed, they all become infantrymen when the need arises. Whatever jobs the team members do, they will be required to work with the team scribe to create the historical record, quantify gains, and create the group presentation of the kaizen event.

The co-leader is the administration coordinator (lunches and breaks) and safety monitor; he or she also runs interference as needed by the team. When things are up and running, he or she can work alongside the other members as directed by the team leader.

One team member is the scribe. As scribe, this person prepares target-sheet updates for presentation, writes standard work as outlined by the team, records events on kaizen "newspaper," helps capture documentation on "before" and "after" time observations, compiles waste check-sheet findings, and, early in the kaizen, takes before pictures to capture the current state that complements the beginning target-sheet numbers. On the last day of the kaizen, this person helps other team members prepare for their presentations and takes after pictures to contrast with the before pictures taken earlier. The scribe also compiles the final target-matrix values from feedback from team members. This person needs a mix of writing ability and some facility with computer applications (PowerPoint, Word, and Excel).

There are normally at least two documenters on the team. One works with the production process and the other works with the "in" and "out" processes that serve the production people. If possible, assign one of the team members as stopwatch operator while the documenter does his job of compiling and notating actions. As documenters, these people are observers and compilers of information and data. They are not debaters of observed methods with the people doing the work, problem solvers on the fly, or spewers of sarcasm. They are not the type to distract the observed workers in conversation. Their goal is to document what is going on by unbiased observations of worker activities and machine-cycle times. These are the people who are good observers and questioners and offer objective sets of eyes.

The other role on the team is the builder. Early on in the kaizen, this role may be asked to help on observations, but usually, by day two, the team's brainstorming will fill in this person's required tasks. The person, who has some "builder hands-on" abilities, will work with other team members to make items needed to set up the total-value flow or cell. After countermeasures are "brainstormed" and decided by the whole team, documenters work on future-state solutions, together with the builder. For creating the level-loading heijunkas, this will mean that this person, supplemented by all other available team members, will make the heijunka boards, posting boxes, and housekeeping shadow boards required. Your maintenance department should be ready to give temporary assistance when required by the builder.

The team leader starts each day with a brief kickoff meeting where team assignments are affirmed and performance in relation to goals is reviewed. The activities requiring action for the day should be captured on the kaizen newspaper form from the prior day's five-minute, end-of-day review meeting. Meeting time should be as brief and as pointed as possible during kaizen week. If it makes sense to do so, a brief review of the highlights of particular Lean points to consider can be covered. This should only be a brief overview—the more in-depth training should have taken place as a preparation event for the kaizen.

The first half day, all team members are busy capturing and documenting the current state. The divided-up team examines all aspects of the targeted flow. Besides watching the actual cycle times and process of making the product, the team members also review the events associated with picking and delivering raw materials; getting and installing tooling, fixtures, and dies required for changeover; monitoring the role of the line stocker in bringing materials to the machine and taking finished product from the machine; observing quality issues, noting maintenance or machine-dependability issues; and marking how product enters into inventory.

The afternoon of day one is the beginning of planning for the countermeasures. The first half of day two continues planning the countermeasures. By the afternoon of day two, the team is already making the changes discussed in the brainstorming. The whole of day three is spent making the changes for the creation of the total-value flow. Day four is spent verifying changes, making revisions to the countermeasures, and quantifying results. Day five is spent making the implemented countermeasures the new standard, summarizing results, and celebrating the victory of the change accomplished. A hearty round of applause at the end of the final presentation should be the recognition for a team accomplishment and the beginning of the new company.

Depending on what the kaizen event is and how typical your company is, the results tend to fall within "normal expectations" in the metrics. Space used can usually be reduced by 50 percent. Travel time and distance can usually be reduced by 90 percent. Cycle times can usually be reduced by 20 percent. Productivity can usually be increased by 20 percent. Work-in-process (WIP) inventory can usually be reduced by 90 percent. Lead time is usually reduced by 90 percent. Crew size is based on "least waste way"—not on standard cost or industrial-engineering, averaged-time studies. Basic visual controls are established—often for the first time. Standard work is created and posted, allowing for consistent process and the ability to cross train. Safety issues are addressed as a part of establishing the total-value flow or cell. Basic housekeeping is addressed and has a metric to maintain. Establishing a total-value flow or cell should hit most of these markers. At the end of the kaizen, the resulting savings can also be dollarized.

Determining goals can be done after the team concludes the documenting-reality portion of the kaizen event. The goals and the documentation process are the results of examining the opportunity present. The documentation process captures reality as honestly as possible. These values become the beginning numbers on the kaizen target-sheet. Against these numbers, stretch goals must be created to stimulate thinking "outside the box." Never sell the collected abilities of your team short. You will continually be amazed at the power of imagination to forge creative solutions during kaizen events. People generally rise to the occasion presented. The catalyst is employee respect and the ever-powerful word of encouragement. If little is expected, little is done.

The documentation of reality can begin immediately after the kick-off meeting. One or more people can be assigned to observe the machine-operator activity and machine-cycle time. As mentioned above, the documenting-reality process is often done in pairs, one person capturing the element steps, and the other manning the stopwatch to capture the time.

The observer should sketch out the layout of the machines on which the products are made, or use a facilities or maintenance plat (ideally, with a scale) showing this information. The layout or plat is required to document the operator-travel activity during the course of making the product. This marked-up layout or plat becomes the "spaghetti chart." As in the element documentation, one or more people can be assigned to this task, one person actually tracing the steps on the plat and the other person documenting the steps, measuring the distance, etc. The foolproof method to ensure you have as accurate a spaghetti chart as possible is to make sure the documenter keeps the pencil or pen tip in continuous contact with the pad, and, thus, never misses a movement from one point to another.

If the current state has products moving from or to other departments in the factory, this should also be captured on the layout or plat. The documenter, who tracks the material handling "ins" of raw material to the machine and the "outs" of the product to other machining processes and ultimately to finished goods, will also use spaghetti charts in the manner described above. Taken altogether, all the spaghetti charts should equal the total distance the product travels in your factory's production cycle. If you have a third person available, he or she can be noting opportunities for improvement, any special conditions or circumstances in the production cycle, material handling issues, etc. The important thing is to have a realistic plan on how to allocate manpower and capture the data.

The operator and machine-cycle observer should use a walking measuring wheel or tape measures to get as accurate travel or distance numbers as possible. If it makes sense, color code the different processes the operator follows in producing the part. For example, black shows the pure, direct production-fabrication flow (even between departments); red shows obtaining and putting away jigs, fixtures, and dies for a particular operation; green shows taking first piece to inspection department; blue shows travel to pickup point for outside or other-department process; etc. (Figures 11.1 through 11.4).

It is very important that the observer does not interfere or impede the operators in any way as they do their jobs. What the documenter is trying to capture is the day-to-day "usual and customary" flow of work activity. The rate of work should be what seven of ten workers should be able to meet in making the product. You do not want observations based on your

15 DAY "TO-DO" LIST

Event #	1	Description:	VO Cell	Date:	8/29/2014

No.	Action to be taken	Person(s) responsible	Date due	Percent complete
1	Welder maintenance plan	Jim S.	9/19/14	25 50 75 100
2	Create standard work for VO II	Tony R.	9/5/14	25 50 75 100
3	Cut conveyor for access	Jim S.	9/5/14	25 50 75 100
4	Fabricate return conveyor	Jim S.	9/12/14	25 50 75 100
5	Redeploy operators	Tony R.	9/1/14	25 50 75 100
6	Hang tool boards	Carlos R.	9/5/14	25 50 75 100
7	Determine what to use open space for	Tony/Todd	9/12/14	25 50 75 100
8	Install and on light	Jim S.	9/19/14	25 50 75 100
9	Install anti-fatigue mats	Jose C.	9/5/14	25 50 75 100
10	Move light closer to folder table	Carlos R.	9/8/14	25 50 75 100

Figure 11.1 A kaizen newspaper.

"worst-case" worker, nor do you want observations based on your hyper-superachiever who only breathes every third minute.

The workers who will be observed should be informed by their management of the kaizen event and told to work in their normal manner. Given worker paranoia, which is a natural outgrowth of the weakening of employee-management loyalty in the global economy, this monitoring could otherwise catch the uninformed operator off-guard. The employee should be reassured of the purpose of the observations, and he or she should be encouraged to perform his or her work in a "normal" manner.

In addition to the spaghetti chart, which gives distance information, the operator and machine-cycle observer should use the "time-observation worksheet" to document the actual elements (the actual steps) that go into the making of the product. There are two portions to the elements—what the operator does and what the machine does. The first part, observing the operator, requires the most effort to document correctly. The second part, observing a machine cycle, is the easiest to document.

When documenting the operator, there are several things to be aware of. First of all, document reality by the simplest noun–verb descriptions for what the operator is doing. This is not the time to try out the company

Time observation form

Process for observation No.	Component task	1	2	3	4	5	6	7	8	9	10	Lowest repeatable time	Comments
	VO #1 (2 per unit)									Observation date 2/23/2014		Analysis number 1	
											Observation time 10:45 AM		Observer R.J.	
1	Find pallet jack (1 every 24)	313 / 313										13	Searching for jack
2	Move material to form (1 every 24)	541 / 228										9.5	Batching
3	Load sheet in fixture	551 / 10	618 / 15	722 / 91	757 / 8	812 / 37	851 / 13	888 / 19	1162 / 12	1193 / 18	1224 / 15	15	Went to tool box, interrupted by quality
4	Cycle start machine and form	558 / 7	626 / 8		763 / 6	817 / 5	857 / 6	895 / 7	1166 / 4	1200 / 7	1230 / 6	6	
5	Place formed VO onto pallet	603 / 45	631 / 5	749 / 27	775 / 12	838 / 21	869 / 12	1150 / 255	1175 / 9	1209 / 9	1239 / 9	9	Making adjustments to pallet × 2, get jack
6	Wait for wip from punch (1 every 24)										2009 / 840	35	Material not available from upstream
	Variation in the cycle												
	Amortized over 24 pieces												
	Time for 1 cycle	119.5	85.5	175.5	83.5	120.5	88.5	338.5	82.5	91.5	87.5	87.5	

Figure 11.2 A time observation form.

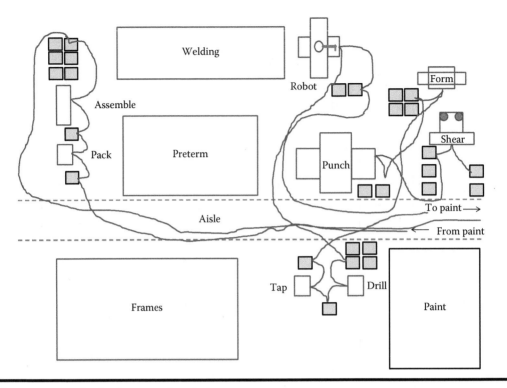

Figure 11.3 The before spaghetti chart.

Key measurement	Goal	Start	Mon	Tue	Wed	Thu	Fri	Percent change	Follow through
Space (sq ft)	50% ↓	7625				→	4125	−46%	7
Part travel distance (ft)	90% ↓	1650				→	330	−80%	
Crew size	Least waste way	7				→	4	−43%	
Cycle time (sec)	20% ↓	1435				→	928	−35%	
Productivity (units/work hour)	25% ↑	1.96				→	3.43	75%	5
Inventory (WIP)	90% ↓	648				→	48	−93%	
Cell created	Up and running by Wed	0				→	1	100%	4,3,9,10
5Ss	First 2	0				→	2	100%	
Standard work	1 VO	0				→	1	100%	1,2
Visual control	1 SW 1 TT Visual Cell Brain Gauge	0				→	2	100%	6,8
Lead time (hrs)	90% ↓	206				→	13	−94%	

Figure 11.4 A completed target sheet.

thesaurus—simple, one-syllable words are the best; for example, drills raw material, saws tube material, pours casting, adds flavoring, blends recipe, etc. Where it makes sense and helps in comprehension, use the company word for verb action or the noun described. The key to the words is to be as simple and as clear as possible.

The second point to be aware of is, you need to capture each element of activity the operator is doing, and break it down into its smallest describable steps. There is no need to get anal retentive here, but sometimes things have more substance than appears on the surface. For example, "removes part from machine" may be more accurately detailed as: locates box wrench, loosens five bolts by hand tool on cam part-holder mechanism, uses small pry bar to loosen from fixture, slides conveyor to left, takes control of A-frame hoist, positions A-frame over part, attaches slings on two lifting points, hoists part, positions 4″ × 4″ lumber on skid, lowers part on skid.

In the example above, depending on circumstances, there could be additional notes and distance measurement to be made. Does operator walk 20 feet one way to his tool box to get his box wrench? Does it take the operator five-minutes to break loose the cam part-holder mechanism bolts? Where is the pry bar … back at the tool box? Does he or she have to get someone to help slide the conveyor? Where is the A-frame hoist relative to the operator? Is there only one piece of equipment in the shop he has to wait for? Where are the slings kept? Where is the lumber for the skid spacer? Etc.

When you are documenting the machine cycle, you want to capture strictly the run times associated with the part. All the activity leading up to the actual pushing of the button to start the machine and the removal of the part from the machine will be captured in the operator observations. On the time-observation worksheet you normally do not need to document what the machine is doing—only how long the machine runs for that particular operation. For example, you do not have to document in detail how the machine cycles: spindle begins rotation, spindle locates focus point, spindle begins cutting metal, spindle retracts, and spindle stops rotation to allow part to be removed. *Nor,* do you need to document what the "product" is doing—awaiting pickup on skid, waiting in tote. On the contrary, note any significant factor—curing or aging times, cooling time, etc.—that causes the product to wait between operations. Simply capture the cycle times the machine is working on the part.

Normally "feeds and speeds" are an attribute of the raw materials you are working with; unless you know otherwise, you can assume they were properly set when the part was routed to the machine. If an element of making the part is operator adjusting feeds and speeds, these are legitimately noted elements in the production process. In a worst case, the documenter should note any questions to be asked later. The documenter will capture the essence of what the machine is doing and the time it takes to do it. An example is: machine mills part, 42 seconds cycle time; machine drills parts, 18 seconds per hole; and machine blends ingredients, 312 seconds per blending cycle. If the documenter sees something worth noting in the machine cycle, he or she must make note of it on the time-observation sheet. An example of this might be that the machine broke down or "stalled" on four of the ten observations, or the existing, "one computer program fits all" CAD-CAM or PLC program allowed the machine cycle to "drill or cut air."

The end purpose of the whole documentation process is to be able to separate the "value added," "non-value added," and "non-value added but currently necessary" steps. When the team begins reviewing all the data and information they have collected during the first days of the kaizen event, they will immediately target the "non-value added" steps for elimination. By cutting the non-value added steps, minimizing part travel, and eliminating space and inventory, the kaizen event will get its immediate gain in productivity. Over time, future kaizen events will tackle the non-value added but currently necessary steps to get the maximum gains.

A successful documentation process requires the documenters to be as meticulous as possible in capturing all the elements and actions of both the machine and the operator. This is why the emphasis on noting operator sequence, part travel, all quality checks, safety practices incorporated into the process, safety concerns, and quantities of inventories in the current state are important. In order to create a future-state process, the documenters need to know as much as possible about the current state with all its stumbles and inefficiencies. What the documenter presents to the group for the brainstorming sessions will substantially help form the countermeasures the team derives.

When making the operator and machine documentation, if possible, the observer will want to watch at least five, and ideally ten, complete cycles. If the documenter is dealing with longer cycle times—one hour or more—try to use at least five observations. What we are looking for is to discover the lowest repeatable time with the required product quality and operator safety.

This becomes our potential given our current machining and producing capabilities. Reviewing a greater number of operator and machine cycle times will also give the observer an insight into the variation and cause of variation at work in the current state. Trying to get an insight into the variation is equally important to determining lowest repeatable production time.

If, in the course of reviewing your documentation, you discover significant equipment-reliability problems or significant quality issues, you may want to deal with these as the focus of a kaizen event before setting up the cell. If your machine only works reliably three days per week or 50 percent of the parts coming off the machines are either rework or scrap, setting up a cell may not get you the gains you think you will get. If your production is based on operator Joe's 20 years' experience of knowing where or when to put the shim in the right place to make the part, you have a bigger problem. You might be better off looking at your part programing, effectiveness or absence of your maintenance programs, or age and condition of your fixtures, jigs, dies, or machines. Your large inventories and excessive overtime (at a significant cost to your company) may be what is keeping you afloat for all the downtime or quality issues you experience. This falls into the silk purse and sow's ear reality check.

Having said this, on the other hand, going ahead and setting up the cell may get you to the root cause of the problem faster and with more pin-pointed focus. By using one-piece flow, detecting and correcting defects, standardizing the process, and not passing any defects to the next operation, you may eliminate issues or determine where the problem actually exists and where you can focus on appropriate corrective action.

If your machine reliability and quality are reasonably consistent and dependable, go with the lowest repeatable time with the required product quality and operator safety. For Lean purposes, we will call this the least waste way. This should be the value from the observations that appears repeatable—after outliers are discounted in a large enough sample. If you have a very small sample, it may be in your interest to extend the kaizen event's documentation period until you know you have a representative sampling. Because the resultant, chosen value will become the new standard, you want it to be as do-able and repeatable as possible.

Do not use industrial-engineering or standard-cost averages. This is a key point. There is a big difference between traditional industrial engineering methods and Lean thinking. Traditional industrial engineers use averages and loss factors (like personnel fatigue and delay factors—typically 15 percent) to determine standards. This tends to build waste into the standard. Lean thinking uses the least waste way, which may require continuous improvement to meet consistently.

We do not want the new cycle time to be based on averages. We want the basis to be actual, observed values—ideally, the lowest value that safely produces a quality product on a repetitive basis. Be aware, also, not to "pad" the values either to the high side or the low side. If you skew it one way or the other, as in a buildup of tolerances in an engineering design, you will be doomed to meeting your cycle times only in optimal conditions. If you pick the least waste way, you have selected a starting point in the fact of observation for establishing your total-value flow potential. We will discuss least waste way more in depth in Chapter 12.

The other reason the selected cycle time is so important is that it will determine manpower in the production cell. Since the total-value flow will be set up to move operators to the work as needed to make the cycle time equal to or less than the required takt time, there will not be a "one man-one machine" mentality when staffing the total-value flow. For example, a worker who runs something through the bending press may then move to the drill press, while the other worker does the welding and then moves to the packing table. We will discuss this point in depth in Chapter 12.

Before we leave the operator and machine documenter, there is one other point we can consider. Some companies use a time-elapse camera to capture the activity when travel distance is minimal. While the camera records the events, the documenter keeps a running record of the activities taking place. This may or may not pay dividends—most of the time the camera captures the machine area sitting idle while the operators are off somewhere else getting tools, dies, hailing a forklift, or trying to find the "expert" to answer their question. This may be overkill, unless someone can articulate a good reason for the need. A good observer with the ability to document in detail and question what he or she sees may be the best answer. In Lean, technology is not necessarily an equal substitute for an engaged person.

The documenter of the machine and the operator should also get accurate measurements of the production areas in use for the product. This production area square-footage value, added to the square-footage value the inventory WIP observer finds, will determine the starting space value on the Lean target-sheet. When determining square footage, simply get the actual areas encompassed by the production area. Do not include any aisle space unless it is specifically part of the production area.

The same type of documentation, the spaghetti chart and the notation on activity, also applies to the person who observes the ins and outs of material to the machines. Using the same type of facilities-layout map or engineering plat as the machine and operator documenter, the materials observer traces and measures the travels of raw materials into the machines and the movement of either finished goods or processed material out of the machines.

Using a walking measure wheel, the observer can get fairly accurate distances. Both distances and actual travel path should be noted on the map or plat. As with the machine and operator documenter, if there are activities that lend themselves to color coding, do this if it helps clarify the activity. An example of this might be: use black lines to show travel of picking from warehouse stock to machine, use green lines to show travel to pickup point for outside processing, use blue lines to indicate travel to different department for secondary operation, etc. Color coding could also be used to show the travel of different product families.

The materials documenter must also determine quantities of WIP inventories that are at the cell—both incoming raw material inventory and outgoing processed inventory. The documenter wants to get a snapshot of inventory quantities and dollars tied up at all the production machines associated with the production cell to be established by the kaizen event. If there is other inventory at the cell, say "rejects" from the machine awaiting repair time availability, this should also be noted. The sum of all the inventories at the targeted machines making up the production path or stored rejects will be dollarized as the beginning dollar value of the current state. Along with quantities of WIP inventory, the materials documenter must also get the square footage that the WIP inventory occupies.

Normally, the materials documenter will have an easier time documenting the line stocker activity. The documenter captures picking time, picking quantities, travel distance, travel path, and travel time. If there are particular issues with any one element, the documenter should make note. An example might be excessive waiting time for fork lift availability, time spent looking for a pallet jack, picking inventory quantity needed from a multiple random-bin locator, etc. The materials documenter should also capture any insights or questions he or she may want to share with the team. From the information provided by the materials documenter and distilled by the kaizen brainstorming session, both standard work and a delivery schedule will be created for the line stocker in the future state.

Once all the documenting of reality is completed, the team will be able to fill out the starting conditions on the target sheet. This will become the baseline against which the team's success will be measured. This is the first step in identifying, quantifying, and dollarizing waste in the process. We will discuss this more in depth in Chapter 12.

For the purposes of the kaizen event, there is no need to dollarize the beginning positions of the kaizen event and then update as the team moves through the event week. If it makes sense, it can be something that is dollarized and commented upon at the final presentation of the kaizen team. For the team starting out on the kaizen event week, talking in terms of dollars rather than square feet, pieces of inventory in WIP or stock, and seconds of production time associated with the objectives of the event tends to be a distraction.

As a byproduct of this kaizen to set up heijunkas and get to level loading as soon as possible, the documentation process should also highlight many areas that should become the focus for on-going kaizen events after the heijunka boards are in place. The most obvious will probably be set up or changeover reduction needs on the machines or lines, or operator-machine maintenance (and preventative maintenance) practices. Do not become overwhelmed when you see all the wastes in your current process. You have lived with them up to this point—you were just not as keenly aware of the problems. This is good. This is an improvement. This means the education and process are working. The kaizen event and the documentation process have given you a map to future improvement and company success.

In the next chapter, we will begin the discussions on deriving the countermeasures to get the total-value flow up and running. Focus—this will consume the afternoon of day one and the morning of day two—will be on two items: team brainstorming of options to create the desired future state, and team understanding of the variations in the observed machine and operator data. The team will create a "percent loading chart" to determine manning for the total-value flow and begin the load balancing process.

Chapter 12

The Percent-Loading Chart

In this chapter, we will begin discussing the results of the documentation phase of the kaizen event and start thinking about takt time and its relationship to cycle time as presented in the useful Lean analytical and visual tool called a "percent-loading chart." The brainstorming of countermeasures to set up the level-loaded, line-balanced production cell will follow in the next chapter.

The documenters have spent the better part of a day observing and recording the elements, times, and distances involved in the current-state process; the key now is to understand what all that information means for the team. Understanding clearly the information and the variations in the information will allow the team to successfully grasp the "least waste way" production cycle and establish an effective production cell layout and process. By the end of the second day, the team should have started bringing into reality some of the creative ideas on how best to set up the production cell.

The first thing the team should do is to record the beginning data positions for the goals called out on the target matrix sheet. This current-state data will be the baseline the team will measure their results against at the end of the kaizen event. The values for square footage, inventories (separately for both work-in-process (WIP) and finished), and part travel distances will probably be aggregate sums of numerous observations and measurements for each value. Take the time to get these numbers as correct as possible. Some of these values (especially inventory) can be dollarized to see tangible savings potential compared to the future state.

Against this current-state data, the team will also establish goals that they want to meet in the course of the kaizen event. As your company does more and more kaizen events, these goal entries will become more obvious. Since this is your first attempt at establishing a level-loaded and line-balanced production cell, we will tell you what reasonable goals should be.

The goals should be as follows: space required by new flow, down 50 percent; part travel distance, down 90 percent; crew size equal to the least waste way (with freed-up workers redeployed to other value-added work); cycle times, down 20 percent; productivity (units per worker per hour), up 20 percent; inventory (WIP), down 90 percent; total-value flow, created; Lean housekeeping—first two steps—things sorted out and set in order; standard work, created; visual controls, created; and lead time, down 90 percent.

The space and distance goals reflect the new configuration, which will result from brainstorming efforts to establish the new production cell. By configuring the cell in a "U" or more compact layout and taking out obvious waste, the operator, doing multiple jobs, will have less territory to cover when going from point "A" to point "B" (remember radius and diameter from geometry?). By moving machines into closer proximity and having inventory available at point of use (where this makes sense), total part distance travel will be substantially less.

The crew size, reduced cycle times, productivity gain, and lead-time reduction goals result from team countermeasures after review and brainstorming of the observed operator elements and understanding of the variations in the documented process. If you think of one definition of Lean as "removing time, distance, and wasted effort from a process," what is left is "value added" or "non-value added but necessary" activity in the most compact time and distance possible at the kaizen time. When all possible waste is removed from the process and the time to do the process is minimized, it follows that productivity (output per operator per unit of time) will improve as cycle times shrink. This is the least waste way (appears in Lean literature as "LWW"): the best way we know how to do things today, knowing tomorrow it should continue to evolve and change for the better. As cycle times shrink and productivity increases, the number of operators needed to man the production cell becomes apparent and fewer than before. This thinking will help meet the operator-related goals. With a rationalized, streamlined process, reduced lead times naturally follow the least waste way.

The inventory goal will be met by embracing the basic tenets of Lean production: producing to takt time, doing it one piece at a time, and doing it at the demand of the customer. Given the seemingly logical benefit of volume-based "comparative advantage" and maximized "price quantity break points" or economic order quantities, the idea of one-piece flow seems counterintuitive. From our experience, the concept of one-piece flow and the perceived need for complicated manufacturing software systems, usually standard-cost based, to run the shop floor seem to be the most persistent mind-sets against starting Lean manufacturing. In Lean, as you are probably starting to understand at this point, the "bigger is better" mantra does not always work.

Most historical manufacturing software systems have also been "batch and queue" systems—counter to Lean practice—which forced inventory onto the factory floor via algorithms controlling replenishment-planned order creation. In practice, both with traditional inventory views and standard cost considerations, we have been conditioned to think "bigger is better" or spread the cost over a larger population. Historically, standard cost systems and industrial engineers have set production lot sizes to offset production time lost to setups and changeovers and drive individual part prices down. Companies have not always understood that what the market is willing to pay for your product minus your cost to produce it equals a margin that may or may not allow your company to stay in business. The key point here is that the market tells you what they will pay for your product—not your accounting, purchasing, or engineering departments.

This all-encompassing computer system approach was "aided and abetted" in the purchasing department by accepted inventory ordering policies, most typically period of supply or economic order quantity, revolving around procuring or strong-arming vendors to give the lowest piece-part cost, rather than looking at the bigger picture of total inventory costs. Traditionally, even "management by objective" and other performance-based concepts have rewarded the purchasing department for efforts to reduce piece price by volume buying and beating up vendors—at the peril of the company's cash flow. When we went through the rationalizing of inventory, we took into account the total cost of inventory and we right sized it to serve the interests of single-piece flow and takt time.

One other note on inventory before we leave—when you are collecting the starting data for the WIP inventory valuation, also get a snapshot of the quantities and dollars of inventory sitting in stock for the part numbers that will be controlled by kanbans due to the new total-value flow. Although you will specifically be measuring WIP inventory at the establishment of the production cell flow during the kaizen, the warehoused inventory will also become a big savings item. For cost comparison calculations, roughly one half of the total kanban card population will be on hand in the future at any given time. This contrasts to the point-of-time quantity and dollar snapshot for the same inventory of parts residing on the shelves at the beginning of the kaizen. Kanbans will result in a reduction of inventory and an improvement of company cash flow. You should collect both numbers (WIP and finished inventories) and dollarize both to see the impact of what you are doing.

The standard work and visual controls in the newly established production cell tend to be revolutionary in most companies. Before Lean, most standard work resided in a dust covered operations or procedure manual or engineering standards and guidelines three-ring binder safely ensconced on the production foreman's lower bookcase shelf. The operator made the product from the routing sheet, an attached bill of material, and a blueprint—all of which, at times, may not have been the latest revision. When most companies with reduced workforces are fighting fires every day, correction and maintenance of records, routings, and bills of material sometimes, unfortunately but realistically, are on a "time available" basis. Alternatively, the engineering change notice process tends to be too "loose" or subject to "cutover" timing problems due to using up existing inventory stocks of complementary parts.

Visual controls, if they existed at all, were more probably red tags dutifully hung on all the rejects awaiting open machine time for rework, rather than positive indicators to help the process. Once performance-assisting visual controls are in place at the end of the kaizen event, cross-training of manpower can effectively begin and variation can be taken out of the process. Visual controls also provide obvious indicators of performance to takt time, relay information designed to assist the production and material handling flow, and supplement the standard work process.

The housekeeping goal probably has more prominence in a Lean environment than in a more traditional factory. In a traditional factory, housekeeping is more esthetic than practical. Sweep up at the end of the day—if harassed by the foreman and if you can find a broom—in case someone important visits the plant. If you doubt this take on traditional factories and housekeeping, take a census of brooms and dust pans in your factory. You will be shocked to discover that typically there might be two or three brooms and one dustpan to service the entire 10,000 square foot facility. If this is not the management "cause of the day," housekeeping becomes a secondary activity of little spontaneous interest. Even if it is the cause of the day, it usually consists of a feeble effort to sweep around the machines, before sprinting toward the end-of-day cleanup and punch-out.

In Lean, housekeeping (also known in Lean parlance as "5S") has an economic grounding and an objective metric for housekeeping that can be scored. Housekeeping is important, because if your work area is not organized and clean, it affects product cost. The first two steps of Lean housekeeping—sort out only what is required at the production cell and set it in order (and remove what is not)—may make all the difference in the world whether or not your operator can function productively. If your operator spends time looking for needed tools, if your operator cannot detect a leaking lubrication line or seal that might lead to serious financial consequences via machinery repair or replacement for your company, if your operator sorts through inventory trying to find the proper components, you have a housekeeping and orderliness problem. In all probabilities, you will have to buy more brooms and dust pans too.

When setting up the production cell, you will not have time to do a full housekeeping event (including all points of a 5S) *and* do the kaizen to set up the total-value flow. What you want to accomplish during the production cell setup kaizen is to get rid of all clutter in the area, and make sure paths are clear for the operator. Establish basic procedures on how and where tools and fixtures should be stored, define permanent bins for inventory at the cell, and clearly mark "in" and "out" drop-off and pickup points for the line stocker. Focus only on the inventory, tools, and equipment called out in the kaizen event, and bring only the necessary items, following proper housekeeping practices, into the cell.

The cleanup and sort can be done on day one of the kaizen event by the team leader or co-leader, while the other members of the team are doing their observations and documentations. The team leader or co-leader should assess the targeted area for general clutter and superfluous equipment and inventory. Designate a temporary location and move all clutter from the area in which the team will be working. Equipment collecting dust, such as old dies, fixtures, test equipment, conveyors and material handling or packaging equipment that is unused and, for all purposes, probably obsolete, should be quarantined in the temporary location. Red tags should be affixed with the name of the supervisor responsible for disposition of clutter and due date for resolution. This action item will become a follow-up "to do" item at the end of the kaizen. Basic cleaning suffices for day one activity. Other housekeeping and organizing activities (the "put in order" of housekeeping) required for the kaizen event will come out of the kaizen brainstorming and be assigned by the team.

Once the team has the new production cell laid out, the balance of the initial housekeeping activities (shadow boards, inventory bins, "ins" and "outs" locations and markings) can take place. The completion of the housekeeping effort (the cleaning and painting, standardizing as required, and setting up the metrics for sustaining) can be a future, logical follow-on (maybe even best as a separate housekeeping kaizen event) to the cell created, once the production cell is up and running and operators are somewhat used to the changes. We will talk more about housekeeping in Chapter 16.

Time-out. Perhaps we should take a moment at this point in the book to see if any readers have developed weak knees or faint hearts about setting up their first total-value flow. The thought may have occurred to some that it would be easier to simply clean up the place, move machines and inventory closer together, and try this modification with existing systems first? You worry because you still do not see how Lean would work with the equipment you have—the centralized paint shop or multi-million dollar "super-machine" you just bought last year, which cost accounting is beating you up to utilize. Stopping or modifying the focus now would certainly silence the growing skepticism in the company—the "legacy creators" who feel threatened at this point and the "answer men" who feel their authority being undermined. For those under pressure, we sympathize. It is time to "buck up" or "cash out." Have resolve or be resolved.

To our point, Lean is *not* batching in shorter distances. Lean is taking time, distance, variation, and wasted effort and resources out of a process. Moving machines together will not get you Lean. The contracted space for an unchanged batch process will probably only get you to gridlock in your factory earlier than leaving things the way they are. A batch system offers little hope for improving your cash flow, reducing product lead times, minimizing space usage, assisting in cross-training workers, or getting to the mixed-modeling, level-loading production cell you desire.

While we are at a "wax philosophical" pause in the book, there are also a couple of other issues you need to think about and discuss. We spoke to this earlier in the book, but it is critical to success. Once you are at the point of moving machines and changing the day-to-day operation of your company, you are committing to change. Change is difficult in the best of cases. Thirty-one percent of the public may check "undecided" in random public opinion polls on topics ranging from religion to politics to global warming, but everyone will have an opinion on change in your factory. You need to make sure you have circumstances and attitudes in place to allow your team to succeed.

The competent people you put on the team are the ones responsible for seeing the kaizen event through. Even as they brainstorm many possibilities, they need to be supported in their efforts and protected from the "naysay-ers" and the former "answer" men who feel their authority status under-mined by the whole thing. One mean-spirited or menacing word can undo everything. An interloping executive vice president—or someone having direct management oversight authority of a team member—can easily put the damper on activities by one flip, negative, disparaging, or discouraging comment. You owe it to the team to make sure this does not happen.

The team must have the authority to make changes. This is another crucial area in which they will need support. They will probably be mov-ing machines, changing job description duties of both operator and line stocker, making decisions on inventory stocking and purchasing, determin-ing cycle times that are not industrial engineer, time-study-average derived, and requesting timely assistance from other departments to get as many of the kaizen goals realized as possible by end of the kaizen week. If they get hamstrung on any of these issues, your kaizen event will probably not suc-ceed. You owe it to the team to make sure they have the authority to make necessary changes.

This civility and respect must also extend to team members' behavior toward each other. Particularly, when the brainstorming part of the kaizen is occurring, everyone should be encouraged to give input and ideas, no criticism of any forthcoming input or idea should be allowed during the brainstorming session, and all input or ideas should be captured and writ-ten down on a flip chart and posted as they occur during discussion of a specific topic. The brainstorming continues, person by person in continuous rounds, until all ideas are exhausted.

Once brainstorming is completed, the group can then review in detail and brutal honesty each of the points presented. As with people in authority dampening creativity by disparaging remarks, team members can also stifle creativity within the team by sarcasm and judgmental snarkiness. The team leader must caution all participants against this before the brainstorming ses-sion begins and be ruthless to stifle it if any example surfaces. Some of the most creative solutions have come from the most unsuspected team member or, on further discussion, from a seemingly frivolous comment. Kaizen aside, civility and mutual respect are valuable in themselves. They are hallmarks of good companies where employees feel positive about themselves, their work contribution, and their company.

The wax philosophical and blood pressure check "time-out" is over, and we are back in play now. We have our goals and actual, documented start-ing positions recorded, so now we can begin our discussions on how to set up the total-value flow. There are several components to these discussions. We must know takt time for the production cell. If there is much variation in the products eyed for the total-value flow, we will have to address that. We will also put together our percent-loading chart based on the review of the documented data. Once we have wrestled with the conclusions of these two items, we will then have some idea of where to begin to lay out the production cell and how to determine the required manpower (Figure 12.1). In Figure 12.1, the dashed line represents the required takt time, and the stacked columns represent times from documented operator element observations.

The percent-loading chart is a stacking of observed operator elements in time, which is then compared to takt time to determine relative position. For example, if the stacked value of the observed operator elements— the elements recorded in the "document reality" portion of the kaizen—is 123 seconds and the takt time required for the product line is 111 seconds, the team will know they need to take a minimum of 12 seconds out of the documented elements to meet the takt-time target. You could also have a reversed situation, though more unlikely than likely, that the takt time is 123 seconds and the stacked value is 111 seconds. In this second case, at the conclusion of your kaizen event, you will probably have added capacity to easily expand production volumes.

When you are talking about both cycle times and takt times, there is a possibility you could have multiples of both categories, depending on chosen

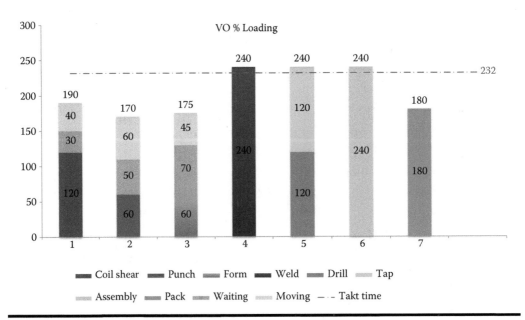

Figure 12.1 The before percent loading chart.

products going through the production cell. Different product lines could have different takt times and share the same production cell equipment. Different product observations could result in different cycle times. You will have to take this into account when you set up your total-value flow. Your total-value flow will have to accommodate all annualized takt-time values for all targeted products in the production cell. (More on this as we go on...)

Takt time, by way of review, is the market-imposed time required for your production cell to produce a product, given your defined, hands-on, actual producing work day and the historical demand (plus anticipated growth) quantity your production cell needs to meet. Cycle time is the sum of all the operator elements from one start of the production process to produce a part to the next start of the same production process. The cycle time the team should focus on in the kaizen is the most repeatable least waste way observations from the documentation cycle for each element. Part lead time, a third "time" definition, is neither takt time nor cycle time. It is the cycle time to produce a product plus time variables due to scheduled backlog, and material and machine availability. For the purposes of the total-value flow, takt time is the important "time" definition to focus on—this is what the production cell must produce to.

If all the product lines are similar from a manufacturing viewpoint (e.g., six drilled and tapped holes versus four or three, or one or two fewer weld points out of a maximum of 12 points, or one or two added ingredients to blend), product differences from a consideration of cycle times may be insignificant. In this case, if the time elements are not significant, you could probably have the same cycle-time value with differing takt times by part number. If products are significantly different (e.g., major or multiple setup issues or one or more significantly different operator elements, etc.), there could be problems running them together through the cell.

Total-value flows are usually set up to handle like products. You can add other products that use the same machines, if they are not too dissimilar. Generally, minor variation can be covered in scheduling rules. If you have so much variation in the products that the variations required are really "major" variations and not "minor" variations, you might think of creating a "standard" cell and a second, "specials" cell. If you have significant "major variation," you also have the option of supplying the dissimilar part to the production cell from a kanban-controlled feeder machine not physically in the production cell. You must know the changeover or setup for each product. Scheduling rules may piggyback minor setups on the back of major setups. If changeovers or setups are too significant and you have no ability to reduce in the short term, it would be best to create a separate cell, or sub-cell, or continue from the current feeder machine and control by kanban signal to and from the production cell. You will have to use your judgment of what works best.

If there are multiple product lines going through the machinery in the proposed production cell, and their individual product processes are like, you may have to recalculate the takt time for the total-value flow to take into account the various blended product totals. Each product will have its own takt time and cycle time, and we will have to figure the cumulative takt value. To do this, we will need to know total annualized volume of all products in the total-value flow and total annualized time available.

Let us assume that all the targeted products for the total-value flow are alike with only minor variations. Figure 12.2 represent the product family annualized values.

The total-value flow must be designed to accommodate the annualized volume per year of 55,120 units or 230 per day (if we assume 240 work days per year). If we posit that the production day is eight hours minus one-half hour for lunch and two ten-minute breaks, the net production day is seven hours and ten minutes or 25,800 seconds per day. Defining the new blended takt time, the total-value flow needs to make a product, at a minimum, approximately one every 112 seconds.

The cumulative, annualized volume in seconds from the documented observations of all the product lines targeted for the total-value flow is 7,446,960 seconds. This sum, divided by total annualized units of 55,120, gives an average cycle time per product (question of setup and changeover aside) of 135 seconds. This value, divided by 112 seconds, determines the theoretical minimum starting number of people needed in the total-value flow manning. This would show 1.2 people. If the team can find and eliminate 23 plus seconds of waste per cycle, we could get down to one operator.

Product	Units per year	Cycle time per unit in seconds	Annual cycle time in seconds	Takt time per day in units
Product "A"	22,000	135	2,970,000	92
Product "B"	15,360	132	2,027,520	64
Product "C"	8,160	134	1,093,440	34
Product "D"	6,000	136	816,000	25
Product "E"	3,600	150	540,000	15
Totals:			7,446,960	230

Given: 240 production days in year

Figure 12.2 "Blended" data to determine takt time for like products.

This should be the goal for the team; otherwise, using two people would waste 0.8 of operator. Sometimes this works out, and sometimes it does not. If you must keep two people in the production cell at the beginning, two things to consider: give the excess "0.8" portion of a worker other value-added duties upstream or downstream within the cell (this may be difficult to do using one-piece flow), and then review other kaizen opportunities to get to one person. Keep in mind, the company and the team still benefit from the real gains made in the kaizen event. The lesson: perfection is hard to achieve, but the pursuit is totally worthwhile in itself. Obviously, the end results of the team's brainstorming enhancements will determine the final number of people needed to man the total-value flow.

If setups and changeovers are significant for specific products in the product family targeted for the production cell, this could be an issue in the total-value flow. Since the purpose of establishing the production cell is to optimize the production of like products, the products targeted for the production cell, for the most part, should share like processes. Since they share the same general processes, setup and changeover should be a "minimal" issue and not a "significant" issue. From our experience, this is usually the case, but there can be oddities in the product features that trigger the setup issue. A conservative course of action might be to target the products with the setup issues on a focused kaizen event to reduce setup or changeover time.

When you have significant setup or changeover issues, a separate, focused kaizen event can normally do wonders to substantially reduce setup time. Taiichi Ohno of Toyota was successful in taking full-day automotive model die changeovers and making them into a single-minute exchange of dies as the ultimate baseline for making setup insignificant in the running of mixed models on the automotive lines. You cannot set up a total-value flow with heijunkas *and* combine that with setup reduction at the same time. Setup reduction gains will have to be left to a future kaizen. A setup reduction kaizen event could be a logical follow-on (the other most promising candidate being operator preventative maintenance) to the establishment of the production cell.

If it makes things easier to size up, you can also create a resource usage matrix to display information about the versions of a single product family or all product families that will be going through the production cell. To do this, the left vertical axis of the matrix should represent frequency of occurrences and the right vertical axis should represent the cumulative percentage of all classes. When you apply these findings to the percent-loading chart versus takt-time consideration, you can then make judgments whether the single production cell makes sense or whether you need a second or "specials" cell. If you are looking at seven different products in the same family to go through the production cell, you may see that two of the products in the same family make up 77 percent of all volume to go through the production cell. You may also discover that of three different product families using the cell equipment, one family makes up 86 percent of all volume. You may not have been aware of this percentage mix otherwise. This type of presentation of data will make your decision process a little easier.

Ideally, you would like your team to allow the cell workers to meet takt time and have a few minutes available each day for other activities. If your team's first pass is typical, it may have a tough time just getting to takt time in the production cell creation. Challenge them to "re-think" things to meet a "stretch" goal. If strictly meeting takt time is the best they can do with the observed elements, they have done their job. The other tasks you will want the operator to do can be done with minimal overtime, but it would be better to have them done within the work day to avoid added expense.

The stretch goal, and an extra creative challenge to the kaizen team, is to not merely meet the required takt time but to take as much waste out of the documented elements as will make it possible to meet production requirements in 85 percent to 95 percent of the defined work day. If you can meet the takt time while loading the total-value flow to 85 percent (most companies start here and reluctantly give ground—much is dependent on the specific process in question) of its day, this leaves time for the operator to meet his takt goals without overtime in the event of some line stoppage or minor quality problem. It also allows operator time for total preventative maintenance tasks, allows operator time for periodic quality training, and, most importantly, allows time for the end-of-day walk-through review with management.

When we talk about the productive work day and time available for the operator to meet takt time, there are several cautionary points you must consider. If your work day includes a half-hour lunch and two 10-minute breaks, for example, you should not use the kaizen event as an excuse to eliminate breaks or shorten the lunch break. Your team must find creative ways to eliminate waste and to meet or exceed takt time without beating up the workforce. Squeezing the employee, along with practices like announcing the layoff of redundant personnel immediately after a successful productivity improvement kaizen, will ensure that your future productivity improvement kaizens will be filled with dolts who have no creative idea for taking waste out of any process—let alone recognizing waste when it stares them in the face. New "team recruits" will leave you wondering how they can find the restroom every day.

Employees will see "take aways" as punitive. They will also view the Lean implementation leader as the "grim reaper," and any goodwill to help him or her will evaporate. As we discussed earlier, if your company is using Lean because it is in a potential "death spiral" and you need to improve cash flow or there is no future for anyone, you should have had an employee meeting and conveyed this foreboding triage situation to your employees. If your company is not in a death spiral, also as discussed earlier, you should have a plan on what to do with employees freed up by productivity improvement gains—seed other kaizen improvement teams, cross-train to eliminate overtime and increase workforce flexibility, put pressure on your highly paid sales force to bring more volume into the factory to fill extra capacity, eliminate the need for temporary employees, eliminate chronic and costly overtime, etc.

Besides being the production requirement demand (historical demand adjusted for anticipated future changes) required by your customer, takt time serves as a baseline for other activities in the establishment of the total-value flow. The cumulative time of the actual documented elements, divided by takt time, will determine the manpower required by the total-value flow. Takt time will be used in establishing the line stocker schedule for servicing the total-value flow. It will be used in determining the timing of inventory quantities needed to service the customer demand. Takt time will also be instrumental in the metric review and visual performance indicators for the production cell. We will discuss all these items in more depth as we go on. The concept of takt time is vital to the idea of level-loading and line-balancing in the total-value flow. In a nutshell, these are attributes of maximizing correct materials and informational flows, and eliminating queues while meeting takt-time requirements.

Just as there were rules for handling kanbans from an inventory perspective, there are also rules for kanbans from a total-value flow takt time and signaling perspective. The team must be aware of these rules as they begin brainstorming. These should be considered standard work and posted at the production cell for the operators. They are as follows:

1. There is no production allowed without a kanban signal.
2. There is no over- or underproduction of kanban quantity allowed.
3. Do not honor handwritten kanban signals.
4. Only acceptable-quality parts count toward fulfilling kanban quantity.

5. Never send unacceptable-quality parts downstream.
6. Period production totals must be recorded on the takt sheet in a timely manner.
7. Reasons why takt time not met must be recorded by operator.
8. Kanban signal quantities can only be changed by materials group or scheduler.
9. Visual indicators must be used in timely manner in production cell.

One other bit of wisdom to infuse the kaizen team members with before they start their analysis of the operator elements and begin setup of the total-value flow is this: "use creativity, not cash." When visitors come to a truly Lean factory, they tend to be surprised to see plywood, corrugation, PVC pipe, duct tape and simple, multi-purpose, easily adapted aluminum or light steel channels everywhere. Everything they see is functional and safe, but it probably does not exude a sense of permanence or luxury. The reason for this is that it is not meant to be either luxurious or permanent. At the very heart of a kaizen is the concept of continuous improvement. What works today can be improved upon or replaced with something more efficient tomorrow. If your company is a food processor or a pharmaceutical company or other process-defined or regulated company, there might be strict material issues you must address and adhere to, but, generally, if something meets the function and *is safe*, encourage the team to consider it.

Once the Lean mind-set starts to dominate a company, employees will more readily recognize waste and agitate for the improvements. Some very advanced Lean companies have done away with dedicated kaizen events—except for special projects or concerns—and replaced them with total-value-flow-based, worker end-of-day brainstorming on problems or opportunities. If you are just starting out, you are years away from this.

In the next chapter, we will consider how to analyze the observed elements and begin to create the percent-loading chart, which will drive the setup of the cell. By the end of the second day of the kaizen event, if not sooner, the team should have started implementation of countermeasures to establish the total-value flow. The key to this process is the ability to identify the waste in the process and to understand the variations observed. By the end of the next chapter, we will have a layout of a production cell.

Chapter 13

Using the Percent-Loading Chart

Common Lean metrics say that 95 percent of all lead time, both in the factory and in the office, consists of non-value-added content or waste. For our purposes, eliminating the waste is the key to establishing a good process in the total-value flow. The documenters, if they did their job observantly, should have recorded the information that will help to identify the wastes. This understanding of variations in the process, and the elimination of wasteful activities and time, will help the production cell to meet the required takt time in a new process. The tool for getting to the new process in the production cell is the percent-loading chart.

The percent-loading chart's starting point is the concept of "lowest repeatable" elements. If the documenter did the observer job correctly, he or she should have timed all the work elements and made notes on an ideal test population of 10 complete production cycles. This number of observations should allow the team to review and pinpoint the element times that seem to be the "most repeatable." By stacking the lowest repeatable elements in a "percent-loading chart," we can see a baseline cycle time that, given other changes to follow, should at least be our minimum, consistent, potential cycle time, and a starting point for refinement of the process.

During the documenting reality process, you will understand the outliers in time elements through observation by noting additional steps added, delays encountered for any reason, interruptions to the process for any reason, and missed steps. All of these make time elements outliers and not to be used for a standard. Using the lowest repeatable observation time, which also provides for safety and quality, you will gauge the magnitude of productivity opportunity at the beginning of the event. The challenge for the team is to focus on eliminating waste and creating a new standard. If the team does a good job during the event of eliminating waste, this improved, observed-baseline reading could potentially become your new standard.

By observing a test population of 10 production cycles, outliers can more readily be identified and excluded from the baseline consideration. Outliers can go either way—they can be optimum values as well as worst case values, and they do not fit the criteria of "lowest and most repeatable" times. If you use only optimum values, which means a step was skipped or proper process not followed, you will be setting the production cell up for failure. It will not be able to produce consistently at that rate. You would never use worst case values, because they embody waste. If you were analyzing the values statistically, you will probably find that the usable time element values are more closely clustered around the mode rather than the mean or median value. As a matter of fact, we would discourage using averages—they tend to skew higher in this situation.

Make a judgment based on the data presented. If all things appear to be equal after outliers are discounted, take the mode value or the third or fourth lowest value as the element time for your team's starting point. If your documenters, for some reasons—equipment breakdown, single-trained operator illness, line-stopping material shortages, etc.—did not make more than a couple of observations, you have the option of suspending the kaizen until you get a representative number of observations, or make a judgment based on limited data and observation during the documentation phase and adjust as needed. If you cannot get 10 observations to document, five complete sets of observations might be considered a base minimum to determine values.

By way of example, we have created a process with "observed" times recorded by a team documenter in the following table. For the sake of simplicity, we are using basic verbs and nouns to denote the activity. In practice, the goal is always to break down elements into "bit"-sized tasks—that is, the "smallest observable." This level of detail allows the documenters to separate the value-added and non-value-added activities more clearly. The spread of times is typical of what a documenter would see. The observations for a single product with the simplified verbs and timed values (times in seconds) are shown in Figure 13.1.

On our current, one-product example, if you posit that the takt time is 1000 seconds and we use one operator, the observed and documented least-waste-way cycle time (least-waste-way times are in red by observed element)

Operation/ Obs #	1	2	3	4	5	6	7	8	9	10	Avg	LR
Coil shear	120	132	154	120	118	117	145	133	120	121	128	120
Move wip						1680					70	70
Punch	87	61	60	110	72	58	60	62	60	62	69	60
Waiting for material						450					50	50
Move pallet										720	60	60
Wait for material		843									70	70
Form	49	33	32	30	36	29	30	30	31	31		
x2	98	66	64	60	72	58	60	60	62	62	66	60
Move to weld										539	45	45
Weld	288	272	248	240	240	240	240	240	238	241	249	240
Drill	24	22	20	20	18	20	19	20	20	20		
x6	144	132	120	120	108	120	114	120	120	120	122	120
Tap	28	22	23	20	20	19	20	20	23	24		
x6	168	132	138	120	120	114	120	120	138	144	131	120
Paint (outside)												0
Assembly	250	242	240	239	241	240	244	278	244	240	246	240
Pack	180	180	180	180	180	278	233	182	181	181	196	180
Total cycle time											1502	
Least waste way												1435

Figure 13.1 Observed times for product A.

is 1435 seconds, the team must be able to find waste eliminations and enhancements to the current process, at a minimum, to meet the takt time of 1000 seconds per unit of product. If, as we stated previously, we want to load the total-value flow at 85 percent to 95 percent of takt time, the team will have to shoot for a stretch goal of reducing the cycle time to 85 percent to 95 percent of 1000 seconds or roughly 850–950 seconds per unit of product. As a company just starting Lean, we suggest that you start with loading to 85 percent as a guideline—you may make it and you may not. You must, however, meet the takt times required. As is typical, secondary kaizen events in the total-value flow will probably get you to the 85 percent loading guideline.

This gap of desired production time (the 85 percent to 95 percent loading) to scheduled production time available (100 percent) covers most production and quality contingency problems, reduces overtime or need for added temporary help, allows for end-of-day review of takt time adherence, and enables regular or periodic operator maintenance of the production cell. It should be noted that the "end-of-the-day huddle" (the five-minute review of takt-time adherence in the production cell) should be taken out of takt time, and regular and periodic maintenance should be done on off-hours and not during time available.

When you are setting up the total-value flow, normally there are two factors that will determine what products you can run in the production cell: element machine run time and setup time. Both are easy to assess for impact on the proposed production cell. Machine run time availability may be a problem you can do nothing about in the short term, but setup or changeover time mismatches have some flexibility. A third factor, manpower availability, should not be an issue for the newly created production cell. (*Note*: A detailed discussion on setting up "make" kanbans and determining appropriate kanban sizes in light of setup and changeover considerations has its own chapter following.)

Machine cycle time may be a physical fact that cannot be improved by adjusting "feeds and speeds." Often times you don't have a lot of choices of where to produce or on what piece of equipment to produce. You need to do the best you can with what you have, or consider acquiring additional equipment. Most companies use what they have, and what they do not have becomes a line on their future capital budget expenditure plans.

If you are planning on moving product from other machines into the production cell, you will need to do the math to see whether you have the machine run time available for all the newly added products. If the targeted machine is maxed out, you may have to consider running multiple shifts. If the machine is operating at its optimum operating values and expanding shifts will not work, you will not have many options in the short term. You will have to add the products to the production cell at a later date when capacity constraints change. You also do not want to overpower or overload the machine beyond the manufacturer's specifications to create a safety hazard. If this is the case, you can leave part manufacture at its existing machine center and control it by kanban cards triggered at the production cell. You will have to do the math to see where you stand.

Element machine time is probably the easiest to determine. If each product line has its own percent-loading chart, it is easy enough to see whether there is any common machine time demand that would prohibit all the targeted products from running together in the same production cell with existing or targeted equipment. By reviewing the percent-loading charts for individual products and extending the pacing-element-observed machine times, we should be able to see whether there will be too much competing demand for any particular machine or asset. Usually the cycle time varies significantly, and a way to handle this is to make the additional processing in a subassembly area or department that feeds the production cell. You do this by adjusting the labor to meet the required cycle time. In essence, you have a subassembly or processing line that feeds the line, and you staff this as needed.

For the common machine elements among the products, summarize the annualized element time for the machine and compare with your production time available.

If setup and changeover times are significant for select products, it might be better to make them in a "special" cell or control them on kanban cards from their current feeder machine. If you control them on kanban cards from a feeder machine, you can choose to do the balance of the operations and assembly and/or pack in the production cell. If you have part numbers that you are considering for the total-value flow, but they have significant setups or changeovers, you can test to see how this will affect your other products as follows.

You know many pieces of data to help you to your answer: (1) the part numbers with significant setup or changeover, (2) the annual volumes for the part numbers, (3) the rationalized kanban card quantities, and (4) the significant setup or changeover time. From these data, you should be able to determine the effects of setup similarly to the analysis you did to determine element machine time demand. Calculate the frequency of setups or change-overs per time period, and, from this, you can get an average setup or changeover value in time to determine whether the product can be added to the total-value flow list of candidates. Keep in mind the resultant time might be "worst case," as if each setup or changeover were done "from scratch" rather than having scheduling rules where minor setups are piggybacked on major setups. Keep in mind, you can always leave the parts, controlled by kanban signals, at their current source and do the downstream operations and packing in the new production cell—if this makes sense. The other option is the "special cell" for the disrupting products.

Special cells usually have a correlation to specific equipment constraints—usually involving onerous setup or changeover issues. In most traditional companies, following standard costing and historical industrial engineering methods and standards, large, high-volume machines, referred to in Lean as "monuments," were the norm. Since the focus was on lowest product cost, maximizing efficiency and utilization to reach maximum productivity was the goal. In monthly management meetings, supervisors and the plant manager were routinely "beaten up" over low productivity and utilization numbers. "Payback" on the machines required they be run constantly. The bigger the lot size, the lower the piece-part cost and the minimal cost of setups prorated over the lot size. Unfortunately, in today's competitive world, when you multiply the lot sizes for the number of parts involved times the extended inventory costs, companies run out of cash and close the doors.

In Lean, profitability comes from maximized flow to meet customer demand and not lot sizing rules mandated by the accounting or industrial engineering departments. Traditional manufacturing and Lean manufacturing philosophies are in conflict on this specific point. Throughput to meet customer demands, on-time delivery, minimized lead times, and minimized inventory become the true measures of profitability in a Lean company.

If you have monuments, you cannot simply replace them and buy new machines—most companies need to "right size" machines over time. If the monument plays a significant role in the total-value flow creation, you will need to get creative on how parts from the volume machine are supplied to the cell. There are two ways to do this, both of which are controlled by kanban signals: (1) set up a buffer inventory at the production cell and pick from this quantity to trigger replenishments at the monument machine, or (2) set up a buffer inventory at the monument and pick from that quantity to trigger replenishments at the large machine. In Lean jargon, these are referred to as variations on the "curtain effect." In both cases, production at the monument would be controlled by quantity and the timing of the kanban.

Given that the monument operator could even be in a different department or different building, it would probably make most sense to leave the buffer inventory at the production cell. In both cases, because setup could be a major issue with the monument, you would be best advised to create several kanban cards' worth of inventory—we would recommend three cards minimum. Each card quantity would equal total-value flow demand for a projected lead time for the large machine to replace the inventory. In this case, assuming raw material is stocked for the part, the lead time on the kanban card should be replenishment lead time plus agreed-upon turn-around time only.

Standard work needs to be written, and "when to run" rules must be spelled out for all parties involved. For example, "card must be run within 24 hours of receipt" or "when operator has received a second kanban card (for part numbers with three-card population), the operator must run the part at next available setup;" or "if the operator only has a single card for part numbers with card populations of more than two cards, the operator has the discretion to run a single card based on the existing work load." Specific work direction must be given to the monument operators who probably will have little other involvement with Lean and are not knowledgeable about how the methods fit together.

This would give some leeway to the monument operator and also acknowledge the onerous setup time required for a small lot on a high-volume machine. Obviously, this is a very imperfect answer acknowledging a mismatch in machine and equipment needs. The key "takeaway" from this discussion is, going forward as a policy for purchasing machines, to have machines right sized to service the needs of the production cell.

If you have parts with outside processing times that will interrupt the flow within the production cell, you can follow the same buffer concept applied to the monument machines. In the case of send outs for outside processing—painting, plating, gun-drilling, annealing, casting porosity testing, laboratory quality checks, etc.—the buffer inventory stock kanban card quantity would equal the lead-time quantity needed, from the production cell to the outside supplier and back to the production cell. This lead time would be the sum of internal processing necessary to send to the outside supplier, plus transportation time to the supplier, plus outside supplier's processing and curing, etc. time, plus outside supplier's processing necessary to send the shipment back to your company, plus transit time en route back to your company, plus receiving time at your company, which ends at the point product is ready to be picked for the production cell. If your suppliers are dependable, have reliable quality, and meet lead times, your container sizes or calculated multiples should be fine. If not, adjust as necessary and/or search for better vendors. For visibility, kanban cards with outside processing should be slotted on the receiving heijunka, just like the purchasing kanbans, and followed up as needed by the materials group.

Manpower to supply the production cell should not be an issue. There are two obvious reasons: (1) existing personnel are making the product at the time of your kaizen event, and (2) your productivity gain from the establishment of the production cell should supply you with freed-up manpower. The only issue you may face is a training issue due to the shuffle of personnel. Keep in mind that you do not need your very best people to populate the production cell—you just need your intelligent, hardworking, average employee. The written standard work should help whoever is assigned to the production cell. Keep this in mind as you move your personnel around.

At this point, we have discussed the takt time, how to deal with "work-arounds" like large, high-volume machines and outside processing, final tests for "tweaking" and choosing the parts projected for the total-value flow, and initial manpower requirements for the total-value flow, so now we can turn to analyzing time and quality variations and elimination of waste. If we do this successfully, the end result of our efforts will be a stacked cycle time that meets our requirements in the production cell.

The key to setting up a level-loaded, line-balanced production cell is to link machines and worker actions to take as much time, distance, and wasted effort out of the process as possible. When all is done, what you should have left to work with are value-added elements and non-value-added-but-necessary elements. You shouldn't expect to eliminate all waste in one, all-inclusive kaizen event—if anything, you will find more waste than you originally thought. Think small, incremental improvement steps versus going for the one "bold stroke"—bold strokes are better tried out at the golf course. Do what you can in the five-day time-frame allowed, remove as much waste as possible, and continuously improve.

The big difference between a Lean company and a traditionally managed company is that the traditionally managed companies generally take the "all or nothing" approach. They want to make their effort and results perfect, and, subsequently, they spend inordinate time planning and developing an activity or project plan, only to find the best plan didn't work as expected. In the meantime, the Lean company implements small improvements right away and continues to build on what works. The Lean company gets on-going, incremental improvements and retains the ability to capitalize on small-change opportunities that arise from their improvements. The traditionally managed company plods along the bold stroke path, and, when expectations are not met and the CEO is walking around with a mad man expression—like Jack Nicholson's in "The Shining"—the executive search group is contacted to replace the culpable executives and managers.

Create the cycle time as if one person alone is doing the production work. This makes it easier to think about how all the elements meld together. When you actually establish the production cell, you will need standard work to cover the actual number of operators assigned to the cell.

With the filled-out, baseline "least-waste-way" percent-loading chart as a starting condition posted where all can see, begin your brainstorming session with the documented elements making up the percent-loading chart. Using the eight wastes discussed in earlier chapters as context, begin review of each element. (It may be most helpful and is recommended to have a preprinted waste checklist as a handout to jog the memory and understanding during the documentation phase.) Review the noted wastes by observed element and classify them on flip-chart paper. The key to this analysis is determining what distinguished them as waste. Start with the most obvious wastes.

In analyzing machine and operator element documentation, one of the keys to watch for is what is happening between documented elements. This is normally a bounty of waste potential. What is the operator doing in the documented element while the machine is cycling? What activity finishes first and for what reason? How soon does the next production cycle begin and what steps precede the start of the production cycle?

What distinguishes waste as waste? Although wastes do not typically fit neatly into a single category, here is a list of types of manufacturing issues that your team will identify somewhere in their list of wastes. It is representative of the discussions and questions the brainstorming will surface. Since waste is so prevalent, keep in mind the list is by no means exhaustive:

1. *Overproduction*: Vendor lot sizes are random and do not match production need? Operator makes extras—"just-in-case" inventory—to cover quality "fallout" or yield problem? Extra processed parts (semi-processed or finished) held or inventoried at the machine? Significant quality issues requiring constant rework?

2. *Excess inventory*: Variations in purchased product? Missing material? Defective material? Purchasing ordered wrong materials, or vendor sent or substituted wrong materials? Purchased materials do not work due to random sizes or quality deviations of purchased materials or variations within the machines? Poor timing of engineering change-notice process creates inventory imbalance?

3. *Waiting*: "Watching the wash"—operator waiting for automated machine or test to complete, or issue report or data? Lack of equipment for lifting or moving materials or finished product? Operator time looking for tools or missing correct tool to do job? Waiting for equipment—pallet jack, forklift, or material mover? Operator waits for help because raw materials too heavy or bulky to lift? Operator waits at tool crib or die crib at changeover time? Operator must sign out for tools and equipment? Waiting for quality personnel to inspect at the source—quality control responsible for making a quality part?

4. *Transportation*: Operator walks distance to tool, fixture, die, or equipment "room"? Operator carries part to next operation? Operator arranges totes—moves full one out of the way and brings empty one and places at machine? Not using a gravity feed option?

5. *Excess motion*: Requires operator "make-it-work" activity? Looking for tools, info, or materials in no set location? Punches leave burrs or blow-out and operator hits with sander or grinder due to poor tooling maintenance? One-size-fits-all machine program processes or machines "air"? No "ganged" or combined machining or manufacturing functions? Lack of material uniformity requires shims or other operator compensation? Operator has to disassemble packaging before use? Unwrap vendor packaging and shrink wrap with a box knife as it comes from receiving department?

6. *Defects*: Operator has "lookup" questions on specs or seeks out clarification on a drawing or print? Seeking out quality control for in-process inspection? No holding fixtures for part? Operator shims dies and fixtures for adjustments constantly? Kitting for hardware—operator filling against bill of materials rather than visual template per kit hardware? Cartons from vendor sticking together? Die cuts not 100 percent formed and operator has to cut out?

7. *Overprocessing*: Constant adjusting of machine stops? Fixture, jig, die orientation issues? Each changeover measured into place by constant checks and measurements? Shut height of presses all different? Use of bolts versus cam levers, blocks, or clamps to hold fixtures or dies? Excessive drill cycle time and smoke, indicating improperly maintained drill bits or improper drill bit for material or wrong material hardness specification? Sophisticated quality control tests over simple tests? Use of calipers and elaborate measurements versus "go-no-go" gauge?

8. *Underutilized people*: Watch for repetitive operator motions that could lend themselves to robotics, *but remember to eliminate waste before you automate!*

9. *Ergonomic issues for operator*: Where are tools? At what height are tools? Is there constant bending to pickup? Reaching or stretching up? Walking to get something? Walking around clutter or other machines? Operator holding item while machine functions? Operator manually lubes taps every 10 pieces? Operator manually deburrs or sands each piece after forming? Manual feeds involving operator? Operator uses torque bar or pipe on box wrench for added leverage when breaking loose bolts? Labels print from sheets rather than continuous rolls? Operator has a problem peeling off label backings?

Keep the above waste examples in mind as you try to pare down the element times presented on the percent-loading chart. If operator time is less than machine cycle time, can he or she do something to eliminate time in a downstream operation element? Keep in mind that your kaizen results might be an interim step compared to the ultimate matching of machines to need. Take things as far as you can in the brainstorming to develop a plan. Before the kaizen event ends, you will have the chance to test all the enhancements you brainstorm.

When you have refined your observed elements as much as possible and your revised percent-loading chart meets your takt time, you will want to start with the theoretical construction of the production cell. This is "theoretical" construction because you should always test your proposed layout with cut-to-size cardboard templates before you start physically moving machines and electrical drops in the factory. When the team establishes the production cell in day three, it will have a chance to run the cell and make tweaks as needed to the process. This is where the rubber meets the road as far as the theoretical construction is concerned. The layout on cardboard cutouts prevents surprises, economizes cursing, and mitigates the flawed effort recognition, forehead-indenting, epiphany moments.

The easiest way to construct your theoretical production cell is to use a plat or layout of the factory floor and create cutouts of machines, fixed equipment, and inventory locations to fit and position to scale. By brainstorming and using cutouts, you have flexibility to visualize and brainstorm benefits of different flows and orientations. Using the actual, "to-scale" plat or layout will also help you recognize potential problems with door openings, support posts, fire hoses, and electrical boxes, which must remain clear and accessible. You will also need to mark aisles and "in" and "out" drop zones.

The production cell should always be designed in a "right to left" or counterclockwise flow (Lean goes with the percentages to favor "righties") and for single-piece flow (make per kanban as used or sold). The production cell should be laid out in a "U" or semicircular fashion to minimize distances between two points. When dealing with the actual work elements to meet takt time, you will discover that workers will move around to different work stations to perform different elements in order to meet the required time. Minimizing distances saves time and operator energy (Figure 13.2).

The production cell should be designed to be flexible, compact, responsive, and populated with focused and dedicated machines. The flow should be as obvious as it is visual. In and out drop zones and inventory bins should be clearly marked and obvious. Bins should be fixed—no random locations—and right sized to hold the kanban inventory population. Although at any given time you will probably only have one-half the kanban population of any given part number on hand, depending on demand fluctuations, you could have all of a particular part number's population on hand. You must have dedicated bin space available for this occasion.

Flow into and out of the production cell and from and onto the aisles should be obvious and unimpeded. Aisles should be clearly marked. When you are marking floors, sometimes it is easier to use colored tape, rather than painting the lines. Use tape for marking in and out material points, home positions for mobile equipment, inventory bins (if skids or barrels), etc. If you use tape and things change, simply scrape the tape from the floor.

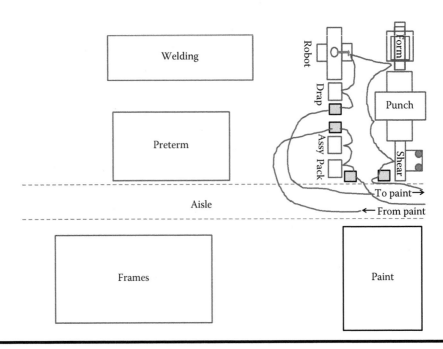

Figure 13.2   The after spaghetti chart.

The production cell should also be designed with flexibility in mind. Since Lean is dynamic, the production cell you set up today may not be the same one that exists one year from now. Your right-sized equipment may be available, or your reduced lead times may have given you a significant advantage against the competition and your volume may have doubled. Since change is inevitable, incorporate this possibility into your production cell.

Put as many things as possible on wheels (obviously common sense applies here) as you set up the production cell. If you have small parts, use gravity-feed shelving units on casters. If parts are heavy or bulky, or they are contained in steel drums, leave them in their container, but mark container home bins on the floor. If it makes sense, leave them on their skid to avoid double handling. If the conveyance or the exchange cart is the kanban signal, it should also have a home bin. Be careful when using conveyor belts or rollers; unwarranted or unwise use of these can become major wasters of time, energy, and money.

Where allowed and safe, use "quick-connect" bus bars and flexible conduit. When your team is considering or recommending changing things like gas lines, electricity and electric connections, sprinkler systems and fire hoses, etc., make sure your team seeks out advice on their plans with the proper on-site authority before proceeding. Lean is not an excuse for ill-advised shortcuts that jeopardize employee safety.

Pay particular attention to ergonomics. There should be rules for heights and weights you want employees to lift or handle or deal with every day. Your shelf and rack height limits for inventory, tooling, and operating supplies should not exceed the height of the shortest person on your team. Weights should be no more than the average worker can safely handle—in no cases should an employee be expected to lift more than 50 pounds on a routine basis without help.

The team should observe tooling positioning in relationship to where the employee in the production cell is working. Tools should be readily available without exaggerated stretching, bending, or walking. Suspend commonly used tools where they are accessible. Use pneumatic or hydraulic tooling or torque wrenches where it makes sense. Fulcrum-extending pry bars and hitting things with hammers to achieve "break loose" generally should be eliminated. Where possible, use "auto-seat" and "auto-eject" mechanisms. Make doing a productive job easier for your employees.

Having tools and equipment in a defined spot—a marked "shadow board" position or defined and marked bin—is part of good 5S practices (housekeeping). Good housekeeping provides the worker with the knowledge of "a place for everything, and everything in its place." It eliminates clutter. It helps with ergonomic issues. It identifies correct tooling. It is an organizing principle. It anticipates where the employee will be going next in the process. It helps reduce time required to do a job. It identifies problems with equipment. Most companies do not equate housekeeping as directly having an impact on product cost, but it does. Organization, housekeeping, and elimination of clutter make an employee more productive. Unfortunately, most companies view housekeeping as nothing more than periodically sweeping the floor and getting rid of the candy wrappers.

Since the purchasing kanbans were established using vendor-standard packaging wherever it made sense, the line stocker should bring parts to the total-value flow ready to be used. The production cell operator should not have to unwrap, count, weigh, or orient materials; he or she should only be picking and using as needed. Inventory should be at point of use, and it should require the user to travel minimal distance to pick. The purchasing person must make sure the vendor delivers product in the proper packaging.

When considering options with setups and changeovers, try to have the operator do as much anticipatory work as is allowable while the machine is cycling. Operator can also use machine cycling time to do operations preparatory to downstream work elements. Where possible and where it makes sense, use cam levers, clamps, and mechanical torque wrenches in lieu of operator's manual use of box or crescent wrenches to secure setup or changeover. Use of set measurement blocks or mechanical stops can help to foolproof positioning time. Having uniform press shut heights and uniform measuring and fill mechanisms can also reduce downtimes due to setup or changeover.

When you are creating fixtures, jigs, and dies, keep the specific design for a specific product. "One size fits all," with interminable adjustment activity, can be pennywise and pound foolish. Likewise, machines should have emphasis on functionality and flexibility. In many cases, an inventory of the maintenance department's "bone yard" can turn up old drills, presses, saws, etc., which can find new life in a production cell where operators and load are balanced. Machines do not have to be the newest or the fastest, be capable of processing the highest volume, or be the latest NC controlled; they only need to help the production cell meet its takt time. Do not add roots and vines to simple machines and operations.

Be on the lookout for opportunities to combine tool usage where reasonably possible. If you have a drill operation followed by a tap operation, try to combine them into a drill and tap operation. If you have a drilling operation with many iterations, think about the possibility of "gang drilling" in one operation. The combinations lack only creativity—drill and chamfer, drill and deburr, cut and deburr, etc. One word of caution: be careful not to overdo this, or it can turn into a monument. If it does not add another unreasonable level of complexity to the situation or require a new level of training or dependance on another source to execute, it might be worthwhile considering. If it introduces undue complexity into the process, opt for the simple instead. One of the key rules of Lean is to simplify the complex and, at the same time, keep your worker as self-sufficient as possible. If your efforts make things more complex, it can also reduce your ability to adjust labor needs based on takt time.

From an engineering perspective, when it comes to NC or CAD-CAM programs, be on the lookout for "one-program-fits-all" situations. It is not unheard of that programs are designed to cover all products. Machine cycling can be observed drilling or milling out "air" where there is no product, or going through a superfluous orientation or check cycle. The engineering efforts should meet the product need at hand. If the operator has to constantly enter codes or keystrokes to make a program function, your team probably has an opportunity for improvement.

When you are to the point of setting up the production cell and you know where the cell will be built, clean up the area as much as possible first. Take all superfluous machinery, equipment, and inventory out of the area. If you are unsure what to do with things, "red tag" them and designate someone to drive a decision (default is department supervisor) for disposition by an end date (default is two weeks). As you start to gain floor space, keep it off-limits to all the usual company packrat suspects. If you want to send a positive message, mark with "reserved for future company growth." Cordon off the area by stanchions. Shrink wrap fixed-shelving units and fixed racking to keep out casual encroachers.

Once the production-cell layout is settled, the team will have to finish off housekeeping efforts and make sure productivity-enhancing visuals are in place. The team will not be able to complete all the housekeeping efforts associated with a "5S" during the kaizen event. The concentration should be on initial cleanup and setting the place in order (shadow boards, machine arrangement, test equipment, etc.) to allow the production cell to begin. Painting machines; sealing floors; reviewing and standardizing handling, storage, and identification of jigs, fixtures, and dies; standardizing housekeeping practices; and establishing metrics will need to be done in a follow-up event.

Stress creativity to the team: generate ideas before spending cash. If the team gets "thinker's block," challenge them to contemplate other sources for ideas. Have they dealt with a similar problem at home? If so, what did they do? Everyone has at least one home remedy involving the use of duct tape. Consider the natural world outside the meeting room: How do the creatures or forces of the natural world do things? Gather food? Communicate? Build nests or dens or dams? Move things or food? Get from one point to another? Bend or stretch? Physical scientists refer to this search for answers in the natural world as geo-mimicry. Is the team aware of any benchmarking with similar industries or competition? Are there any other analogies from life like the problem at hand? Very few things in life are unique, and we humans are a most adaptive and resilient bunch. If you were on a desert island and your life depended on surviving with the resources you have, what would you do and how would you do it? We guarantee you someone would have an idea for a plan of attack.

We are never underwhelmed by the outcomes of kaizen events. We have seen the most ordinary-seeming people do the most extraordinary things. The key is creativity and discounting the obvious. Following is an example of an idea put forth by an unusually quiet and reserved team member whose high-school-picture caption probably said, "The person most unlikely to have any new ideas."

In a setup reduction kaizen for a large tonnage press, after the team had made some progress but continued to struggle with how to reduce the time to the desired one-minute goal, the soft-spoken inventory clerk team member suggested a "what if": that they use some of the excess roller ball-bearing conveyors in the factory to make an apron connected to the side and rear of the press at the table height to store the dies and allow the operator, unassisted, to slide the particular dies as needed into and out of the machine. Light bulbs went on at the suggestion. This was the breakthrough they needed to get to the single-minute exchange of dies for this machine. Who woulda thunk?

If you have monuments, odds are you are not going to get rid of them any time soon. From the kaizen, an intermediate plan and a longer-term plan can be taken into account in your budgeting process to right-size things. Accept them and work around them as best as you can. You still have to service your customer. Do as much as you can do as quickly as you can do it. Your successful kaizen has opened eyes, and the seeds are planted for your future.

In this chapter, you have heard suggestions and ideas on how to present and analyze the percent-loading chart data. You also have reviewed wastes by type of waste, and you can apply this discussion to eliminate waste from the observed, documented elements to get to the required takt time and cycle time. You have listened to a discussion on tips to improve layout. The team should be brainstorming and laying out the production cell corrugation cutouts. The area is in the process of being cleaned and cluttered items are being red tagged. In the next chapter, we will discuss factors that go into determining manufacturing kanban signals.

Chapter 14

Dependent-Demand Manufacturing Kanbans

In this chapter, we will discuss all the questions that need to be resolved in order to create effective kanban signals for dependent-demand (the fabricated "children" of the parent part number bill of material) manufactured parts. The discussion revolves around answers to questions involving stocking level for the parent part number; actual net production time available at the feeder machine; setup and changeover times per part number; run time on calculated kanban quantity for dependent component; actual net time available for setup and changeover; modifiers such as manufacturing "multiples," "minimums," or ABC classifications; and actual testing and tweaking of data to ensure the applied math works and passes a "reasonableness" test.

In keeping with one of the goals of this book—"keep it simple, stupid"— we are assuming that most smaller companies and stand-alone manufacturing divisions do not have statisticians setting their inventory levels. By following along with the given examples and spreadsheets, any reasonable person with good analytical skills should be able to set up the manufactured kanbans. Keep in mind, there is no one answer for setting inventory levels. Also keep in mind, whatever levels you set are interim values that will change as your company pursues further kaizen events that increase productivity. In keeping with one of the other goals of this book, pick "best guess" inventory levels to start now, and learn and improve as you go.

When you are establishing kanbans for dependent-level manufactured-part numbers, you must make sure that whatever value you settle on will provide enough dependent components to satisfy the parent-level kanban signal by kanban card. For example, if you have kanban cards for the parent part number to make products in signals of "20," you need to make sure your dependent-demand-manufactured parts are equal to or greater than "20" on the kanban card—if quantity used per parent is "1 per." If the parent uses "3 per" in the bill of material, the dependent-demand signal must be equal to or greater than "60." If the parent uses "0.5 per" in the bill, the dependent-demand signal must be equal to or greater than "10."

This relationship applies to all the manufacturing and purchasing part numbers at every level of the bill of material when the parent level is controlled by kanban signal. This relationship may not always be as cut and dried as the examples presented. In some cases, you will have to make more because of the raw-material quantity, electricity required per batch, excessive setup and changeover times, etc. For example, if you need 15 parts stamped from a sheet of 16-gauge steel and one sheet makes 45, you will probably make the dependent-demand in "45s" to eliminate handling of partially processed raw material or to avoid substantial scrap of the unused portion. In this case, you would probably create two cards for 45 pieces each for the dependent component or set up a visual order point in the bin triggered when one sheet's worth of product reaches the reorder point marker. This same logic applies to containers of reagent-activated resins, processed food additives, chemicals for a dip tank, etc.

If you are going to fabricate parts in the production cell directly from some raw material and incorporate them into the finished product in the production cell in the finishing steps, they will not need kanban cards. They simply start from some raw material and end up as the finished good. In traditional engineering bills of materials, these might be "phantom" part numbers—transitory part numbers used by engineers to help clarify how parts are made, but they are not kanban candidates, as they will never be "stocked" per se. The raw material, the part number the "phantom" is made from, on the other hand, will be kanban controlled.

For example, if you punch, bend, drill, and tap two pieces of metal to make left- and right-hand flanges for a finished good in the production cell, the value-added work is simply viewed as process steps to make the final product in the production cell—you would not assign kanban designations for the transitory right- and left-hand flange phantom-part numbers fabricated and consumed in the production cell in the creation of the finished good. On the other hand, any raw material or partially fabricated part number supplied to the production cell—from either the warehouse or the feeder work center—will need to be kanban controlled.

A	B	C	D	E	F	G	H
				C times D			E divided by 240 workdays
Product	Part number	Product family parent level annualized volume	Quantity per in bill of material per end unit	Annual volume in parts needed for annual demand	Cumulative volume	Percentage of total volume through machining center	Daily usage need in production cell
1 Product A	1243	22000	2	44000	44000	48%	184
2 Product B	6512	15360	1	15360	59360	65%	64
3 Product C	5698	8160	2	16320	75680	83%	68
4 Product D	8745R	6000	1	6000	81680	89%	25
5	8746L	6000	1	6000	87680	96%	25
6 Product E	4523	3600	1	3600	91280	100%	15

Figure 14.1   Parts supplied from a dedicated machining center for production cell.

On the example finished-good part numbers used in this book, which will be made in our theoretical total-value flow, we will assign part numbers, requiring kanbans, for parts supplied to our production cell from a dedicated machining center. Figure 14.1 shows volume data for the six part numbers. The parent-level part number volume is given, followed by the extended "quantity per" volume of the dependent part number required from the machining center.

In order to size the kanbans properly, we will need to know particular information about our part numbers—part run times, part setup or change-over times, workday production time, and workday time available for setup or changeover per day. Once we know the relationships among all these numbers, we can derive a kanban quantity for our card and derive total number of kanban cards needed. Once we derive the kanban quantity, we will also need to review the data in light of common sense minimums, maximums, multiples, or other multipliers that will change the derived number. We will discuss these fully in this chapter.

The current example assumes that the machining center that supplies the total-value flow is dedicated to the production cell. By this we mean that, by and large, the overwhelming majority of the parts produced in the machining center are destined for the production cell. In some companies, this is not always the case. You could have a machining center that fabricates parts for many product lines, some of which go to production cells and are controlled by kanbans and others of which go to non-kanban-controlled traditional manufacturing machines and work centers. We will discuss both scenarios in this chapter.

A	B	C	D	E	F	G	H
			Given	C times D	E times 240		
Product family "XXX"	Part number	Daily usage need in production cell	Run time per piece in seconds	Total run time in seconds per day	Annualized run time required in seconds	Cumulative run time required in seconds	Percentage of total run time through production cell
1 Product A	1243	184	28	5152	1236480	1236480	41%
2 Product B	6512	64	22	1408	337920	1574400	52%
3 Product C	5698	68	28	1904	456960	2031360	67%
4 Product D	8745R	25	48	1200	288000	2319360	76%
5	8746L	25	48	1200	288000	2607360	86%
6 Product E	4523	15	120	1800	432000	3039360	100%
				12664			

Figure 14.2 Analysis of part numbers in terms of run time through machining center.

Figure 14.2 captures the run time information for the kanban parts coming from the dedicated machining center.

This data chart shows us that the daily requirement for the six part numbers being supplied to the production cell requires 12,664 seconds of run time (less than four hours of run time) in the machining center to satisfy the daily requirement of parent-level demand in the production cell. On the surface, it would seem as if the machining center could supply the daily needs handily, but important pieces of information are missing before we can jump to that conclusion. We need to know setup and changeover time between part runs, available work time in the day, and time available each day for setup and changeover. The data table in Figure 14.3 fills in part of the missing information.

In this table, we have supplied values for setup or changeover time for each part number. In real life, when you are putting your own table together, these would be observed or timed values from the machining center. We can see that the setup and changeover time required to run all the parts is 14,400 seconds, and the average setup or changeover time is 2400 seconds. When we add this information to the prior data table, which showed daily run time of 12,664 seconds, we now know that we require 27,064 seconds per day to be able to set up or change over and run every part number required for the total-value flow. Now we need to look at time available—both as production time per day and as time available for setup and changeover per day.

	A	B	C	D	E	F	G	H	I
							C times F	Given	Sum of setup time divided by 6
	Product family "XXX"	Part number	Average machining run time per part	Quantity per year required to service demand	Time per year in seconds required to service demand	Quantity per day required to service demand	Production time required per day to service demand in seconds	Setup time per day in seconds to run kanban card equal to daily needed qty	Average setup time in seconds per day for all parts
1	Product A	1243	28	44000	1232000	184	5152	3600	
2	Product B	6512	22	15360	337920	64	1408	2400	
3	Product C	5698	28	16320	456960	68	1904	3600	
4	Product D	8745R	48	6000	288000	25	1200	600	
5		8746L	48	6000	288000	25	1200	600	
6	Product E	4523	120	3600	432000	15	1800	3600	
					3034880		12664	14400	2400

Assume 240 workdays per year

Figure 14.3   Determining average setup time for all parts in dedicated machining center.

In our theoretical company, our workday is eight hours, but our actual production time is seven hours and 10 minutes. Thirty minutes are allowed for lunch period, and there is one 10-minute break in the morning and a five-minute break in the afternoon. Five minutes are allowed at the end of the shift for clean up of the area. To determine actual production work time available, take the extended clock-time day and net out all non-production-work periods and convert to seconds. This will give you time available in seconds.

In our case, seven hours and 10 minutes equals 430 minutes times 60 seconds equals 25,800 seconds. This is our productive workday time available in seconds.

We know what our run time for all parts per day is: 12,664 seconds. If we subtract this run time from our productive-workday time available in seconds, the difference is time available for setup or changeover. In our case, 25,800 seconds minus 12,664 seconds equals 13,136 seconds available for setup or changeover available per day for our six part numbers. In order to set up or change over and run every part every day, we will need 12,664 seconds run time plus 14,400 seconds available for setup or changeover each day. Since we only have 13,136 seconds available for setup or changeover, we know we will not be able to run each part completely every day.

When we set up a relationship of time available for setup and change-over to time required for setup and changeover to make all parts, the result is 13,136 divided by 14,400 or 0.91 setups or changeovers per day per part number. When the number of year production workdays is multiplied by 0.91, the result is the number of setups and changeovers per part number per year. In this case, the math is 240 times 0.91 equals 218 setups or changeovers per year per part number. If we take one of the part numbers above, 1243, as an example, we can determine kanban size by dividing total annual required volume, 44,000, by 218 opportunities for setup or changeover: 44,000 divided by 218 equals a kanban size of 202. This is a preliminary number, which needs to be reviewed for reasonableness of quantity. If the number meets the reasonableness test, we will probably have a kanban population of two cards times 202 pieces each for a total of 404 pieces. This should cover the reciprocal of 1 divided by 0.91 times 2 or allow kanban coverage for the parent for 2.19 days until the cards complete the setup and run cycle. To test this, we multiply the 184 required per day for part number 1243 times 2.19. The answer should equal 404 pieces. It does. (An alternative way to look at the above results is: change the number of setups for the highest volume parts (from 0.91 to 1) at the expense of the lower volume parts in exchange for carrying slightly more inventory for the lower volume part number. If this makes sense, rework the numbers for kanban quantities for the lower volume part numbers. Do what works best for your company.)

When we say you need to review a number for the reasonableness test, this is what we mean: sometimes there are modifiers that need to be made to a number to minimize waste with a raw material, to meet or take advantage of handling or packaging opportunities or problems, to maximize process efficiency, or to gain the advantage on space or equipment issues. Generally, these are more in the vein of minor adjustments rather than wholesale abandonment of principle.

Most of the adjustments fall into the category of a minimum, a maximum, or a multiple. In the earlier example of 16-gauge-steel sheets, the sheet yields 45 pieces without extra handling or scrap, and this reasonably should become the minimum or multiple for the kanban card. Other examples, which probably revolve around standard packaging for raw materials, would be the reagent-activated resins, chemicals for a dip tank, processed-food additives, etc. Multiples might figure into the equation if handling or storing the product becomes an issue. If you put 4,500 pieces of something into a tote, but you have to wait 45 minutes to get a forklift or crane to move it, it might make more sense to take the kanban card of 4,500 pieces and divide it into thirds of 1,500 pieces each so that a material handler with a pallet jack can readily move the tote from the machining area to a pickup or inventory bin area. In this last case, two kanban cards of 4,500 pieces would become six kanban cards of 1,500 pieces.

If you have a part, for example, that requires time in an oven or drying facility, or you require a significant electrical source for parts you are electro-plating or electro-discharge machining, your cost in energy or process materials for running individual small batches of parts may be prohibitive. As in the case of the totes above, you may have to have multiple kanban signals. This allows the operation to be run when a certain number of kanban cards are present.

There are many examples of modifiers that might be required to get to the correct kanban card quantity and the correct number of kanban cards in a population. There is no one absolutely correct answer. You have to look at your own factory situation. In some cases, you will have to deal with details that are not always neat and tidy. You may even have to work with your vendors to get their packaging to meet your kanban needs, if you cannot adapt to their quantity or their quantity does not pass your reasonableness test—that is, their packaging represents three months of inventory on a shelf. How you answer the question is how you deal with the reasonableness test of the kanbans.

If you are not so fortunate to have a dedicated machining center to supply parts to your production cell, you will have to recalculate kanban cards, taking into account the volume from all parts, kanban and non-kanban, going through the machining center. For your machining center, until everything is scheduled by kanban, the kanban-designated part numbers will be controlled by kanban cards, and, your non-kanban part numbers will be controlled by whatever system controls the non-Lean, shop-order scheduling. In this type of situation of mixed systems, you will probably need to have scheduling rules in place for the foreman to follow for the kanban items. We will discuss all this in the paragraphs that follow.

In the following table (Figure 14.4), we have introduced non-kanban-controlled parts along with the kanban-controlled parts fed to your production cell from a non-dedicated machining center. We have given them values for annual demands, setup and changeover time, and run times per part number. In many companies, this situation of mixing kanban-controlled and non-kanban-MRP controlled will probably be the norm when starting out on the Lean journey. As a company progresses in the Lean journey, machines tend to be more "right sized" and fitted better to the production cell. Since your company cannot just run out and buy new machines, you make the

	A	B	C	D	E	F	G	H	I
				C divided by 240 workdays	Given	E times D	Given	F plus G	Sum of G divided by 20 part numbers
	Product	Part number	Annual volume in parts needed	Quantity per day required to service demand	Average machine run time per part in seconds	Run time required per day's demand in seconds	Setup time per day in seconds to run kanban card qty equal to day's need	Setup and run time per day for average quantity in seconds	Average setup time per day for all parts
1	Product A	1243	44000	184	28	5152	3600	8752	
2	Product B	6512	15360	64	22	1408	2400	3808	
3	Product C	5698	16320	68	28	1904	3600	5504	
4	Product D	8745	6000	25	48	1200	600	1800	
5		8746	6000	25	48	1200	600	1800	
6	Product E	3600	3600	15	120	1800	3600	5400	
7	Product F	non-kanban A	12000	50	28	1400	1200	2600	
8	Product F	non-kanban B	12000	50	28	1400	1200	2600	
9	Product F	non-kanban C	12000	50	12	600	600	1200	
10	Product G	non-kanban D	12000	50	22	1100	1500	2600	
11	Product H	non-kanban E	11000	46	24	1104	1800	2904	
12	Product I	non-kanban F	9000	38	32	1216	1200	2416	
13	Product J	non-kanban G	4000	17	40	680	600	1280	
14	Product K	non-kanban H	3000	13	38	494	1800	2294	
15	Product L	non-kanban I	2000	9	22	198	1800	1998	
16	Product M	non-kanban J	1800	8	24	192	1200	1392	
17		non-kanban K	1800	8	24	192	1200	1392	
18		non-kanban L	1800	8	24	192	1200	1392	
19	Product N	non-kanban M	1500	7	32	224	2200	2424	
20	Product O	non-kanban N	1200	5	42	210	1800	2010	
						21866	33700	55566	1685

Assume 240 workdays per year

Figure 14.4 Determining average setup time for all parts in non-dedicated machining center.

product on the machines you have. Even with mixed-use machining centers, we can still get to our goal of supplying the production cell via kanban signals (Figure 14.4).

When you do share a machining center with both kanban and non-kanban part numbers, there will probably be a need for scheduling rules to ensure the kanban-controlled part numbers flow as needed to the production cell. Since the kanban cards are sized to complement the finished goods shipment schedules, any disruption to the kanban card flow could idle the downstream production cell and set up past-due orders to the customers.

Kanban cards will need to be run on a first-come, first-served basis or when a certain number of kanbans are accumulated, triggering the need to run the parts. Since shared-resource kanban cards are created taking into account the setup and changeover and run times of both kanban and non-kanban-controlled part numbers at the machining center, you have acknowledged the time commitment in the machining center to the kanban parts; you are not asking for anything over and above normal inventory history production. In the shared machining center we are describing, you will also have to have a heijunka board—even a simple series of boxes showing a slotted sequence of what to run next—to help better see kanban cards awaiting production. Any passerby should be able to understand what cards are awaiting at the machining center. The cards should not be filed with the balance of your computer system's printed shop orders in the department's "hanging files" or file cabinets. They must be visible. People in the machining center, both workers and foremen, must be instructed in how to handle the kanban cards and what the rules are for when to run the kanban cards.

When we look at the data presented, we can break it down into the data required to allow us to set our kanban quantities.

- First of all, we know our annual production time available, net of breaks and lunch periods: 25,800 seconds per day times 240 defined workdays equals 6,192,000 seconds per year of production time.
- Next, we know our run time per day required for all part numbers: 21,866 seconds per day times 240 workdays equals 5,247,840 seconds per year of required run time.
- When we subtract run time from total production time, we can determine time available for setups: 6,192,000 minus 5,247,840 equals 944,160 seconds per year available for setups and changeovers.
- When we take seconds available for setup or changeover and divide it by average setup time, we can determine average number of setups or changeovers we can perform in one year at this center: 944,160 divided by 1,685 equals 560 total setups or changeover potential in average year.
- In order to determine what this is for our individual part number, of part numbers to be setup or changeover: 560 potential setups divided by 20 part numbers equals 28 setups or changeovers per year per part number.
- When we take the above information and apply it to one of our example numbers in the table, 1243, we can derive the kanban quantity per card and the total number of kanban cards needed: Annualized volume of 44,000 divided by 28 average set-up or changeover opportunities equals a kanban signal of 1,572 pieces per signal.

Since we will always have two kanbans—one being picked and used and the second being fabricated, the total kanban population will be 1,572 pieces per card times two cards equals 3,144 kanban population.

In this case, each kanban card will equal 8.6 days' worth of usage (1,572 divided by 184). With two kanban cards in circulation, the average inventory on hand at any given day will be 1,572 pieces.

There are other ways to look at the data from the tables. You can define some of the kanban-controlled part numbers with an "ABC" inventory classification and set the cards accordingly. If the "A" classed inventory is the highest volume (most probably, stocked kanbans) level and the "C" category is the lowest volume level, you can decide to run A inventory daily and C inventory weekly. "B" classed inventory, the middle production volumes, can be run twice per week. In a similar manner, you can designate inventory by "turns desired" and rework the tables in this manner. By reserving time in your equations—using daily, twice-weekly, and weekly values—you may better compensate for more "irregular" than "regular" demand patterns. Use your collective judgment to tweak as needed.

The important point is to work from your historical data augmented by current marketing plans for new products being phased in and older products being phased out. The various rankings of demand history showing cumulative percentages show you data in different perspectives: volume of parts required, dollarized volume of parts required, volume by inventory classifications, etc.

You can look at the data in many different ways, but the point of collecting the data and reviewing it is not to reach a state of "paralysis by analysis." The important point is to make kanban cards and start. Go with your best estimates, and drive the stake in the ground. The saving feature with kanban cards is that they can always be changed as data warrants. You will want to periodically review the card data in light of sales history after the first six months just to make sure you are on the right track. As you go along, your materials and marketing people will gain insight and an intuitive understanding of when you should review your card populations or change the individual part number.

As your company travels its Lean journey, you will realize the gains to be made by reducing inventory. One of the most powerful contributors to reduced inventories will be the setup or changeover time reduction on the machines. By eliminating setup and changeover as an issue, your company can pursue single-piece production flow at the request of the customer. This is the ideal result of Lean efforts.

	A	B	C	D	E	F	G	H	I	J
	Inventory at ten turns per year							Inventory with two kanban cards		
Product family "XXX"	Part number	Inventory cost per piece		Annual volume in parts needed	Current inventory turns	Average inventory on hand given turns	Extended part number population average inventory cost	Kanban quantity per card	Extended kanban population inventory cost for two cards	Average kanban inventory cost on hand (half of total card population)
1 Product A	1243	$	3.50	44000	10	4400	$ 15,400	202	$ 1,414	$ 707
2 Product B	6512	$	4.00	15360	10	1536	$ 6,144	71	$ 568	$ 284
3 Product C	5698	$	4.25	16320	10	1632	$ 6,936	75	$ 638	$ 319
4 Product D	8745	$	5.00	6000	10	600	$ 3,000	28	$ 280	$ 140
5	8746	$	4.00	6000	10	600	$ 2,400	28	$ 224	$ 112
6 Product E	3600	$	3.50	3600	10	360	$ 1,260	17	$ 119	$ 60
						9128	$ 35,140		$ 3,243	$ 1,621

Figure 14.5 Inventory level comparison kanban controlled versus ten turns per year.

Figure 14.5 shows an example of traditional inventory valuation versus kanban-driven inventory valuation using the part numbers from our dedicated machining center feeding our total-value flow.

As you look at the data in the table, what is abundantly clear is the relationship between setup and changeover and inventory levels. A second significant factor is the source that drives the inventory build signals. In traditional MRP-type manufacturing environments, algorithms in the programs drive the demand based on some assumption in the reorder code—economic order quantity, inventory reaches a minimum order point, period of supply to be ordered, etc. In our rationalized example, the actual customer demand—as evidenced in the deposit of the kanban card in the posting box—drives the production activity.

As you struggle with the whole question of setup and changeover, you will discover a significant gold mine of potential productivity gain. If your setup and changeover time were cut in half, how would this affect your calculations? If your setup and changeover time went from one hour for a part number to one minute for a part number, your setup and changeover factor would cast your inventory, scheduling options, and cash flow in a whole new light. You would place your company in a "stockless" inventory position where most part numbers are made per demand. All the time formerly spent on setups and changeovers could be committed to sales growth. This could be the next best kaizen effort staring you in the face: setup and changeover reduction on your pacing machine.

To bring the whole point home about setup and changeover and its relationship to inventory, and to demonstrate other benefits of Lean, we have

Given	Given	Given	Given	Given	Given	Given	([(C\$6/G6)*B\$6] *1.2)	(D/3600) * F	L/7.1	([(C\$6/240) *15]*M6)
A	B	C	D	E	F	G	K	L	M	N
Part number	Inv cost per piece	Annual volume in parts needed	Setup or changeover time in seconds	Setup cost @ $100 per hour	Dedicated machine setups per year	Inv turns per year	Total average inventory costs with 20% holding costs included	Annual hours of setup time	Production days lost to setup time	Potential sales lost due to setup at $15/unit FG price times daily demand rate
12345	$ 5.00	50000	7200	$ 200.00	10	10	$ 30,000	20	2.82	$ 8803
			3600	$ 100.00	20	20	$ 15,000	20	2.82	$ 8803
			1800	$ 50.00	40	40	$ 7500	20	2.82	$ 8803
			900	$ 25.00	80	80	$ 3750	20	2.82	$ 8803
			600	$ 16.67	120	120	$ 2500	20	2.82	$ 8803
			60	$ 1.67	240	240	$ 1250	4	0.56	$ 1761

Assume 240 workdays per year

Figure 14.6   Setup and changeover comparisons and resultant cost savings and sales advantages.

created another table. Study the table above, which shows data on one part number, 12345. This part comes from a feeder machining center to a production cell. Assume, as you look at the data, that this part number is the pacing item for its product line. Also, as you look at the table, note how the setup costs become almost negligible as the turns increase with the introduction of the one minute setup and changeover. This will probably seem counterintuitive (Figure 14.6).

In this table, we have assigned values for part number 12345 for inventory cost, annual volume, and different setup or changeover times. We have also assigned an arbitrary cost of 100 dollars per hour for setup. With this data, we can set up a baseline of 10 inventory turns per year to derive annualized setup costs, as well as average inventory dollars and quantities on hand. To the inventory dollars on-hand figure, we have also added a multiplier of 20 percent to cover costs of inventory: financing of inventory loans, square footage and racking or rented trailers to house the inventory, depreciation of warehouse and equipment, containers and totes to hold the inventory, monies (actual cash flow or reserves) for excess and obsolescence and purge and rework orders, material handling equipment based on square footage and type of racking and shelving required, insurance on the inventory, etc. In many companies, the true cost of inventory is hidden in the total numbers. We have also posited that the parent-level finished good that part number 12345 goes into sells for a per unit price of 15 dollars.

What can we learn from the relationships presented in the table? First of all, as noted above, as the setup time lessens, the cost of the setup lessens, the inventory valuation decreases, and inventory turns increase. Second, as the total inventory decreases, the total cost of inventory decreases and cash flow increases. This translates into less warehouse space required to house materials, less material-handling equipment, less money tied up in financing product on the shelf, minimal exposure to purge and rework costs, less risk to excess and obsolescence charges, etc. Thirdly, by turning the setup downtime into productive machining time, simply by reclaiming the formerly "lost" hours, this company can add an extra 7,000 dollars per year in sales for this one product alone without adding manpower or overtime (sales department take note—Lean can create sales opportunities for you!) What is not measured is improved lead time—another benefit for the customer and the sales department—or an intangible like the effects of improved housekeeping and orderliness on worker behavior. For all these reasons and more, setup and changeover focus should be very high on your kaizen list after you start up your total-value flow. Inventory is wasteful and costs you money and time. The optimum lot size is one piece made at the request of the customer. This is a lesson traditional standard cost accounting, with all the added trappings of labor reporting, cannot teach you.

If you are thinking in the standard cost mind-set, the assumption was that the setup had to be amortized over the lot size run. The larger the lot size, the less the percentage of setup cost each part bore, and, thus, the product costing looked better. On the actual manufacturing side, the larger the lot, the easier it was to keep machine and manpower utilization and efficiency numbers up, resulting in better productivity numbers. With better looking product-costing numbers and high machine-productivity numbers, why do companies go out of business for lack of profit and cash flow?

The second pang of the counterintuitive nagging is the little voice telling you that you cannot reduce your setups ... you have tried, and your industry or your company or your product is just too unique for significant gains in this area. Prior management may have bought super-duper, world-class machines, which you cannot replace and which have taken on the subservience and obeisance once accorded to Greek gods. Your company is a process company, where run time is in days or weeks and setup is second to quality or pass-through issues in the refined or blended product. You are a machine shop, where every part you make is different. To you we say, every business can benefit from a review of their setup and changeover process. Most companies will get significant gains from the review. Many of the gains come in the preparation leading up to the setup. Many more come from the organization and housekeeping required for efficient setups. Some companies will get less by way of gain, but they will get a better documented knowledge of their process and better insight into the need for standardization and housekeeping in their whole process.

Chapter 15

The Total-Value Flow with Standard Work and Visuals

In this chapter, we will discuss implementing the enhancements the team came up within the brainstorming sessions. We will also discuss creating standard work based on manning and ensuring visuals are in place, and we will start thinking about the required metrics to monitor total-value flow performance going forward. When you have completed this chapter, you should be aware of the mechanics and process to allow you to set up your own total-value flow with minimum outside help.

First things first. If we are going to set up a production cell, we need to know how many employees we will need to man the different elements that make up the cell's production. In the course of this book, we have discussed everything required to derive the answer. Using the example for determining the "least-waste-way" observations as a starting point in our brainstorming in the prior chapter, let's fill in some theoretical data on annual volumes and length of workday, and determine the required manning.

In the prior chapter, we posited that the takt time was 1,000 seconds per produced unit. We also challenged our theoretical kaizen team to get to a stretch goal equal to 85 percent minimum of takt time as a cycle time. In our example, the enhancements they envisioned resulted in a cycle time of 928 seconds (see chart, which follows). This is typical of results. Some kaizen events easily meet or exceed the goal; others fight for every inch of waste elimination—it depends on the process and machinery involved in the change. Keep in mind that there is another focused kaizen event specifically targeting the welding operation, which quite possibly will allow

Kaizen documentation for making product "A"			
Element observed	Least waste way time from documented observations	Least waste way after brainstorming and waste elimination	Description of brainstorming enhancement
Coil shear	120	110	Use mechanical stops by product in lieu of measurement
Move wip	70	0	Change layout to facilitate 1 pc flow
Punch	60	46	Use mechanical stops by product in lieu of measurement Anticipate portion of setup during shearing operation
Wait for material	50	0	Change layout and level load
Move pallet	60	0	Move machines in close proximity and use 1 pc flow
Wait for material	70	0	Change layout and level load
Form for two	30 60	46	Use pressure clamps and orientation hole in material to more easily seat and hold material
Move to weld	45	0	Move machines in close proximity and use 1 pc flow
Weld	240	240	Needs own future kaizen event—many possibilities
Drill (per hole) for six holes	20 120	148	Combine drill and tap operations. Modify slower older manual drill to "gang drill" the six holes at one time Eliminate separate tap operation
Tap (per hole) for six holes	20 120		
Paint	Two days at outside painter	Two days at outside painter	Subcontract operation kanban controlled and visible on receiving heijunka board
Assembly	240	208	Pneumatic wrench in place of manual torque wrench Better use of visual templates for kitting hardware
Pack	180	130	Better placement of tools (ergonomics) and gluing equipment Install print-on-demand label maker/computer at packing to eliminate sheets of labels with troublesome-to-peel backings formerly printed in office
Least waste way (sec)	1435	928	

Figure 15.1   Kaizen document for making product A.

the opportunity to further reduce the cycle time to reach its stretch goal (Figure 15.1).

For the purposes of your kaizen, if your team can only meet the takt time goal for the cycle time, they have succeeded. You have covered your production needs to service the customer, but other training, maintenance, spontaneous brainstorming sessions on the problem of the day, etc., will have to be scheduled and backfilled on overtime or during the production cell's low-demand times. This is an acceptable alternative if your team has exhausted all its possibilities. If they have not, keep the team focused on reaching the stretch goal.

From the chart, note the team achieved a cycle time—based on the least waste way, "brainstormed" improvement—of 928 seconds. This is down from the initial, "un-brainstormed" 1,435 seconds observation they initially reached. This is an improvement of 35 percent. In addition, the team has identified an additional improvement resulting from a follow-on welding kaizen to reach or exceed the goal. Keep in mind that Lean has an ideal goal, never achievable but always the object of the pursuit: eliminating all waste activities. You should, therefore, view the gains as part of an on-going, never-ending pursuit of perfection.

For our example, let us suppose that we need to make 110 units of product per day at 928 seconds per product and our net available work time (after lunch and breaks are excluded) consists of seven hours and 10 minutes, which leaves us a takt time of 232 seconds. To calculate the numbers of workers required, use the "least person rule." Take the cycle time (928) and divide by the takt time (232) and the result is four workers (man power days) to man the production cell.

Note we did this by loading each operator to 100 percent of takt time. In the Lean world, we do it this way as the least waste way, which is counter to traditional industrial engineering using various allowances. If we decided to use a 90 percent value of takt time and recalculated the number of operators, we would get 928 divided by (232 times 0.9) equals 4.44 operators.

The calculations rarely work out neatly and evenly divisible. That is not how life works. When you end up with fractions of employees, you may have to round up, short term, to the nearest whole employee number and accept that you have one extra person. Using the concept called the least person rule, we would load the first four operators to the chosen number (in this case 90 percent of 232 or 209 seconds) and leave 92 seconds for the last operator. You would then look into adding value-added steps from downstream to fully load this operator temporarily until you can eliminate the additional waste and move from 90 percent to 100 percent. In addition, note that the team targeted the welding element for its own kaizen event, and this will probably result in productivity gain and the need for fewer headcount. Since, by any measure, there should be a significant productivity gain, you should still be ahead of the game in terms of headcount.

Keep in mind that Lean is one of the most flexible manufacturing systems going. It allows you, by means of standard work, to add personnel to the total-value flow in times of peak need. In times of inconsistent demand, it allows you to run the cell part of a day to meet all demands and then place the production cell workers in another cell where demand is peaking. Flexible workers meeting fluctuations in customer demand tends to fly into the face of traditional "keep-the-machines-and-the-people-busy producing" philosophy. You want the workers to keep the machines producing, but you want flexible workers working on the machines where there is real customer-driven demand; Lean does not keep workers "busy" for the sake of giving them something to do.

Looking at the chart, it is obvious that the welding operation is the pacing operation in the manufacture of the product. Since the team noted the need for a kaizen event, they obviously recognized the possibilities of significant improvements in quality or productivity or both. Perhaps, better fixtures could cut the welding time in half. Perhaps, there is a robotics-application aficionado on the team who believes that automation could be introduced relatively cheaply into the process to get better quality yields or productivity gains. *Be warned: you want the team to think in terms of creativity before capital!* Robots have a way of taking people hostage by assuming and demanding a life of their own. In most cases, adding robotics to an unrefined process will only add problematic layers to the ultimate solution. Refine the process first through completion of many kaizens before thinking about robots. Eliminate all waste before automating any process! Bottom line, the welding answer will require the next kaizen team to review all possibilities.

Since a kaizen event must be targeted and specific in scope, the team cannot set up the total-value flow *and* do in-depth analysis and change to the welding element. This is a case, short-term, of living with what is at hand. Design the production cell work flow around the pacing 240-second welding operation. Since the team derived the cycle time at 92.8 percent (928 seconds per unit of product) of the takt time, some give back will still allow the team to meet the takt time requirement of 1,000 seconds.

Looking at the data presented in the "after enhancement" graphic, if you were to set up a four-man production cell to handle the 110 production units per day, this might be a manning option: the first person operates the coil shear, punch, form, and some pack; the second person welds; the third person draps and assembles; and the fourth person assembles and packs. There are many variations on how to assign duties to the workers (Figure 15.2).

Looking at this same example, if production dropped to 55 units per day, you could operate the total-value flow with two workers: the first person operates the coil shearer, punch, form, weld, and packs, while the second person draps, assembles, and packs. Since your historical takt time, requiring four workers, is probably going to be your norm, this will probably be how you will run the production cell the majority of the time. The two-person manning simply shows the flexibility that comes from looking at the elements of work and moving personnel to point of need (Figure 15.3).

Determining how you balance the workload is the hardest part about setting up the production cell. Sometimes, it is not neat and tidy. The

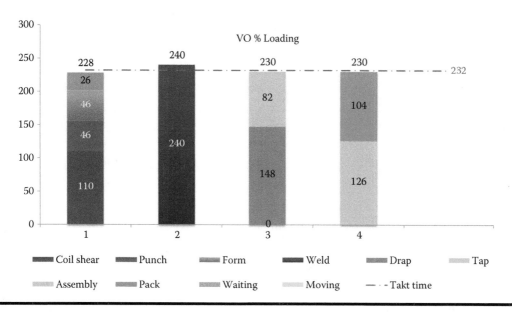

Figure 15.2   After percent-loading chart (4).

percent-loading chart is probably the easiest way to view the stacked elements. It may also point out that machine-cycle time is a fact of physics you have to work around. Keep in mind that operator waiting time while the machine cycles may be an unnecessary waste. The operator may be able to start the cycle and then move on to the next element while someone else

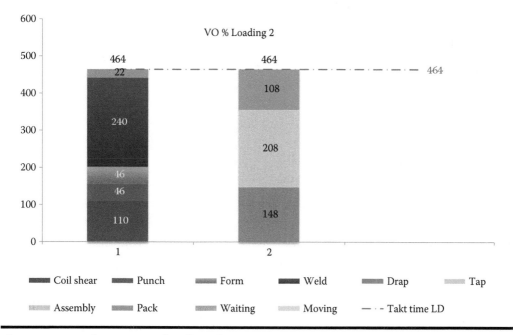

Figure 15.3   After percent-loading chart (2).

attends to the machine after the cycle is completed. Your team's creativity will have to come up with a solution.

Although Lean is flexible, there are two, non-negotiable, cardinal rules to follow when you are running your production cell and allocating man power: (1) do not run the cell to keep workers busy if all customer-driven demand (as represented by kanban card) is satisfied; and (2) insist that takt time be met even if you only have enough demand to run the cell for a few hours per day. Never allow the cell to stretch four hours of kanban-signaled demand into an all-day project. Takt time must be met on a period-by-period basis.

If you have no work for the workers, have them do a "5S" (housekeeping) activity: paint the machines, work on other follow-up items required in the production cell, use the time for technical training and quality improvement, or work on "to do" lists or other value-added work. By not allowing any backsliding, you will instill the proper discipline and expectation in the employees and the supervisory staff. If you are entering into a slower production period and uneven production is a possibility, you should have this talk with supervisors about your contingency plans.

You should have standard work available and posted for various manning allocations. Each employee should know what is required and how production responsibilities are allocated. Each employee should also understand that, as a team, they are responsible for meeting the period-by-period, posted kanban-card schedule.

When you create your standard work, try to balance the written word with pictures and images that convey the work to be done. In many of our factories, workers speak many primary languages, and English as a second language can be a struggle. Do not expect your employees to understand, in detail, the written English. Take a clue from the international traffic symbols and tourist guide icons that are becoming more prevalent. The use of emoticons, icons, and symbols can be as effective as the expression, "One picture is worth a thousand words."

Express numbers in math with arrows showing tolerances, radii, and measurements. Determine whether you will be expressing numbers in metrics or fractions. Use "balloons" and "arrows" on samples of posted documentation to show relationships or where a numerical table applies. Keep in mind, many of the workers who have come to this country grew up in a metrics-based math system. Whatever you decide, be consistent and have easy-to-read conversion charts and other aids posted as needed. Sometimes, side-by-side examples of work being done—with a bar through the wrong method—is worth many poorly written English paragraphs. Get creative.

Run your examples by your nonnative English speakers for their opinions. If you were to ask your kaizen-team members individually how they would communicate a message with minimal or no words to a foreigner, what would they come up with?

The production cell should have all the information required to make the products designed to run through it. This means that quality standards and metrics, as well as engineering work standards, specifications, and prints, should be maintained in the production cell. If it makes sense, you can laminate your prints and other critical documentation in minimal-mil sheeting (or not), just as you did your kanban cards, to prolong their use life. If there is some reason it does not make sense to do this, have your scheduler deliver complete documentation for making the product to the production cell when he or she slots the kanban card schedule.

Lean places primary responsibility for quality and workmanship of product with the operator who made the part. "Inspecting quality in" can become a needless time-waster when the operator is waiting for an inspector to come approve what the operator has already produced. The expectation should be that the operator can and will make a qualitatively and functionally acceptable product.

Some products, however, require expertise or sampling analysis beyond the scope of the ordinary worker. If there are severe liability risks, records may reside only within the responsibility of the quality control department. If controls are not so severe, operators may be able to fill out inspection data for their own production. If quality requires an inspector, there may be ways to mitigate time and paper requirements for the inspection process. Some companies paste an inspection-log, preprinted label on the back of the kanban card to record inspections made when that particular kanban card was processed. The inspector fills in specific data, and the card continues to circulate. When the kanban record-inspection label is full, the scheduler reprints another kanban card and the inspector keeps the original card or pastes another preprinted label over the Xeroxed, full label and the card continues to circulate. If this satisfies your inspection requirements, this might be a possibility for your company. Problems can arise when kanban cards become lost.

When you keep primary documentation and drawings at the cell and production is by kanban cards printed from a kanban database that could be different from your main computer system, you will have to establish controls to make sure bill-of-material and process-change information is communicated immediately and directly. One of the easiest ways to do this is to change your engineering-change-notice or quality-control-change-notice process to include sign-offs from both the production cell supervisor responsible for maintenance of up-to-date production drawings, standards, and quality acceptability and test criteria, and the materials person responsible for maintaining the kanban-part number database and printing the replacement cards.

Since kanban deals with minimal and rationalized inventories, bills-of-material changes are considerably less onerous than in traditionally run factories. With traditional, low inventory turn, large lot inventories to use up, cutovers in bills of material are and were usually a problem. Someone had to be vigilant to make sure the old materials were "used up" and the newer materials were ordered at some calculated future date based on a sales forecast that was always wrong. The effect of this was to make the change-notice process "a work of art" rather than an immediate "cutover" effort. In traditional companies, most engineering changes, 99 percent of the time, came with a "use-up" disposition for existing mounds of inventory parts (in deference to the accounting department fiscal hawks), and, in effect, the actual bill change would not take place for months. Even worse, if the materials department had to order more "matchup" components in order to use up an expensive, superseded component, the change-order process started to take on a life of its own.

In Lean factories, rationalized inventories usually result in relatively immediate card changes, with minimal inventory issues. By visually marking the new cards containing the change-order information and following proper first-in-first-out picking methods (pick right to left, top to bottom, and front to back), older inventories tend to be used up without a problem. On the other hand, if the change notice is mandatory and immediate, the change is effected by printing and replacing the kanban cards and quarantining the remaining kanban-part populations; another example of where the disciplines in Lean methods pay off.

When you set up the production cell and start producing to takt time, timeliness of response to problems in the cell assumes paramount importance. Sometimes, this can be a major culture-change challenge in a traditional factory. In traditional factories, work tends to get into a queue by department and is worked on according to some mysterious timetable and selection process—"loudest screamer first," "the boss wants this," "top of the pile," "it's Tuesday and my head hurts," "this looks easy," etc. In the worst cases, walls, which tend to numb urgency, physically separated the person working on the problem and the person awaiting an answer. When the fact of customer-driven demand drives the equation, things need to change.

Everyone in the building needs to recognize that the production worker, the advocate for the voice of the customer in this situation, needs support, and, if the line is stopped, the support needed is now.

Many Lean facilities have visual signaling systems that trigger a response when a worker in a production cell is stopped by a problem. If the event is on the production floor and all parties to resolution of the problem are within sight, the worker can simply turn on a light (strobe, flashing, rotating, or otherwise) to signal a problem. First responders—a quality person, a line-support engineer, and the supervisor—put whatever they are doing on hold and go to the source of the light to determine what needs to be done. If required responders are not within visual sight, predetermined sounds or musical signals can be triggered by the worker having the line-stopping problem. In Lean jargon, these are known as "andon" lights and signals. These visual signals can easily be something ordered and installed as a follow-up item at the end of the kaizen event establishing the production cell.

In some factories, the different production cells or specific machining centers have different and exclusive aural signals that the production workers trigger in the event of a line or machine stoppage. We grew to hate "The Yellow Rose of Texas" (midi-synthesizer tune version), when that unmistakable eight-bar theme played repeatedly, signaling a problem on a particularly troublesome machine. We knew which cell (one of our cells) had the problem by attribution of the tune only to that particular cell. We envied the personnel who only responded to "I Dream of Jeannie with the Light Brown Hair" or "Beer Barrel Polka" (not our cells). We rarely heard them play, but, when they did, it was a moment of schadenfreude, "guilty pleasure."

The kanban signals to make product get to the production cell from the scheduling heijunka board controlled by the production control department. As kanban cards are pulled by the line stockers and turned in to the posting boxes scattered at strategic locations around the factory, the scheduler will periodically make rounds and pick up the deposited cards. The scheduler will slot the kanban cards on the production-control-scheduling heijunka board into a time slot by day for production or in the unscheduled box. Like the production and line stocker workers, the scheduler also follows his own standard work and scheduling rules.

Following the scheduling rules, when it is time to schedule the production cell and those specific kanban cards, the production control person will take the kanban cards from the production-control-scheduling heijunka and slot them into the scheduling heijunka at the production cell. Normally, the scheduler takes the minimal number of cards to the cell that allows it and the supporting line stockers to function. Usually no more than a rolling two- to four-hour window is placed and maintained on the production cell heijunka. If you can reasonably reduce this further, do so. If the scheduler keeps the kanban cards on the scheduling heijunka until the last possible moment, this gives maximum scheduling flexibility to the scheduler.

A point of human nature is this: if you do not want people to have the opportunity to screw up a process, do not present them with the opportunity to do so. Give information to the production cell personnel and the line stocker as to what product will be made in what sequence in the shortest window required. Keep in mind that the slotted kanbans are also the pick signals for the line stocker to bring the next job's materials to the production cell. (We will talk more about the line stocker a little later.) Have a rolling window of slotted cards at the production cell to ensure a smooth, uninterrupted transition between shifts for cell workers, line stockers, and supervisors.

The production cell heijunka board use can be very simple in function. Since the documentation and standard work to make the product resides in the cell, the kanban card will be the only document that needs to be brought to the production cell and slotted in the appropriate sequence time-period box to create the schedule for the production cell. By limiting the number of cards at the production cell and not bringing one or two shifts' of cards at a time to the production cell, the scheduler can also change the schedule by moving cards if customer requirements change. The "frozen window" within which nothing can change should be minimal. The cell should be working on one kanban card and the line stocker should be bringing the material for the next kanban card. These should be the limits for any frozen window wherein change is not allowed. If the line stocker's picking time or the physical distance things have to move is significant, the frozen window should be modified accordingly. Bottom line, you want to leave the production cell as flexible as possible to address an emergency or expedite situations as they arise.

The construction of the production cell heijunka board can be simple and relatively inexpensive. You simply need boxes or strong, alligator-type clips to hold the kanban cards in the appropriate time period in which it is scheduled to be made. Clear acrylic boxes are our favorite. We would suggest 8–12 boxes, each labeled with an hour numeral (leave off the "a.m." or "p.m.") to be used in a "rolling" fashion. They can be bolted, glued, or otherwise attached along the sides of the structure (some type of tri-pod, flip-chart-type holder) holding the "takt sheet" on which production schedule performance is recorded.

The takt sheet is a most crucial document for the production cell. It is the written schedule. It is the results of performance to the schedule. It is the documentation of reasons why a schedule was not met. It shows very visibly and at a glance how the production cell is performing. It is the basis of metrics for performance and quality at the cell. It is the historical archive, which can suggest ideas for future kaizen events. Takt sheets are not used and thrown away—you can see precedents or repetitions of problems and identify possible solutions from the historical patterns (Figure 15.4).

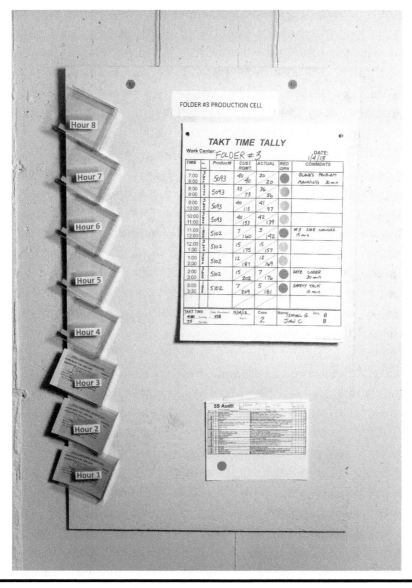

Figure 15.4   Production cell takt board with hourly scheduling boxes.

The production cell operator or lead person, not the cell supervisor, is responsible for filling out and maintaining the takt-sheet data in a timely manner. When the production cell begins to work on the next kanban card, the production cell operator or lead person records part number information and required quantity for the period (as represented by slotted kanban cards that the scheduler slots per time period). When the time period is up, quantities reported completed, in the ideal world, should equal the scheduled quantity.

If there is some quality or production problem with equipment or documentation or material, and the schedule per period was not met, the operator or lead person writes in the quantity of what they did produce and states the reasons why the schedule was not met. If the schedule was not met, the same person puts a red dot after the numbers. On the other hand, if the schedule is met per period, the operator or lead person puts a green dot after the time slot reporting the numbers. This allows, at a glance, anyone to see, without involved conversation, on a walk through the plant, how the production cells are performing in "real" time.

In most production cells, the takt sheet, the cell documentation and standard work, and the slots for the kanban signals are all in the same general place. Sometimes, these are as simple as a lumber, "A"-frame structure on wheels with acrylic boxes on the sides of the structure holding the takt sheets. Pockets and plastic holders, on the back of the takt-sheet A-frame structure, hold documentation and prints. Visuals used for production and cell standard work should be posted for the workers to see at all times. In the cases of things posted at the production cell, it is recommended to laminate them with a minimal-mil plastic to protect them and prolong their useful life.

If you have an expediting problem now, once you create the cell for the product, that problem should go away. As long as the production cell is not locked into some arbitrary and capricious frozen window situation (in traditional MRP-type environments, foremen always complained about a lack of a frozen window), production is controlled by simply moving cards from one time period to the next. If the sales department gets a call from a customer needing product, expediting becomes a matter of making the product at the next available slot. Customer service and on-time delivery with short lead times replace expediting. If you exist in an environment where every shop order has a "red flame" on it (or more than one if it is "really hot"), or your day is consumed by administering to and placating a "hot list," or most of your staff is being treated for hemorrhoids and depression from sitting in interminable "shipment-status meetings," your life should be in for a big improvement.

The line stocker has a crucial role with respect to the total-value flow. If you think of the production cell as performing to "takt time," think of the line stocker as the "sweep hand" of the clock that keeps them in rhythm. The line stocker also has a schedule to meet and standard work to guide him or her. The line stocker's charge is to take the next kanban card from the production cell heijunka board, pick parts per kanban card information, pick the parts per proper Lean picking methods, deliver picked parts to the production cell, locate the picked parts in the proper bin or "in" drop-off point, orient the product for access and use by the workers as stated in the standard work, pick up finished subassemblies or products and take to their proper bins or shipping lanes, and, then, repeat the cycle as long as there are kanban cards to process.

As you can see by the above paragraph, the line stocker function is crucial to the success of the total-value flow. The person who performs this job must be somewhat disciplined to do all that is expected in a timely manner and correctly. In some companies, material handling positions are deemed to be the lowest skill and wage level and targeted to the newest employees or employees performing at the low end of the bell curve. Armed with the knowledge of the importance of the position to meeting takt time, you can now fill the position accordingly. If this were baseball, the line stocker would be the catcher. He controls the game. Whoever you put here does not have to be your best employee; he or she only needs to be disciplined and able to follow the standard work.

The line stocker services the total-value flow on a schedule defined by standard work. Just as the overriding theme in Lean manufacturing is "just-in-time" production to the demand of the customer, the same principle applies to the line stocker. If the production cell is working on one period's kanban card, the line stocker should be picking the next period's kanban card. Batching multiple future-kanban cards in the picking or picking multiple periods of cards to "get ahead" are forbidden to the line stocker. Whatever time the line stocker might think he or she is saving by doing so, the production cell loses in the resulting clutter and confusion with the mixed orders. The line stocker must understand that the convenience of the production cell workers, and not his or her convenience, is what takes precedence when the workers are making product to takt time.

The key to the success of the line stocker is the presence of defined home bins for all inventory parts. This permanent bin location is printed out on the kanban card. The bins are also sized only to accommodate the kanban population for that particular kanban part number. There are no "excess" or "overflow" areas built into the bins—this defeats the idea of the rationalized and right-sized inventory to support the total-value flow. Defined bins will normally be half empty if the cards are functioning properly and demand is consistent with historical patterns. However, the bins acknowledge the possibility that demand could temporarily shift, and all kanban-controlled parts could be sitting in the bin at the same time.

The bin locations may be at point of use in the production cell or in a warehousing area. If inventory is common to many products, it may make sense to leave the inventory in a warehouse (along with the supplier-triggering kanban) and use withdrawal-replenishment kanbans between the production cell and the warehouse. If inventory is peculiar to only the production cell, it may make sense to stock inventory at point of use. Regardless of how you set up the inventory bins, be mindful of clutter and discipline and control issues. Bins must be clearly labeled and bin-numbering protocol obvious and intuitive. Since bin numbers will print out on kanban cards, they must also be maintained and permanent until updated with new bin locations in the computer—never use or allow random bins.

People tend to think of bins, more or less, as something akin to a shelf location. Bins can be more than shelves. Bins can be areas between dividers on flow racks. Bins can be portioned-off areas on racking. They can be marked-out areas (recommend applied tape initially) on the floors for totes and barrels or warehouse-exchange carts. Bins can be "egg crate" type or "honey comb" type structures with multiple compartments. However, you devise your bins, make sure there is some defining location-protocol label for the location.

If you use color codes on the cards to match to the bin locations or stand-alone area markers or signs, make sure your visuals are obvious and can direct any person, with minimal orientation to your warehouse or production cell, to find the inventory. Visuals can be signs (two sided or tricornered for sightlines) suspended from the ceiling joists, cones marking aisle identifications, color coding to the card for particular inventories or bins, stanchions detailing bin information, colored "bean bags" on skids or in bins to show what to pick complete first, etc.

We will talk more about metrics in the next chapter, but, briefly, we do want to mention one aspect of housekeeping that is crucial and primarily centers around the day-to-day activities of the line stocker: the handling of kanban cards. First of all, when you are starting up the total-value flow, the biggest challenges you will have will be threefold: (1) not to lose kanban cards, (2) not to pick and turn in the kanban card prematurely, and (3) not to make inventory for previously "lost and replaced" kanban cards that someone finds and drops in the posting box.

If you lose the kanban card, nothing will be produced or bought, and you will probably experience a stockout problem at an inopportune time. If the kanban card is turned in prematurely due to not following picking protocol or the same kanban cards (original and replacement for original) get scheduled, the produced inventory will not be able to fit in the sized home bin assigned for the part number. As much as everyone tries in the initial start up, there will be some lost cards. Once the procedures and methods are understood, lost cards, in our experience, become a non-issue. The second issue of turning in cards prematurely is either a housekeeping issue with the bins and card attachment or line stocker picking error. This issue should also go away after initial orientation and learning curve is completed. Just make sure you fix the housekeeping problem, if this is the primary causal factor.

If you establish a system that limits who can touch kanban cards, and train the individuals involved to understand that the kanbans are like money, this will be a great start to avoiding problems. All personnel involved in the process must understand that it is the kanban card that triggers replenishment activity, and whoever touches the kanban cards controls the replenishment action associated with the card. If the card is not turned in, nothing is produced. If duplicate cards are turned in, excess inventory, without a home bin, is produced. If cards are turned in correctly and in a timely manner, the system runs like it should.

Line stockers must make sure they pick inventory following the picking protocols: they pick right to left in the bin, from the front to the back of the bin, and from top to bottom. If they follow these protocols and pick each bin location completely before moving on to the next grouping controlled by kanban cards, overproduction will be avoided. When the end-of-shift walkthrough takes place, this is one thing the group should be on the lookout for. This will become an objective metric on how well the line stocker is doing his or her job.

When line stockers pick kanban cards that they will be taking to the posting box or when they pick kanban cards from the production cell heijunka board for the next order to fill, there is a tendency to want to put the kanban cards into the rear pocket of one's jeans. What typically happens next is that the line stocker discovers the cards when he is getting undressed at home, and the closed loop of the kanban cards is broken. To combat this common occurrence, give some thought to a defined container (if on a pallet jack or forklift) or kanban clothing modification like a waist belt with pouch (if the person walks) to define a specific place for the kanbans to go while in transit. Not having a prescribed place to put the kanban cards in transit is a common source of problems for Lean–kanban startup ventures.

The "found" kanban card resolution is the easiest to fix. Post a rule and make sure everyone understands that if you find a kanban card and are not sure what to do with it, give it to the materials person or the scheduler; do not drop it into a posting box. By checking the serial number or "card x of y cards" information for the part number or doing a quick kanban-card cycle count, the materials or production control person should be able to determine it is a duplicate and dispose of it accordingly.

We also hate to write the words to this paragraph, but, unfortunately, this can happen from time to time with companies finding cultural change difficult. Some disgruntled workers will deliberately sabotage the Lean start up. This is very minimal, in our experience, but it does happen. If you find and prove someone subverting the goals and progress of the Lean–kanban start up, you will need to think about your response to the situation. As managers, all things equal, we would terminate any employees—at any level—doing this, but you will have to address the issue in the context of your personnel policies and precedent. Just be aware of this possibility.

At this point, we have covered creating kanban cards for products targeted for the total-value flow. We have discussed how to document reality in the kaizen event. We have observed the role of the percent-loading chart in analysis of observed data. We have calculated the takt time required in our total-value flow. We have brainstormed countermeasures to reduce cycle time. We have calculated manpower required to staff the total-value flow. We have discussed ways to balance and load the factory via the various heijunka boards. We have discussed how the scheduler, materials group, and line stocker interact with the total-value flow. We have discussed proper locating and labeling of inventory. We have done much, and, by the end of the next chapter, you should have all the information you need to begin your first kaizen event to transform your factory. 5S and other housekeeping exercises are good, but you are now at the point to take the next substantive step. Hang in there, we are almost done.

Chapter 16

Tying Up Loose Ends in the New Total-Value Flow

As you have probably correctly concluded by this point, Lean manufacturing rises or falls on the unfailing discipline of the workers and their adherence to defined process, standard work, and team efforts. To the casual observer, this sentence may sound like a very repressive and depressing statement that ultimately sucks the life out of employees as individuals and turns workers into automatons or "Frankenworkers"—unquestioning rote workers bereft of individual contribution and imagination, prodded to produce ever more for the "company," as if in some Aldous Huxley or George Orwell novel setting. To be fair, when we first read about Lean in the early 1980s, we thought it would be imagination-stifling and onerous to work in this environment. At the least, it somehow seemed "un-American" and an example of cultural collectivism foreign to and incompatible with the American sense of "rugged individualism." When we understood it in the context of "worker empowerment" and actually experienced its rationality in practice, we changed our minds.

If you think about traditional companies, the workers on the line (and, by extension, everyone on the factory floor side of the wall), who physically made the product that paid everyone's salaries, usually got the least amount of respect. The engineers who created the design and the technician who did the CAD-CAM drawings rarely entertained the opinion of the people who did the job every day, when it came to making the product better. The machinist who made the product and intimately knew the machines he worked on every day—and their capabilities—could not possibly have a correct opinion on why a blueprint turning radius could not be met or a specified tolerance could not be held. Drawings were finished and "checked off" to management as completed and then "thrown over the wall" to manufacturing to figure out as best they could do. Similar types of institutionalized contempt were felt by other departments (not to unfairly single out the engineering department) against the worker who made the product.

To make things worse, in most companies, nonexempt or hourly workers were viewed as the adversaries to management. Peaceful coexistence came at a price of rigid contract rules that stipulated how far each side could go in pursuing their interests. The rigidity of work rules institutionalized waste into the daily norms. Throw in office politics on top of everything, and, in many companies, you had the "Wild West," with everyone on their own, six guns blazing in all the "turf wars," fighting over the institutionalized wasteland. Management meetings became witch hunts to punish the most vulnerable and whomever was lowest on the food chain—most efforts focused directly toward whomever was handy to divert attention from one's own problems. Opinion and lack of objective and verifiable fact and metrics blurred the conversation. Lung air capacity and deft employment of the correct catch phrase usually won the day. If we were cynics, we might ask: "Where was empowerment to anyone—let alone 'worker empowerment'—in all this?"

Discipline is a habit reinforced over time. It does not have to be associated with paternalistic and nineteenth century sounding adjectives like "harsh" or "stern." It can have positive or constructive aspects. It does, however, have to be reinforced daily and measured objectively against some criterion, with feedback to the employees involved. If people do not know discipline matters, they will tend to indulge the path of least resistance. From our experience, most people want to know how they are doing, as long as the reported results are not accompanied each time by punitive actions or demeaning words, filled with subjectivity, or measured against a standard that cannot be clearly articulated. From our experience, most people will try to improve and meet the expected metric, if they know someone thinks their day-in-and-day-out efforts are important. In many ways, the concept of discipline seems to be related to the concept of self-respect and the concept of having a sense of purpose.

In Lean methodology, individual workers are responsible for their work and the quality of the work. They are expected to meet takt time when they produce the product. By extension, they become the voice of the customer when they are producing to the demand of the customer. Because they have this responsibility, they also have the right to say, "Hold everything;

something is wrong here." If something is wrong with the process, they participate on the kaizen teams that come up with the enhancements for the problem resolution.

Through their use of imagination and efforts to define creative solutions, the workers have the power to improve their lot in work life. With this element of control over their processes comes the sense of empowerment. With empowerment usually comes buy-in. Now, instead of someone who works at a company, they have a more immediate sense that they *are* the company. If they are treated fairly, they respond even more. In Lean, they are judged by objective metrics: did they or did they not make quality products and meet the takt-time expectation? Bottom line, they will willingly produce more without all the frustration of looking for things or waiting on others or suffering from ergonomic issues, futilely begging management to address a process issue, or trying to fit 10 pounds of work into a five-pound bag at the insistence of some screaming, irrational supervisor.

After the creation of a successful total-value flow, we have yet to encounter workers who staff these units yearning to go back to the "good old days." In the rationalized total-value flow, they know what workmanship and quality standard is expected. They know their work is valued. They know they can contribute to improvements on future teams. They understand that the undue stress of unreasonable expectations has been mitigated. These "rehabbed" workers will become your best Lean salespeople among your workers.

Metrics are the enforcement tool that drives the Lean process. For the total-value flow, plan on a daily end-of-day walk-through with involved workers and supervisors, responsible materials and scheduling personnel, the line stocker servicing the production cell, responsible quality personnel, and depending on need and involvement, a representative from the maintenance area. On the walk-through, review production to takt time—note the "red" dots (where they did not make the takt-time schedule) and the "green" dots (where they did make the takt-time schedule). Were the dots placed and the takt sheet updated in a timely manner? Or, were they batched and placed at the end of the shift? Make sure reasons for misses are discussed and documented on the takt sheet. If training issues are involved for the miss, hold the supervisors accountable for educating the worker. If the supervisor is fuzzy on the answer, educate the supervisor. If the supervisor is the impediment, get a new supervisor.

Review the housekeeping—Are things where they should be? Is there clutter? Is the place swept and things put away on the shadow boards or in the appropriate bin? Is there too much inventory (overproduction)? Why did this happen? Are there rejects? If so, for what reason? Have causes for rejects been captured on the takt sheet? Is there leftover line stocker material at the cell? Why is this the case?

In the beginning of the total-value flow, you may have to invest more time in the walk-through than in the ensuing months when the total process matures. If done correctly, a 10-plus-minute walk-through from the office to the cell to the warehouse should be sufficient during the startup phase. Keep your questions and observations direct and to the point. The purpose is to educate all workers involved in Lean, to ensure the appropriate documentation took place, to see that metrics are recorded, to see that visuals are used, to monitor housekeeping, to monitor use of safe work practices, and to record information that may lend itself to future improvement events. Solve what problems can readily be solved, but remember, the purpose is not to discuss and resolve every problem immediately (obviously, safety issues have their own level of importance). Even after Lean is firmly established, have a walk-through every day involving the same personnel as above. This is part of your company's cultural change, and it reinforces the value of Lean and employee involvement and feedback. This is also part of the respect—your time and attention—you owe your workers.

The daily walk-through should end at the bins where the kanban-controlled inventory is held. Review the visuals that direct the line stocker to the defined bins. Are they clear and self-intuitive? Is only one bin being picked at a time, and is the picker following the correct protocols for picking inventory (right to left, top to bottom, front to back)? If these protocols are not being followed, you will have excess inventory produced and, subsequently, no place to put it in the kanban-population-sized bins. How is the housekeeping in the warehousing areas? Soda cans and candy wrappers on the shelf? Has the area been swept?

There are several ways to capture the daily walk-through in metrics. Using the standards cited and the questions proffered in the preceding paragraphs as a model, create a checklist of five or ten items to check and score every day. We would recommend including housekeeping with the total-value flow checklist rather than as part of the greater multi-departmental housekeeping score (Figure 16.1). On the tour, after the discussions, calculate the score and post it in a prominent place for all to see. Use visuals for each checklist item—green for compliance and red for noncompliance—so it becomes obvious to passersby how the total-value flow is doing. As we stated earlier, if employees understand something is important enough to be

5S Audit				Production cell	Auditor	Date / /		
5S	**No.**	**Checking Item**			**Evaluation criteria**	**0**	**1**	**2**
Sorted	1	Parts and materials			*No unnecessary* stock items or work in process—"everything belongs."			
	2	Machines and equipment			*All* machines and pieces of equipment are serviced and ready for production.			
	3	Jigs, tools, and molds			*All* jigs, tools, molds, fixtures, cutting tools, and fittings are serviced and ready for production.			
	4	Visual control			*Necessary and unnecessary* items can be distinguished at a glance, and visual metrics used.			
	5	Documentation			*All* engineering, quality, and production documentation is current and to latest specification.			
Straightened	6	Materials			*All* material is presented to the operator at the point of use, in correct quantities, and in the order of standard work.			
	7	Labeled shelves and stored items (material, documents, tools, jigs)			*All* shelves and items in storage are labeled clearly. Documents are labeled clearly as to contents and responsibility for control and revision.			
	8	Quantity indicators (expensed and stocked materials)			Inventory control indicators are *evident* for maximum and minimum inventories.			
	9	Bulletins and announcements			*All* departmental, divisional, and corporate bulletins and announcements are updated and orderly.			
	10	Jigs and tools			Open storage of *all* jigs and tools is well-organized for ease of extraction and return.			
Scrubbed	11	Floor			The floor is always clean and shining to help identify leaks or problems.			
	12	Machines, equipment, and fixtures			Machines are kept clean and painted.			
	13	Cleaning responsibilities			Cleaning activities are governed by standard work and rotated among workers assigned to the production cell.			
	14	Housekeeping mindset			Workers understand need for housekeeping and maintain an orderly work area during production hours—understand both "clean" and "check."			
Standardized	15	Ventilation			The air is clean with no obvious smoke or odor and all filtration devices are functioning and in use.			
	16	Lighting			The angle and intensity of illumination are appropriate.			
	17	Area Layout			Minimizes the work required to maintain the first 3Ss by insuring waste cannot accumulate over time.			
Sustained	18	5S Audits			*All* audits are posted in the area.			
	19	5S Audits			Audits are conducted by the supervisor (1/week), manager (1/month), and site director (1/quarter).			
	20	Discipline, rules, regulations, respect			A *disciplined* system of control and maintenance in place, standard work procedures and regulations are strictly observed, and mutual *respect* among workers and management is in place.			

Key: "0" is unacceptable "1" is generally acceptable but some nonconformance noted and must be resolved in timely manner "2" is unconditionally acceptable

Figure 16.1 A typical housekeeping check sheet and grading criteria.

scored and management is taking the time to score it daily, they will adjust their behavior accordingly. Metric enforcement is one of the key responsibilities of management, and the recording must be fair, objective, and based on *fact* and not opinion.

This is a behavior changing metric—*management cannot delegate this activity.*

Be brief in the review (maximum of five minutes) and give "attaboys" when workers do it correctly. Celebrate the positive changes. If things are not as they should be, talk about the reasons why they are unacceptable and why they must change. Approval should never simply be silent expectation, and the beatings should never continue until morale improves.

We would also recommend that you have a daily meeting with your operations and materials supervisory personnel and appropriate members of the sales, marketing, and engineering departments to review the prior day's metrics at the beginning of each new day. This will keep nonmanufacturing departments updated and involved in day-to-day progress and problems. This meeting should be a metric summary, by day, month to date, and year to date, of production cell presenteeism (scheduled manning), adherence to schedule, on-time delivery, a quality-control metric covering rejects, and review of current production cell lead times. Either materials or operations management, preferably operations management, should conduct the meeting. The meeting should be focused, and it should be a clearinghouse for information exchange. If marketing or sales have information to share on market plans, sales emphasis, or customer feedback, this should be succinctly discussed in this meeting. If other issues arise, treat them in their appropriate venue. If administered competently, this meeting should project results on a screen, and, 10 minutes later, people should be returning to their jobs better informed and ready to start their day (Figure 16.2).

Metrics should also be discussed in periodic, plant-wide meetings with all employees. If companies changing to Lean are open to the idea, reviewing quarterly financial reports makes a complementary topic for the presentation of the operational metrics. It is human nature to want to know "how is our team doing?" Metrics should also be posted in an employee-frequented traffic area for all to see. Self-intuitive charts and graphs for simple, themed topics such as "on-time delivery," "productivity in dollars per employee," "reject rate as percentage of total production volume," "reduction of lead times by product line," "sales dollars shipped per employee," "housekeeping," "plant safety," etc., are easier to understand than verbiage. Include goal lines. If it makes sense, include both production-cell data and company-summary data.

Date: 3/17/14			Daily production meeting
Measurable	Result	Reporting	Comments
Presenteeism %	98.5%	MA	OK
Past due lines #	56	JK	
Open orders #	27	JD	ETA 3/20
Plan to actual performance			
P1	80%	Jose	Crosstraining JR
RunW	100%	Jose	
SE	77%	Jose	Welder #3 down time
Wash	100%	Fidel	
Paint1	92%	Fidel	
Paint 2	100%	Fidel	
FCM	93%	Tony	
HFM	89%	Tony	Component issue
Chassis	83%	Tony	Missing bracket
Materials report			
IN Trouble #	3	JM	BLOBS again
Big orders/horizon			
	1	MB	LTO from AX starting in 2 weeks
Quality %			
Defect percentage %	93%	EF	Welded flange not in spec
Houskeeping audit			
Cell audits %	3	TM	OK
Other issues			
	1	GH	Scheduled shut down this weekend Fri (pm)–Sun

Figure 16.2   A daily production meeting.

Once the templates are set up in the computer, reporting the data becomes a non-issue. Try to capture enough of the historical values of what is being measured so that there is a baseline for comparison of Lean to former practices. If the company has profit sharing, the employees will pay particular attention to the results.

Looking at the bigger picture for a moment, your new Lean company should think "Lean" when you are setting management goals in the future. In many companies, management performance objectives run counter to companywide interests. We are aware of a set of management objectives in one company that rewarded the purchasing manager (purchasing was a separate department from materials) for improved purchase-price variance as a goal to reduce product cost. The purchasing manager achieved his goal through bigger lots at the expense of the inventory manager's goals for total inventory and inventory turns. Likewise, some manufacturing supervisors are rewarded for maximizing productivity by maximizing utilization of equipment and machinery and achieving maximum efficiency—which may also affect the inventory's goals for total inventory and inventory turns when unnecessary product is made ahead of time.

An example of a Lean management objective might consist of a shared engineering-materials-purchasing goal to reduce product costs by 2 percent per year. This puts the burden on all three departments to work together to find ways to reduce costs, which is compatible with the top management goals of increasing inventory turns to "X" times per year. Buying bigger lots, constantly beating up vendors, and competitively bidding for price reductions may not be the answer to achieve this goal. Engineering may have to look at product design, process requirements, or material content within existing design. Is the product designed with an unnecessarily high engineering safety factor? Could some materials be taken from sides or webs of structures and still maintain perfectly acceptable safety factors? Has engineering designed in or introduced "non-standard" materials or fasteners into the product? Can a higher content of lead be introduced into machined product to help increase tooling life and decrease cutting, milling, or drilling time? Purchasing may have to get the vendors involved to discuss the new design or solicit their suggestions for cost reductions. Peripheral issues like packaging and handling or vendor distance (any local sources?) and transportation costs may be a fertile source for cost reductions. Even your company's constant, historical expediting with a vendor could have driven their costs higher—the rationalized kanban inventory should allow this to become a negotiable bargaining chip. In this example, all three departments need to take into account total product costs as possibilities for reduction.

Your new company will require flexible workers with accommodating job descriptions to get the maximum benefit from Lean. If you have a union shop with strict job descriptions, strict division of labor, and many labor classifications with restrictions on who can do what, you will need to have discussions with the union representatives and union stewards about what you are trying to achieve with your Lean plans. If you make a case for attempting to grow the business and improve it against the global competition for the sake of trying to promote a better future for the employees who currently work there, you will probably have a sympathetic audience. If you are using Lean to get rid of people rather than grow your business, you will probably not get cooperation. Unionism and American manufacturing endured one of their worst periods in history from 2001 to 2009, when Bureau of Labor Statistics shows American manufacturing lost almost six million manufacturing jobs. Instead of getting rid of manufacturing personnel, motivate your sales and marketing people to fill the new-found capacity in your factory with sales orders. You should be able to produce substantially more product with the existing workforce you had before you started Lean.

While job descriptions should be broadly written and defined, specific skill levels and capabilities should be chronicled and posted. Keep track of who can weld, who can do set ups on what machines, who can paint, who can mold, who can operate a brake press or punch press or turret press, who operates material handling equipment, who can do NCR programing, etc. In some cases, you may have to have subsets of capabilities, for example, proficient in welding steel but not aluminum, or paints water-based paints only, etc. This information will come in handy when your plant foremen are having a manning meeting to decide how to cover vacations or schedule overtime needs. In some companies, this is the beginning of the "skill-based pay" incentives for employee development. Unlike subjective employee reviews or nebulous employee "improvement plans," this will document, for all to see, who has what skill and who needs to get more skills if they want to advance within manufacturing. This will also tell management, at a glance, how to prioritize cross-training to cover exposures in skill levels. If something does not happen because someone goes on vacation, this is the first place to start training (Figure 16.3).

With the changing world economy, most unions are aware that strict job descriptions and rigid work rules are not going to allow a company to compete and be successful in today's world. Oddly enough, some of the most successful Lean implementations can be found in the historically most unionized companies and countries in the world—one only needs to look at the domestic auto industry or the country of Germany. In some situations, worker councils from unionized companies assist in the day-to-day management of companies. Bottom line is that unionism and Lean do not necessarily preclude their ability to work together. Communicate. Build trust. Involve. Educate on mutual benefits. Request their help. Share praise and reward. Point out risks of not changing. These are the positive actions for getting workers on your side.

We have discussed job descriptions and manpower, and now we should discuss the kanban cards, which drive the heijunka process. Two points of discussion usually arise with regards to kanban cards: (1) how often do you change kanban cards for individual part numbers, and (2) how can you mitigate effects of "lost" kanban cards. Since the heijunka board and, by extension, all manufacturing processes are driven by kanban cards, these are two excellent questions. We will answer them in the following paragraphs.

First of all, it is rare that all kanban cards will become problematic and have to be replaced en masse. Since they are based on historical demand, this tends to temper and smooth fluctuations in card replacement. You will

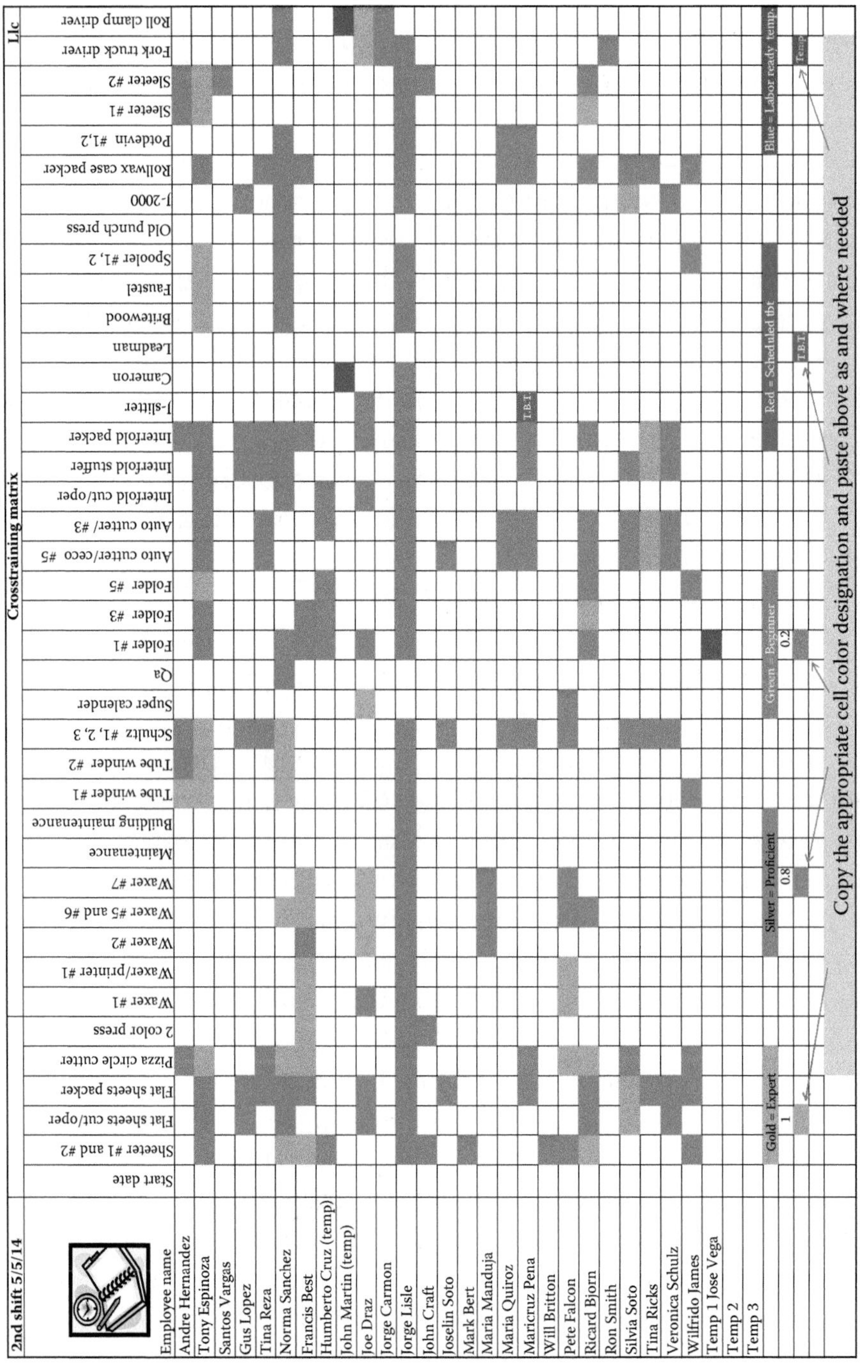

Figure 16.3 A crosstraining matrix.

have to replace all verified lost cards and pay particular attention to newly introduced products or dying products, but it is rare that your demand will change so suddenly as to invalidate the information that went into the make-up of your entire card deck.

Once you start up your total-value flow and have had several months of smooth operations (allow four to six months to smooth things out), you may want to review your kanban cards. To do this, the materials manager should convene a meeting with the sales, marketing, an operations representative, and production-control personnel to review shipment history. If the cards are behaving within normal variations, we would suggest leaving the cards as they are. If you see a trend in shipment data, ask questions. If new products are beginning to take off, pay close attention to the data. If old products are nearing the end of their life cycle, note the new shipment patterns and modify the cards accordingly. The ultimate decision on card changes should be among materials, sales, and marketing, with marketing getting the tiebreaker vote. The sales department has a tendency to go with the last phone call as the baseline; marketing has the macro-responsibility for the longer view of the corporate product plan.

There is no reason to get nervous with your kanban deck and to be constantly tweaking it. The numbers, even at the periodic reviews, are based on the longer historical view of actual shipment data. Unless something is drastically out of line or someone knows something has catastrophically changed, the odds are on the side of history. Change only the cards you need to change, but, when you do change them, retrieve all the card population and replace with new cards. In some cases, this will require bin resizing or modification. When you are replacing lost cards, replace only that specific card that makes the part number population whole again.

When you start up the production cell, until everyone gets used to handling kanban cards, you will have lost cards. You can set up a kanban card cycle count program to monitor your card handling during the startup. The cycle-count check sheets count cards in heijunka boxes, posting boxes, defined bin areas, and in pickup and drop-off areas. The kanban cards should have "card x of xx cards" information printed on them, so the counter must make sure to find and count all the cards that make up the card population. For example, part 123 has four cards, and the individual kanban cards will have printed on them, "card 1 of 4 cards," "card 2 of 4 cards," "card 3 of 4 cards," and "card 4 of 4 cards." If the kanban cards also contain a serial number per card, the counter could, alternatively, check off each serial number as he or she finds it.

If you cycle count kanban cards, we would recommend that you do this only on a temporary basis. As the initial problems are corrected, personnel will become more attuned to the value of kanban cards and they will not lose them. (We touched on this earlier, but a brief review is worthy of the effort.) Insist on defined holding places or wardrobe accouterments (defined acrylic boxes on forklifts, bandolier or belt pouches for line stockers, etc.) for securing the kanban cards while they are in transit. For the first three weeks, the back pocket of Levis will be the culprit involved in the lost cards. Try to ascertain why the cards were lost, and foolproof the process where possible. Give feedback to employees in the areas involved, and solicit their suggestions for improvements. If there is any deliberate sabotage involved, deal with it through your personnel policy.

After three weeks, lost kanban cards will start to become less and less of an issue. As you progress in your Lean journey, kanban cards can be replaced with kanban containers themselves, right sized, which become the kanban signal for replenishment when taken to the production cell. Do not establish the kanban cycle-counting position as a full time job—this will be unnecessary and wasteful in the longer term. Plan for a typical three-week tenure.

When you are setting up your total-value flow, do not forget to educate and get the sales force involved in the Lean change. Most sales personnel view Lean as something manufacturing is doing that does not involve them. This, as we have said previously, is not the case. Sales are directly involved in the Lean conversion and the conversation, and they must have enough knowledge to use the Lean conversion as a sales advantage when they talk with customers.

When the idea of minimal inventories is mentioned to salespeople, visions of deteriorating customer service and thinner commission checks immediately pop into their heads. The mantra will become deafening: "I cannot sell from an empty wagon." Lean and "sales advantage" are counterintuitive terms that do not go together. The sales force needs to understand the concepts of Lean in order to sell it effectively to their customers.

Your Lean inventory and support levels are structured from historical shipment data for your core products. Your inventory safety factor should be able to cover two to three successive shipments at a high shipment-percentile-level quantity. If, for some reason, you cannot ship items from stock, you have significantly shortened the lead time to ship what you have to make. For this reason, your company should be able to satisfy your normal customer demands and your normal customers.

The sales force should also focus on selling the company's core products—sell what is on kanban. Too often, salespeople get side-tracked dealing with "one-off" products as higher margin opportunities. If all the costs associated with these oddball products are not captured, your company could be fooling itself. Salespeople should sell products that reflect the core competency of the company. This is why you are setting up the total-value flow. These are the tried and true products on kanban.

If your sales manager decides to override your established policy and ship everything in stock to satisfy one abnormal demand, thereby knowingly putting all subsequent customer orders—including established and consistent customers—at lead time, that is the prerogative of the sales department. In the past with MRP-type systems, it was always a research project to be able to pinpoint which customer would suffer when the schedule was tossed upside down for expediting. How things are scheduled in the factory ultimately is a sales choice, and expediting conforms to the laws of physics in the factory. Where sales can orchestrate their will in the prioritizing of cards awaiting to be slotted on the cell heijunka board, the production scheduler can point out the affected orders that will be displaced. We are now at real-time scheduling with real victims named.

The limited-time offer (LTO) process, where orders are quoted and shipped at lead time (although significantly reduced lead times), was specifically designed to protect the loyal customer who calls every day for your product. If every order your company receives is an "expedite" and "cannot wait" situation, your sales person is out of control and out of touch with your customer. If your company has historically been driven by expediting, Lean provides the best type of expediting—producing the product with the minimal amount of lead time. As you track your lead time improvement by production cell, this should be posted and everyone made aware of it. Within a typical factory where historical lead times were in weeks or months, within one to three years of continuous improvements, they should be in days or hours. This should be the first sales point for your sales staff.

The second sales point should revolve around selling the reduced lead times as an advantage to your customer. If you are shipping product as needed to the customer on time and with no backorders and at a shipment service level of 98 percent plus, over time your customer will realize that he can lower *his* inventory levels because he now buys from a competent and on-time supplier. It may even be that the outlier quantities on some of your products were due to lumpy, self-defense order quantities from specific customers—timely and consistent deliveries can overcome the fear and distrust of past missed-order history and help customers balance out their cash flow better. (One of the interesting ironies of dealing with the customers of a poorly delivering supplier is that they tend to place bigger and bigger order quantities because they know they have a problem getting any product on time—needless to say, especially in a non-Lean company with excessive setups and changeovers, this only exacerbates the problem.)

We will relate a story of a successful mutual Lean application for a company and one of its primary customers. In the pre-Lean arrangement of these two companies, the customer held six- and seven-digit dollars of inventories from this supplier in their distribution centers. Orders were placed all at once—usually at the end of the month (late suppliers always beg for more lead time). Orders tended to be lumpy demand with outliers blended in with normal inventory. The vendor shipped product at a fulfillment rate of 60 percent to 70 percent. Freight became an issue, because orders were shipped "as product available" if order not shipped complete and on time. The supplier constantly expedited internal orders. The daily product meetings discussed the "hot," "hotter," and "hottest" orders. Communications with the customer revolved around meetings to discuss intransigent freight issue positions, poor delivery performance, threats to find a new supplier, and customer insistence on seeing the supplier produce a "performance improvement plan" to atone for all their corporate sins. Bad blood was a byproduct of poor supplier performance. The emasculated management staff of the supplying company urged the sales group to find "better customers."

To add to this sorry story, each fiscal year, the customer, per the agreement allowed by the sales department, was able to return for credit a certain percentage of product that did not turn. This product was warehoused in short-supply, precious space, and quarantined awaiting future return to the customer or eventual scrap by the internal accounting department in the annual "excess and obsolete" available reserves throw-out campaign. When inventory was not being returned for non-shipment, a smaller percentage of product stood the possibility of being returned due to engineering change-notice activity on mandatory recalls. These recalls—although infrequent, but noticeably irritating to the customer—usually resulted in another subheading being added to the "customer improvement plan" for the next emasculation meeting with the supplier. Not a pretty picture.

To make a long story short, the supplier company knew it had a problem and started on the Lean journey. This customer, being a major customer, had its products targeted for a heijunka-driven, kanban-controlled total-value-flow kaizen event. Over time, the supplier company was able to reduce lead times, improve quality by installing foolproof methods into the process, and become a reliable, on-time supplier. They soon requested and received weekly orders from the customer. The supplier brought the customer into the factory to learn about their improved methods.

Over time, with the consistency of shipment history, the customer reduced his inventory. More inventory reductions followed until the supplier had this customer's product on a demand-driven, kanban-signal system. Ultimately, customer inventories dropped to minimal levels to cover high service-level demands over minimal replenishment lead times. This helped the customer's cash flow. Eventually, the supplier negotiated a program to ship some product from the supplier's factory as pass-through product bearing the customer's paperwork and logo packaging. Everybody won. Cash flows improved all around. On-time performance and reduced lead times carried the day. The need for expansion space was nixed at the distribution site. The supplier became a crucial partner in the customer's business model. Talks became friendly, and the supplier management stopped talking like castratos and began smiling.

The moral of the story is this: your salespeople need to understand what is going on in the factory and be able to sell the change to your customers. Customers, like salespeople, get nervous when they hear their suppliers are "going Lean." We have often said that Lean is "counterintuitive." It is like saying that "less is more." How can this be? Your sales force needs to be able to answer this question and articulate the mutual advantages. This should be their homework.

Another issue we should discuss is the need for a computerized and integrated system for Lean. There are many Lean and "kanban" software systems out there. Many are disguised manufacturing requirements planning (MRP)–enterprise resource planning (ERP) type systems that merely replace shop orders with printed kanbans. You will have to do homework, ask questions, and be wary of software sales pitches. Some work relatively well and others not so well. The methods and processes explained in this book, as you should understand by now, work with minimal computer "system" involvement.

In the methods described in this book, computers are used as part number databases and for card printing. Computers gather shipment data and aid order entry. Computers have purchasing and vendor data. Computers execute order-picking and shipping paperwork. Accounting costs are actual-period expenses. Kanban inventory levels are relative to a defined population and normal card fluctuations, and they can be calculated outside a computer framework. Workers report their own status on production and quality. Schedulers sequence work on heijunka boards. There are no super computer wizards looming in the background.

If you have an existing MRP system, the Lean processes and methods in this book can probably peacefully coexist with it. Use MRP-system modules for sales input, order creation and pick list generation, engineering bills, process sheets, shipment invoicing and history, purchasing vendor information and history, and accounting payables and receivables. Shut off or ignore the inventory control, production control, shop floor control, capacity planning, and inventory transaction and labor-reporting-dependent accounting modules.

If you go with a computerized kanban/Lean system, there will probably be hidden costs. First of all, you will have to purchase the Lean software license with its annual renewal costs. You will probably add additional personnel to support the system—either in the IT or cycle-counting areas. Administering and "patching" or "customizing code" tends to create its own bureaucracy, as well as budget and time lines. More levels of involvement, conflicting opinion, and vested interests are introduced into your company. Time exponentially expands for the researching, interviewing, selecting, coding, installing, debugging, and parallel testing prior to launching of the new system. The lay people and your workers who should be in control of their circumstances are made onlookers on the sidelines to the slow pace of installing and troubleshooting the new technology. Their autonomy is replaced by a phone call to the IT department.

You can begin the methods and processes described in this book one total-value flow at a time. You can probably begin the change as quickly as your available time allows. Various groups in your company can be working on their piece of the startup database creation and bills of materials files concurrently. Best of all, the experts who schedule and make your products remain the experts responsible for seeing the creation and start up through. No hired mercenaries or levels of obfuscation here. The people responsible for their own fates control their own fates. Give them the understanding and guidelines, the expectation, and the power to effect change, and stand back. Prepare to be overwhelmed, you cynic. If your choice is to be underwhelmed, spend your money on a computerized Lean system.

When you get your first total-value flow up and running and your team has completed its presentation on the kaizen event, celebrate your victory. Find some money in your budget to have sheet cakes and balloons brought in, or spring for pizza for everyone. Make some noise. Clap. Make sure everyone understands this is the turning point for your company. Today is the first day of the rest of your company's life. Acknowledge and praise the personnel who assisted in the first total-value flow. *Acknowledge your workers for the "job well done."*

After the euphoria has died down a bit and business in the production cell resumes, make sure that management is actively seen as taking a genuine interest in what is going on there. Walk through the area and look at the takt board periodically during the day. Give a "thumbs up" for the "all is well" moments. Give a word of encouragement for the red dots on the takt sheet. At the end of the day, make sure management leads the end-of-day review of the total-value flow. It must be a mandatory performance for workers involved in or serving the production cell. Keep focused. Ask pointed questions. Keep the review as brief as possible. Do this every day. Do not delegate this responsibility to subordinates. As a manager, you owe this time to your employees.

Good luck!

Chapter 17

Competition and Continuous Improvement

A Story

John Madigan

I first walked into a factory during the summer of 1965, after I graduated from high school. That summer factory job at Butler Manufacturing in Galesburg, Illinois, a unionized, blue-collar, rail-road-and-factory town, was my first step to fulfilling my hopes for the future. I still remember the smell of the oil and solvents, which covered the waiting-to-be-fabricated, silver-colored, coiled rolls and black-banded, stacked bundles of steel. It was the same palpable, unmistakable smell that prior generations of factory workers had smelled.

Butler's factory in Galesburg no longer exists. Eight hundred middle-class jobs went away, a casualty of the outsourcing and global economies that made their way to my home town three decades after I worked there. The local paper chronicled its protracted, sleepless-night, worry-filled death, and published its obituary. Butler's memory is now only secondhand and referential to newer generations. Galesburg's attempt to replace Butler's—and the other 5000 middle-class wage factory jobs that also left—is a medium-security prison. "Hope" has a different meaning in a prison town.

As the U.S. population ages, the "boomers" are not the only ones experiencing memory loss. Our country is also losing its memory—of our once world-dominant manufacturing sector. Worse, we are losing the memory of what manufacturing contributed to our people and communities, because of its ability to trigger innovation, wealth creation, and dream fulfillment. Our manufacturing base, which fueled the economy that built the middle class and made this country great, is threatened by foreign competition.

According to Bureau of Labor Statistics data, the United States lost approximately six million manufacturing jobs between 2000 and 2009 (roughly one third of our manufacturing base). We are not economists, but with manufacturing plants closing and middle-class-wage jobs going away, there seem to be correlations among the disappearance of manufacturing, the declining middle-class wages, the erosion of our tax base, and a continuing lowering of our standard of living. Unlike what a lot of experts say, the job loss was not all due strictly to productivity increases and robotics. A lot of good suppliers went out of business, because their customer manufacturing base moved out of country.

Newscasters and pundits talk of the "creative destruction"—the recurring cycle of inevitable change where innovation drives out the old thinking—that is occurring in our economy. Since the 1980s, "experts" have spoken in succession about the eclipse of the "smokestack- and steel-manufacturing" economy and its eventual replacement by the coming "service- and transportation-based economy" … and then the coming "knowledge-based economy" … and then the coming "finance- and financial service-based economy" … and now, a "consumer-driven economy." What we have ended up with is a financial mishmash of a model which cannot sustain a vibrant, middle-class-supporting standard of living. Where the historical manufacturing base created wealth and broadly supported the middle-class wage, the other models simply recirculate existing wealth. In the longer view, we all get poorer. Consumer spending, repackaging debt and risk, or selling one's labor without producing anything does not create wealth. For the most part, the "destruction" not only came before the "creativity" but also displaced creativity.

We need to reflect on how we created the wealth that benefitted all classes. The fundamentals have not changed since Adam Smith's time. Domestically, you add value to some raw material—land, ore, seafood, commodity, or a technological idea—that you then sell. The accepted wisdom is that one manufacturing job supports six other jobs—suppliers, secondary operation providers, transportation companies, caterers, and service providers. If you do the math, the six million lost manufacturing jobs have directly or indirectly affected 36 million plus workers and their families. If our theory is correct, that accounts for a lot of tax-base erosion, lost opportunities, and broken dreams. This is the "jobless recovery" everyone sees—multinational corporations with foreign manufacturing operations are flush in money, the stock market is reaching new highs, and the middle-class, wages shrinking, is undergoing extreme stress just to stay afloat.

We are taught to think that globalization means the inevitability of outsourcing jobs to cheap labor markets. People talk about this as if it is a "fait accompli." We do not think this is necessarily true. We think Lean processes and theory can provide a path to restored economic health for our country and the minimizing of "outsourcing." Because of the continuous-improvement and waste-elimination manufacturing philosophy and methods of Lean, kaizen-driven activities are causing labor costs to become insignificant in comparison with the high costs of oil, transoceanic and transcontinental transportation costs, the inflexibility of long lead times, costs of borrowed capital to finance inventory to fill the pipeline from offshore sites, costs of separation of research and development from the factory, and maybe the most expensive of all, the risk to intellectual property.

Unless the cheap-labor-chaser manufacturers continue their race from country to country, other factors such as the political pressures of rising wages in the producing countries, ecological pressures on air and water and energy, and the continual propping up of currencies will exacerbate their problems in the future. There is a price for *cheap*. There are no altruists among the multinationals. There is also no allegiance to employees or countries.

A generation ago, labor costs could be as much as 30 percent or more of product cost; today, from waste elimination and process improvement and the application of technology, that cost is a single-digit percentage of product cost. For this reason, many companies, in fact, are rethinking their outsourcing strategy. Companies who sell where they manufacture and source where they manufacture, will have a competitive advantage. Smart companies of the future will only "offshore" to sell offshore.

It is a given that competition is a reality. The trick is how to compete. We say you compete by using Lean as a strategy and manufacturing philosophy. Lean has a blueprint on how to do this: energize your workforce. The philosopher Friedrich Nietzsche captured the point we are making when he said, "He who has a 'why' for something, can endure any 'how' of that 'why'." When communicated properly, the Lean message gives the empowered workforce the "why." The involved and energized workforce supplies the "how."

The key is that the message must be articulated and supported at the top and then promulgated all through the organization. Employees must understand Lean is important, waste is job threatening, and management must act like Lean is important. Once the employee-populated kaizen events start, they will understand their role in the company's future.

Following accepted Lean methods and processes, employees and kaizen team members will be the ones who really drive the change. This is the real, customer-responsive creativity and innovation, not the false chimera of hoped-for creativity in the "creative destruction" theory. Not surprisingly, morale will improve, creativity and innovation will flourish, and the will to compete will thrive. You might even see laughter and unmitigated joy back in your workplace. People want to be part of the solutions. Lean metrics will give them the affirmation, fact-based, they seek. Lean can be a "win-win" for all. If employees have a stake in profit sharing, all the better for motivation.

As consultants, we have gone into companies in various stages of "Leanness." As you walk through these companies, you get a sense of how deep the employee engagement is. Some are superficially "Lean," and it shows. Some have exceptional employee buy-in. In this latter group, it shows in employee enthusiasm about their Lean accomplishments. Even when language differences do not allow effective communication, this enthusiasm translates into smiles of ownership or authorship and gestures of scope of change. If Lean is top-down, and all the "Lean-ing" is done by consultants and black belts, there is a different atmosphere and outcome.

We went into a large Midwestern facility of an allegedly "Lean" company. The six-digit square foot building served multiple purposes. Thirty percent was used for manufacturing, 30 percent was used for distribution, and 40 percent was used for receipt, sorting, testing, and quarantine of defective transoceanic container loads of materials needed to make the company's product. This building served as a hub to ship approved product to their final manufacturing and distribution sites. The "Lean" portion was limited, in this building, to the final assembly of the product and the distribution warehouse. Upon mentally calculating costs of waste, we have to question whether or not the company was truly "Lean." From our experience, if the company was truly "Lean" and empowered by employee involvement, "waste-aware" employees would have questioned the wisdom of this situation.

Contrast this facility with the formed wire product manufacturer we spoke about earlier in the book. In the manufacturer's limited-space building, the transoceanic container loads of the cheapest priced, formed wire product the company finished threw the factory into an uproar every time a new shipment arrived. On one of the kaizen events, team members focused on the waste this caused in the factory. Having an understanding of the value and potential of Lean, one of their follow-up activities from a kaizen event was a "what if" idea that led to a search for a domestic, Lean-oriented, formed wire manufacturer. They reasoned correctly that a Lean supplier might be more flexible and open to trying to make their wire forms. They found a supplier 150 miles from their factory! Deliveries were twice weekly. They were not the cheapest supplier, but the amount of waste they eliminated in terms of handling, overtime, and missed schedules was more than a bargain. This was a change driven by the employees who had to deal with the wasteful situation.

The moral of the story is: in order to compete, you have to start. This is the message we have been preaching in this book. Pick a product that can be successful, do the mapping exercises, rationalize the inventory, create the kanban cards, balance the labor to meet takt time, and measure results. You want a success story. You want to create an incubator "learning lab" to teach other employees. You want to instill discipline and metrics. You want to create opportunities for your employees. You want your employees engaged and driving the continuous-improvement activities. You want to increase productivity to free up workers to increase the speed at which you populate other kaizen teams and tackle more problem areas.

There is always the danger you will want to put together an elaborate plan, spend months finalizing the plan, and then go for the "bold stroke" and get all the gain at once. Somehow, this seems to be ingrained in the American psyche. Home run hitters make substantially more money than single hitters do! This is a mind-set you need to get over, if you want to gain the maximum benefit from Lean. Lean is continuous improvement and the accumulation of smaller savings over time. To illuminate our point, here is a story of bold stroke versus continuous improvement.

A major company had two plants, one in Mexico and one in the Midwest, which had identical designs and equipment. Both had powder-coat-paint booths to finish their metal products. The standard color was black, but more and more customers were requesting other colors. This posed a problem, because it took 6.3 hours to change over the paint booth to paint the new color. Because of the changeover time, the company built up the black-colored inventory level, by overtime and weekend work, to cover the down-time required for the new color changeover.

The management team in the first plant (Mexico) found a company that made quick-change paint booths and decided to order one. The cost was $375,000 with a lead time of 24 weeks. The second plant planned to order one, but, because of the capital budget situation, it did not want to do so until the beginning of the new budget year. As time went on at the Midwest plant, the customers did not care about their capital budget problems and started to complain about lead time. Buffer inventory was getting out of control, so the vice president of operations asked for a continuous-improvement team to look at what could be done to improve the lead times, until the new paint booth could be ordered at the beginning of the new budget year.

A kaizen team was formed, and the team was trained in quick change-over concepts (in Lean, single minute exchange of dies or SMED principles). The team spent one week working on the project and came up with a significant number of improvements, resulting in a 64 percent reduction in paint booth setup time to bring the changeover time down from 6.3 hours to a little over 2.24 hours. In order to achieve this and significantly improve the operation, the kaizen team spent only $65. In addition to the 64 percent reduction, the team identified additional opportunities to reduce the change-over even more, and a second kaizen event was planned. The second kaizen team did as well as the first, and the improvements were of such a scope, using changes to existing equipment, the company decided to forego purchasing a new paint booth. After conducting four kaizen events and spending only $17,000, the team reduced the setup time from 6.3 hours to 23.4 minutes!

The Mexican sister plant processed their capital request, ordered the quick-changeover powder-coated paint booth at a lead time of 24 weeks. In time, they received and installed the equipment and went through the learning curve on how to run the new equipment. The entire process took a little over nine months. The first month in operation, the setup time took a little over four hours. The second month, it went down to 1.95 hours. The third month, it bottomed out at 41 minutes—which was a little longer than the manufacturer's claim of 20 minutes. They are still working on achieving the 20 minutes. The total cost was $375,000 (Figure 17.1).

Your company's manufacturing is important. Our country's manufacturing is important. We need to do all we can to preserve, sustain, and cause it to prosper. It has to be so good as to allow your company to compete with the rest of the world. We think Lean is one of the answers that will allow your company to compete.

Setup reduction

Paint booth	Oct	Nov	Dec	Jan	Feb	Mar	Apr	May	Jun	Jul	Aug	Sep	Savings	Cost	Benefit
Kaizen ($17k)	6.3	2.24	2.24	1.22	1.22	1.22	0.76	0.76	0.76	0.39	0.39	0.39		17,000	
K savings labor	0	2027	2027	2537	2537	2537	2766	2766	2766	2951	2951	2951	28,816		
K savings material	0	3265	3265	5266	5266	5266	5743	5743	5743	6127	6127	6127	57,938		
													9078	86,754	17,000	$69,754
Bold stroke ($375)	6.3	6.3	6.3	6.3	6.3	6.3	6.3	6.3	6.3	4.1	1.95	0.68		375,000	
Bs savings labor	0	0	0	0	0	0	0	0	0	2280	4509	5826	12,615		
Bs savings material	0	0	0	0	0	0	0	0	0	1098	2172	2806	6076		
														18,691	375,000	−$356,309

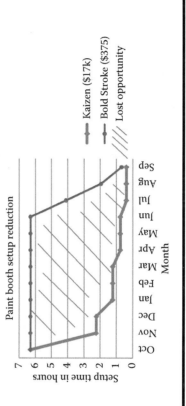

Figure 17.1 Continuous improvement versus bold stroke.

We have come to the end. We hope we have educated and inspired you to do something. Just keep in mind: a person of conviction, with a plan, is a majority. Remember to think big, but continuously improve in small, cumulative steps. Start somewhere.

Again, good luck. Don't forget to celebrate your victories.

Recommended Readings

Cunningham, Jean E., and Fiume, Orest. *Real Numbers: Management Accounting in a Lean Organization*. Durham, NC: Managing Times Press, 2003.

Maskell, Brian H., Baggaley, Bruce., and Grasso, Larry. *Practical Lean Accounting: A Proven System for Measuring and Managing the Lean Enterprise*. 2nd ed. Boca Raton, FL: CRC Press (Taylor and Francis Group), 2011.

Solomon, Jerrold M. *Who's Counting? A Lean Accounting Business Novel*. Fort Wayne, In: WCM Associates, 2003.

Emiliani, Bob. *Better Thinking, Better Results*. Wethersfield, CN: The CLBM, LLC, 2007.

Goldratt, Eliyahu M., and Cox, Jeff. *The Goal: A Process of Ongoing Improvement*. 4th revised ed. Great Barrington, MA: North River Press, 2014.

Byrne, Art., and Womack, James P. *The Lean Turnaround: How Business Leaders Use Lean Principles to Create Value and Transform Their Company*. New York, NY: McGraw-Hill Books, 2013.

Liker, Jeffrey K. *The Toyota Way: 14 Management Principles from the World's Greatest Manufacturer*. New York, NY: McGraw-Hill Books, 2004.

Index

80/20 rule, 38

A

Abnormal demands, 13–14
Absolute waste, 4
Accounting managers, 12
Administratively necessary activities, 5
Aggressive company, 114; *see also*
    Kaizen event
All-encompassing computer system
    approach, 135; *see also*
    Percent-loading chart

B

Batch and queue systems, 135
Bin locations, 190
Black box answers, 38–39
Bold stroke, 107, 116, 154, 215, 217
    continuous improvement, vs., 217
Brown paper, *see* Butcher's paper
Butcher's paper, 59; *see also* Current-state
    process map

C

Capital improvements, 50
CFO, *see* Chief financial officer (CFO)
Change agents, 3
Change-notice process, 184; *see also*
    Standard work and visuals
Chief financial officer (CFO), 13
Cloud burst, 62, 69
Company
    aggressive, 114
    organized, 50
Competition, 211–218; *see also* Continuous
    improvement
Computerized kanban/Lean
    system, 208
Continuous improvement
    bold stroke, vs., 217
    competition and, 211–218
    creative destruction, 212
Cooperative effort, 13
Core product sales, 205
Creative destruction, 212; *see also*
    Continuous improvement
Crosstraining matrix, 202; *see also*
    Total-value flow
Current-state process map, 55; *see also*
    Future-state process map;
    Process mapping
    cloud bursts, 62
    completed, 61
    decision point, 60
    details of action in process, 63
    determining content of notes, 62
    initiation, 60
    mapping exercise, 55
    marking department's role in
        activity, 60
    metrics of documented, 63–64
    necessities and supplies, 59
    point of, 62
    role of team leader, 61–62
Curtain effect, 10
Custom, *see* Non-stock end

Cycle-count check sheets, 203–204; *see also* Total-value flow
Cycle counting, 98; *see also* Kanban card
Cycle time, 141
  machine, 150

D

D&B, *see* Dun and Bradstreet (D&B)
Decision point, 60; *see also* Current-state process map
Deliver reliability, 15
Demand; *see also* Dependent demand derivation
  analysis, 18
  pattern, 23
Deming, W. Edwards, 2
Dependent demand derivation, 43; *see also* Dependent-demand manufacturing kanbans; Inventory rationalization
  capital improvements, 50
  coding in kanban database file, 44–45
  combining kanban and non-kanban usage, 47
  cost to inflated lead times, 48
  data files, 43
  kanban files and programs creation, 44
  kanban population determination, 47, 48
  lead time, 14, 48, 153
  lead-time-dependent part numbers, 53
  modifying computer systems, 43–44
  MRP systems, 44
  need for rationalized inventories, 50–51
  negotiation with vendor, 52–53
  organized company, 50
  parent and dependent child part numbers, 44
  piece-part price, 53
  planning bill to aggregate dependent demand, 45
  purchasing policy with inventory cost, 49–51
  quantities on kanban cards, 45
  setting reorder quantities, 49

vendors and sourcing, 53–54
working with vendors, 51–52
Dependent-demand manufacturing kanbans, 163; *see also* Dependent demand derivation
  analysis of part numbers, 166
  average setup time determination, 167, 170
  data in kanban cards, 171–172
  inventory level comparison, 173
  kanban cards, 169–171
  modifiers, 169
  parent-level kanban signals, 163–164
  productive workday time, 167
  setup and changeover comparisons, 174
  setup time vs. setup cost, 174–175
  sizing kanbans, 165
  supply from dedicated machining center, 165
  time for setup and changeover, 167–168
  value-added work, 164
Dun and Bradstreet (D&B), 63; *see also* Current-state process map

E

ECNs, *see* Engineering change notifications (ECNs)
Economic order quantity (EOQ), 49
Element machine time, 150
End-item part; *see also* Kanban signals
  numbers, 37, 38, 41
  review, 25, 26
Engineering change notifications (ECNs), 80; *see also* Kanban card
Enterprise resource planning (ERP), 1, 207
EOQ, *see* Economic order quantity (EOQ)
ERP, *see* Enterprise resource planning (ERP)
Expediting as waste, 22

F

FDA, *see* Food and Drug Administration (FDA)

Feeder machine, 10
FIFO, *see* First in first out (FIFO)
First in first out (FIFO), 10
Food and Drug Administration (FDA), 5
Ford, Henry, 2
Freed-up labor, 115
Future-state process map, 55, 62, 65;
　　　see also Current-state process map
　analysis, 68–69
　cloud burst, 69
　computer systems, 70–71
　goal, 67, 68
　group discussion, 66
　heijunka–kanban process, 72
　initiation, 70
　inventory and kanban cards, 73
　Lean production cells parallel to
　　　MRP system, 74
　MRP-type systems, 70–71
　note classifications, 66–67
　process, 65
　productivity reporting, 72
　purchasing, 72
　shipping, 72
　standard work documentation, 73
　system interfaces, 73–74
　waste but necessary, 67–68
　waste elimination, 68
　waste vs. value-added content, 66

G

Group leader, 58

H

Headcount reduction, 114
Heijunka, 27; *see also* Future-state
　　　process map
　-driven cells, 9
　–kanban process, 72
　setting up, 132
Heijunka boards, 32, 83, 85, 93; *see also*
　　　Kanban card; Kanban–heijunka
　　　card-flow process
　building, 110
　cost, 96

hourly schedule boxes, 95
　receiving, 94
　scheduled subassemblies, 96
　scheduler placement, 97
　scheduling heijunka, 94–95
　scheduling rules, 97–98
　scheduling with posted standard work, 85
　size of receiving, 94
Home bins, 189–190
Housekeeping, 136–137, 190–191, 195;
　　　see also Total-value flow
　check sheet and grading criteria, 197
　efforts, 161

I

Improvement activity worksheet, 108
Inventory
　bins, 100–101
　effect, 12
　kanban cards, and, 73
　level comparison, 173
　review, 25–26
　review frquency of, 28
　safety factor, 204
　stock, 27–28
　-stocking decision maker, 24
Inventory rationalization, 12, 14, 21,
　　　33; *see also* Kanban cards;
　　　Kanban signals
　demand pattern, 23
　end-item part review, 25, 26
　expediting as waste, 22
　frquency of inventory review, 28
　heijunka board, 32
　inventory review, 25–26
　inventory-stocking decision maker, 24
　kanban classification, 27
　kanban population, 28
　Lean factories, 184
　link to customer, 22
　minimal-inventory system, 27
　need for, 50–51
　order interval review, 26
　people interchangeability, 32
　product family sales data, 24
　reasons for inventory stock, 27–28

Inventory rationalization (*Continued*)
    required change in perspective, 22
    sales-history review, 26
    SKU, 28
Involving upper management, 16

J

Job descriptions, 200–201; *see also*
    Total-value flow

K

Kaizen; *see also* Kaizen event
    document for making product A, 178
    newspaper, 124
    presentation meeting, 112–113
    team, 105–107, 178
    week, 112
Kaizen event, 3, 105, 177; *see also* Reality
    documentation of kaizen event
    aggressive company, 114
    freed-up labor, 115
    goals, 110–111
    headcount reduction, 114
    heijunka boards, 110
    improvement activity worksheet, 108
    McGyver shop, 110
    objectives, 113, 109
    planning, 116
    preparation for, 107
    productivity gains, 114
    rules of, 11
    takt time, 111–112
    target sheet, 109
    team-member acknowledgment, 112
    time for, 107
    training in Lean and kaizen, 108
    waste elimination, 116
Kanban, 4, 27; *see also* Kanban cards;
    Kanban signals
    ABC analysis of product line A, 36
    classification, 27
    coding in database file, 44–45
    database, 79
    –heijunka process, 32
    inventory level comparison, 173

non-kanban combined usage, and, 47
    population, 28, 47, 48
    sizing, 165
    startup data analysis, 35
Kanban cards, 10, 28, 77, 95–96, 152–153,
    169–171, 201; *see also* Heijunka
    boards; Inventory rationalization;
    Kanban; Kanban–heijunka card-
    flow process; Kanban signals;
    Total-value flow
    acknowledgment sign-off
    requirement, 80
    assembly stock, 31
    attachment method, 102
    bin location, 99–100
    classifications of, 78
    color variation, 31
    cycle counting, 98
    database maintanence, 98
    data in, 171–172
    defined bins, 100
    format, 30
    handling cycle, 82
    handling of scheduled, 98
    information on, 30, 31, 79, 81
    inventory bin visuals, 100–101
    to keep track of, 83
    matchup, 103
    materials and size, 78
    non-stock, 29
    notification to ECN or PCN, 80
    parts of, 79
    posting box, 82
    processing for replenishment, 102–103
    in production cell, 84, 88–90
    production control person and, 82–83
    purchased, 90
    quantities on, 45
    reorder point visual, 84
    review of, 203
    rules, 81, 99
    scheduling heijunka board, 85
    scheduling rules, 85, 86
    shipment, 90
    standard work and instructions on, 85
    stocking part numbers, 101–102
    stock kanban cards, 29

stopping points for, 83
takt board with scheduling boxes, 87
transfer kanbans, 101
types, 34
walk-around, 103
Kanban–heijunka card-flow process, 77;
    see also Kanban card
heijunka boards, 83
kanban database, 79
level-loaded schedule, 77
scheduling heijunka board, 85
Kanban signals, 33, 185; *see also*
    Kanban; Kanban cards
80/20 rule, 38
black box answers, 38–39
classifications of orders, 34
end-item part numbers, 37, 38, 41
initial data analysis for kanban startup
    quantities, 35
kanban ABC analysis of product line A, 36
MRP-type programs, 37
non-Lean factories, 34
parent-level, 163–164
part number-specific shipment data, 40
production's internal customer, 35
rationalizing inventory, 33
safety stock, 38
sales department and reduced
    inventory, 39
service-level approach, 39
setting inventory levels, 34
shipment data, 35, 39
Kickoff meeting, 121, 122
Kraft packaging paper, *see* Butcher's paper

L

Late order, 14, 91
effect, 15
Lead time, 14, 48, 153; *see also* Dependent
    demand derivation
agreed-to, 90
buyer-padded, 103
cost to inflated lead times, 48
-dependent part numbers, 53
kanban population and value per day
    of, 39

ordering pattern and, 26
part, 141
productivity, vs., 39
rationalizing inventory and, 26
selling reduced lead times, 205
unreliable, 15
Lean, 1, 2, 3, 17, 179; *see also* Lean
    methodology; Waste
abnormal demands, 13–14
as accounting change, 12–13
accounting managers, 12
against, 17
benefits, 16
champions, 7
as cooperative effort, 13
deliver reliability, 15
engineering department in, 22–23
ill-advised product designs, 23
involving upper management, 16
late order effect, 14–15
learning lab, 7
management objective, 200
mentors, 7
misconceptions about, 21
on-time delivery, 14
origins of, 2
preferred provider, 15
priority customer, 13
production cells parallel to MRP
    system, 74
profitability in, 151–152
rationalized inventory, 14
sales department in, 15–16, 22
salesperson in, 13
tackling nay sayers, 16
takt time, 17–18
teaching company, 17
Lean methodology, 193; *see also*
    Total-value flow
computerized kanban/Lean
    system, 208
individual workers, 194
management objective, 200
metrics, 195, 198
MRP system, 207, 208
need for integration, 207–208
production meeting, 198, 199

Learning lab, 7, 9
Least person rule, 179
Least waste way (LWW), 122, 129,
     133, 134
Level loaded, 77; *see also* Kanban card
Limited time offer (LTO), 13, 27, 34, 78,
     205; *see also* Total-value flow
Line stocker, 189; *see also* Total-value flow
  bin locations, 190
  home bins, 189–190
  housekeeping, 190–191
  kanban cards, 191–192
  picking protocols, 191
Link to customer, 22
LTO, *see* Limited time offer (LTO)
LWW, *see* Least waste way (LWW)

M

Machine cycle, 127; *see also* Reality
     documentation of kaizen event
  time, 181
Made to order (MTO), 27, 34
Management by objective (MBO), 50
Management performance objectives, 199
Manufacturing issues, 155–156; *see also*
     Percent-loading chart
Manufacturing requirements planning
     (MRP), 1, 32
  parallel to Lean production cell, 74
  system, 44, 207, 208
  -type programs, 37
  -type systems, 70–71
Mapping exercise, 55; *see also* Current-state
     process map
Market-driven production, 18
Materials documenter, 131
MBO, *see* Management by objective
     (MBO)
McGyver shop, 110
Minimal inventory system, 11–12, 27
Modifiers, 169
Monument, 152
  asset, 3
MRP, *see* Manufacturing requirements
     planning (MRP)
MTO, *see* Made to order (MTO)

N

Necessary activities, 5
Non-Lean factories, 34
Non-stock end, 27
Non-stock kanban cards, 29

O

Occupational Safety and Health
     Administration (OSHA), 5
Ohno, Taiichi, 2, 5
One-piece flow, 134–135
On-time delivery, 14
Order interval review, 26
Origins of Lean, 2
OSHA, *see* Occupational Safety and Health
     Administration (OSHA)

P

PCNs, *see* Product change
     notices (PCNs)
People interchangeability, 32
Percent-loading chart, 133; *see also*
     Total-value flow
  all-encompassing computer
     approach, 135
  analyzing machine and operator element
     documentation, 154
  batch and queue systems, 135
  before, 140
  brainstorming, 139
  challenge to team, 161–162
  cleanup and sort, 137
  current-state data, 133
  cycle time, 141, 154
  drilling operation, 160
  ergonomics, 159
  goals, 133–134
  housekeeping, 136–137, 161
  inventory of maintenance
     department, 160
  Lean, 138
  Lean vs. traditional company, 154
  manpower to supply production
     cell, 153

manufacturing issues, 155–156
observed times for product A, 149
one-piece flow, 134–135
one-product example, 148
outliers in time elements, 147–148
production cell, 133, 157, 159
program function, 160
setting up total-value flow, 140
setup reduction kaizen event, 143
setups and changeovers, 143
after spaghetti chart, 158
standard work, 136
starting point, 147
takt time, 141, 142, 144–146
team members' behavior, 139
tooling positioning, 159
visual controls, 136
Permanent bin location, 99–100, 189
Picking protocols, 191
Place holders, 82; *see also*
   Kanban card
Preferred provider, 15
Priority customer, 13
Process mapping, 55; *see also* Current-state
   process map
approach, 56
core group and departments, 57
days allocation, 57
group leader, 58
key rule for, 58–59
planning, 56
time for, 57
Product change notices (PCNs), 80; *see also*
   Kanban card
Product family sales data, 24
Production
meeting, 198, 199
unit throughput, 11
Production cell, 9–10, 183; *see also* Percent-
   loading chart; Standard work and
   visuals
construction, 157
heijunka board, 186
manpower to, 153
operator, 159
parts from dedicated center, 165
products in, 149–150

rules for running, 182
setting up, 133
takt sheet, 186–188
Productive workday time, 167
Productivity
gains, 114
reporting, 72
Product-line candidate, 10
inventory build, 11
Purchasing manager, 199; *see also*
   Total-value flow
Purchasing policy, 49–51

R

Rationalized inventory, *see* Inventory
   rationalization
Reality documentation of kaizen event,
   117; *see also* Kaizen event
builder, 121
co-leader, 120
completed target-sheet, 126
cycle time, 130
documenters, 120–121
documenting machine cycle, 127
goals and, 122
kaizen newspaper, 124
kickoff meeting, 121
machine layout, 123
material documenter, 131
planning countermeasures, 122
purpose of, 128
reliability and quality issues, 129
roles of team members, 118–119
scribe, 120
setting up heijunkas, 132
spaghetti chart, 123, 126
square footage determination, 130
takt-time value, 117–118
team leader, 119–120
time-elapse camera, 130
time-observation worksheet,
   124, 125
traditional industrial
   engineering, 129
Replenishment activity,
   102–103, 191

S

Safety stock, 38
Sales department, 35
    in Lean, 13, 15–16, 204
Sales-history review, 26
Scheduling rules, 185–186
Scribe, 120; *see also* Reality documentation
        of kaizen event
Service-level approach, 39
Setup time
    determination, 167, 170
    setup cost, vs., 174–175
Shared equipment, 10
Shingo, Shigeo, 2, 88
Single Minute Exchange of Dies
        (SMED), 216
    computerized and integrated
            system, 207–208
    computerized kanban/Lean
            system, 208
    individual workers, 194
    Lean management objective, 200
    metrics, 195, 198
    MRP system, 207, 208
    production meeting, 198, 199
SKU, 28
SMED, *see* Single Minute Exchange of
        Dies (SMED)
Spaghetti chart, 123; *see also* Reality
        documentation of kaizen event
Standard work and visuals, 177; *see also*
        Total-value flow
    balancing workload, 180
    change-notice process, 184
    color codes, 190
    expressing numbers, 182
    inventories in Lean factories, 184
    kaizen document for making
            product A, 178
    kaizen event, 177
    kaizen team, 178
    kanban signals, 185
    Lean, 179
    least person rule, 179
    machine-cycle time, 181

    after percent-loading chart, 181
    primary documentation and
            drawings, 183
    production cell, 183, 186
    rules for production cell and man power
            allocation, 182
    scheduling rules, 185–186
    takt sheet, 186–188
    use of pictures, 182
    visual signaling, 185
    welding operation, 180
Standard work documentation, 73
Statistical information, 43; *see also*
        Dependent demand derivation
Stock kanban cards, 29

T

Takt sheet, 186–187; *see also* Standard work
        and visuals
Takt time, 17–18, 111–112, 141, 195; *see also*
        Kaizen event
    percent-loading, vs., 144–146
    value, 117–118
Target sheet, 109
Taylor, Frederick W., 2
Teaching company, 17
Team leader, 119–120
    role of, 61–62
Team members' behavior, 139
Time-elapse camera, 130
Time-observation worksheet, 124, 125;
        see also Reality documentation
        of kaizen event
Total-value flow, 141–142, 146, 177, 195;
        see also Lean methodology;
        Percent-loading chart; Standard
        work and visuals
    computerized work, 207–208
    core product sales, 205
    crosstraining matrix, 202
    cycle-count check sheets, 203–204
    daily production meeting, 198, 199
    element machine time, 150
    housekeeping, 195, 197
    inventory safety factor, 204

job descriptions, 200–201
kanban cards, 152–153, 201
line stocker, 189
LTO process, 205
machine cycle time, 150
management performance
    objectives, 199
mapping, 9
monuments, 152
MRP system, 207, 208
mutual Lean application, 206–207
products in production cell, 149–150
profitability in Lean, 151–152
purchasing manager, 199
review of kanban cards, 203
sabotaging Lean startup, 192
sales force and Lean change, 204
selling reduced lead times, 205
setting up, 140
setup and changeover times, 151
takt time, 195
tying up loose ends in, 193
walk-through, 196
waste elimination, 147
Toyota Production System, 2
Traditional companies, 193–194; *see also*
    Lean methodology
Transfer kanbans, 101; *see also* Kanban
    card

U

Unavoidable waste, 4
    retention of, 5

V

Value-added work, 164
Value addition, 3, 4
Vendors, 51–52; *see also* Dependent
    demand derivation
    negotiation with, 52–53
    sourcing and, 51–54
Visual signaling systems, 185, 190; *see also*
    Standard work and visuals

W

Walk-around, 103, 196
Waste; *see also* Lean
    absolute, 4
    defects as, 6–7
    elimination, 3, 68, 116, 147
    excess inventory as, 5–6
    excess motion as, 6
    expediting as, 22
    lost opportunity as, 7
    overprocessing, 7
    overproduction as, 5
    possibilities, 3
    sources of, 5
    transportation as, 6
    unavoidable, 4, 5
    underutilized people as, 7
    value-added content, vs., 66
    waiting time as, 6
Wasteful but necessary situation, 67–68
WIP, *see* Work-in-process (WIP)
Work-in-process (WIP), 122